WHAT'S YOUR SPIRITUAL QUOTIENT?

How to Respond to Life's Toughest Issues With Spiritual Intelligence

MARK A. BREWER

DESTINY IMAGE® PUBLISHERS, INC.
P.O. Box 310, Shippensburg, PA 17257-0310

"Speaking to the Purposes of God for this Generation and for the Generations to Come."

This book and all other Destiny Image, Revival Press, Mercy Place, Fresh Bread, Destiny Image Fiction, and Treasure House books are available at Christian bookstores and distributors worldwide.

For a U.S. bookstore nearest you, call 1-800-722-6774.
For more information on foreign distributors, call 717-532-3040.
Reach us on the Internet at www.destinyimage.com.

ISBN 10: 0-7684-2675-8
ISBN 13: 978-0-7684-2675-5

For Worldwide Distribution, Printed in the U.S.A.
1 2 3 4 5 6 7 8 9 10 11 / 12 11 10 09 08

Dedication

To my remarkable wife, Carolyn, who has a "spiritual intelligence" beyond anyone I have met. And to our children, Vanessa, Paul, and Rachel. Decades of learning from some of the greatest schools has taught me one thing: Often the greatest teachers are those closest to you. These have been my treasure and ever growing teachers from God.

Mark A. Brewer

Endorsements

Dr. Mark Brewer has been a friend, a brother, and a mentor to me for more than 30 years. His spiritual counsel has proved invaluable, time and time again. His book, *What's Your SQ?* is true to form. Mark's thesis about spiritual intelligence is a testament to his own life—a life marked by worship, study, discernment, and seeking wisdom at every turn.

Governor Bill Ritter
State of Colorado

Pastor Mark Brewer has written a gem. *What's Your SQ?* crosses denominational divides in revealing God's position on some of the toughest issues we face in today's culture. Can the Christian unhook a loved one from life support? How should Christians respond to homosexuality? Do we really need to tithe in the 21st century? What about divorce and remarriage? Dr. Brewer delves into these and many other questions by going to the best source of all for the answers—the Bible. If you want a refreshing and balanced teaching on how modern Christians can increase their Spiritual Intelligence, if you want God's wisdom on life's toughest issues, then *read this book!*

Dr. Robert H. Schuller
Founding Pastor
Crystal Cathedral, California

Quite simply, Mark Brewer makes old truth fresh, he makes universal truth personal, and he makes hard truth attainable. But he does all of this without reducing truth. He doesn't present the Christian life as simple or easy. He presents it as doable if we are spiritually smart. His treatment of spiritual intelligence enables us to take the grand truth of the Gospel and apply it to every corner of life. Mark Brewer writes about spiritual intelligence as one who, in abundance, has spiritual intelligence. This is a great book.

Bill Robinson, President
Whitworth University
Spokane, Washington

In our contemporary world that includes a multiplicity of societal alternatives and has seen the rise in the elevation of relativism, humanity has become like a boat on the massive waves of life, left without an anchor. The need for not just an anchor but also a rock to which one can fasten that anchor in our sociably unpredictable and unstable world is imperative. The average human is searching for some form of absolutes to serve as a stabilizer and guide to regulate our decisions. Dr. Mark Brewer in this landmark work provides practical and relevant answers to some of the waves that seem to crash over our lives every day. Every issue he addresses is relevant and necessary, and I hope you will read this book and benefit from its timely wisdom.

Dr. Myles Munroe, Chairman
Bahamas Faith Ministry International and
International Third World Leaders Association
Nassau, Bahamas

A battle rages for the mind, heart, and spirit of a contemporary society caught in the tension between God's love and compassion and His demand for justice and obedience. Dr. Mark Brewer challenges the reader as he confronts the toughest issues facing society today—issues that most ignore, many deny, and only a few even acknowledge. With biblical boldness and compassionate sensitivity, Brewer moves into these controversies armed with four sentinels of spiritual intelligence as he seeks to dig up the mine field of theological and philosophical debate. You may agree. You may disagree. But prepare to be confronted, challenged, and even changed as you join him in tackling the tough topics of today's society and their impact on the emerging church.

Dr. Kenneth C. Ulmer, Senior Pastor
Faithful Central Bible Church
Los Angeles, California

As someone who sits regularly under Mark Brewer's preaching, he had already helped to boost my spiritual intelligence to a pretty high level. But reading this book sent it up several more degrees! Dr. Brewer makes it clear that having a high spiritual intelligence quotient does not mean having all the answers—it means being able to struggle with the questions with a deep confidence in the truth of the Gospel. This book is a wonderful gift to all of us who need guidance in the struggle.

Dr. Richard Mouw, President
Fuller Theological Seminary

Mark Brewer is called and gifted by God and has impacted lives for Christ all over the world. This book will bless all who read it and I highly recommend it. As you live life in a fallen world, you will find strength, insight, laughter, and joy through Mark's words.

Dr. Jim Dixon, Senior Pastor
Cherry Hills Community Church
Colorado

There is nothing more foolish than an answer to an unasked question and nothing more powerful than an intelligent response to the real questions people are asking. Here is a book that defines the true meaning of intelligence and then uses that gift to respond to the most urgent questions people are asking. Mark Brewer is one of the very finest communicators in America today. He is an outstanding preacher, and as you will experience in this book, he is an impelling author who has listened intently to people, their deepest concerns and issues, and writes with one-on-one intimacy and integrity. You'll not want to put this book down and you will want to give copies to your family and friends.

Dr. Lloyd John Ogilvie, Chaplain
United States Senate

Table of Contents

PART II
20 Tough Issues and How to Respond With Spiritual Intelligence

Foreword

I remember that when I first came to faith in a significant way, although I knew I needed and wanted a relationship with God, there were two big hurdles. The first one was intellectual. I was in a university where anything about God was laughed at as if you had to put your brain in the freezer in order to believe in Him or the Bible. Thinking people just did not believe those things, or so I was led to believe. So, every time I longed to know God in my heart and mind, it was difficult to get those two together. I was stuck.

The second hurdle I faced was that it seemed that the lifestyle of a lot of Christians I knew was weird. They were so *not* connected to the culture that I lived in, and couldn't seem to relate in some significant ways, that I thought to be a Christian was to go live on a compound somewhere and not go to the Spring Homecoming Formal. For me, that was out of the question. So, in my circles there weren't many Christians who seemed "normal" about how they looked at things. And on other issues of daily life, they seemed just a bit too out of the loop for me to join.

In a real sense, the term "fundamentalist" fit them to a tee. They had no "fun" and not a lot of "mental." I am sure that they were sincere, but I knew something was wrong with the picture of a God who did not fit with what we know about philosophy and science, and could not relate to real life and its issues. After all, if God created this world and this life, shouldn't belief in Him allow us to think and function here?

It was in the middle of that quest that God led me to some "spiritually intelligent" Christians, and I remember feeling like my heart, mind and soul had found a home; they could all exist together, in one body. I knew also that that kind of integration was what the Bible talked about as well. We should be able to love God with all our heart, mind, soul, and strength. He said so. And there is nothing better in life than when all of those come together.

For that reason, I am privileged to introduce you to Mark Brewer's *What's Your Spiritual Quotient? How To Deal With Life's Toughest Issues With Spiritual Intelligence*. It gives me now the same benefits that I have found to be important since those early days of faith for me. Except more.

First, this book will show you that you do not have to be a brainless superstitious anti-thinker in order to be a Christian. In fact, it shows you the opposite: there are compelling arguments for our faith and the positions that believers in Jesus take on important issues. You may not agree with everything, as we all have our different thoughts and views on many issues. But you will know that thinking people *think* about these issues of faith, as opposed to "not thinking at all."

Second, you will get to know that to be a person of faith, you can be a normal person also. Mark's style, and his own thinking is not like some weirdo on a compound somewhere. The lifestyle message comes through: believe and be normal. So, you can still go to work and have your friends, *but* bring more to the party than before.

Third, you will get to know a lot about these important issues. He takes us through them one by one, and the different dynamics, facts, and issues that come to play in each one will make you think, and you will learn. He will help you to form your own conclusions, as a good teacher does.

And last, he models not only what he thinks, but also a *way of thinking*. Too many times Christians are unapproachable, rigid, and difficult to dialogue with about these kinds of issues, which I think is why he entitled it "toughest issues." Often, these are the ones that divide relationships and even churches. But Mark shows us a kinder way to speak, and his concern comes through.

So I invite you to read, think, learn, and be at home with this book. It will serve you as you think about these things for years to come, as these are the kinds of issues that we tend to revisit over and over. Thank you, Mark.

Henry Cloud, PhD
Los Angeles, California

Introduction

How many times have you said something like, "My head tells me 'yes,' but my heart tells me 'no'." Or maybe, "How can this be wrong when it feels so good?" Or how about, "I've weighed the pros and cons of what to do, but I'm not feeling peace about either direction." Or maybe, "I really want to do this, but all my friends tell me 'no'." And here's a classic—typical advice given by well-meaning friends—"It doesn't matter what you do, as long as you're sincere."

With all the changes happening today, with all of the conflicting opinions flying back and forth, how could you ever know what is truly the *right* thing to do? More importantly, how could a book written thousands of years ago have anything to say to help you today? With all of the "voices of reason" telling us that they know what's best for you, how can you really know?

This book was written on the hinge of frustration—mine and others. For theologians and ethicists, certain parts of this work may prove frustrating. But is was not intended to be an exhaustive examination of the various issues that perplex this generation; only a "spiritual primer" in how we can make wiser choices in our everyday lives. So, if you will stick with me for a few pages, I want to show you exactly how you can determine the best methods for choosing wisely in every single situation that you encounter in this bittersweet, wonderfully painful journey we call life.

PART I
SPIRITUAL INTELLIGENCE

Introduction

Some of the younger members of the team could hardly believe what they were hearing. They had all liquidated their assets and invested everything they had on this mission. They had traveled together for months, overcome horrible resistance, and just when the goal was in sight, the leader said, "We're changing directions." It might be understandable to adjust because of lack of clarity or some new overwhelming obstacle, but these were devout, seasoned, brilliant, tough-minded leaders. These men had the vision and resources to accomplish their mission. Why were they not pushing forward? Because the Spirit of God had forbidden them. From doing what? From preaching Christ in Asia (see Acts 16:6-12).

To add to the strangeness of deciding not to preach Christ to the lost, the men who were deciding this were none other than the apostle Paul, along with Luke, Silas, and Timothy. How did they know the Holy Spirit was holding them back? As Paul would say later, "We have been given the mind of Christ" (1 Cor. 2:16). The Spirit of God was leading and guiding His people, and He was doing it by four Heaven-sent sentinels given to guide and guard His people.

As the story would unfold, this band of travelers were about to take the Gospel to Europe and dramatically affect the history of the entire world. The thrilling truth is that each one of us can discover and use this kind of wisdom for the journey of our own life.

HOW DO I KNOW WHAT GOD WANTS?

We live in unparalleled times. Times that Jesus warned us would come. Is the world going to get better or worse? Jesus said "absolutely." He answered that question in Matthew 13, Mark 4, and Luke 8 when He said the wheat and the tares would grow together. He was teaching His followers not to focus on uprooting all the evil in the world, but instead to plant the good. Why? Because it is possible to sometimes confuse the good with the bad. It's God's job at the harvest to divide and separate the two.

Yet there is something else behind this unique little parable of the sower: the remarkable inference of Christ that evil would get worse while the good would get better. We are living increasingly in the best of times and the worst of times, as Dickens put it. Good and evil, beauty and ugliness, life and death, all flourish right next to each other. Neither good nor evil seem to be getting the upper hand in this struggle of the ages.

There is so much good today. The wonder and beauty of life itself, along with new inventions and creations, is mind boggling. People are even reaching out and caring in powerful and loving ways never seen before. More people are volunteering to help others than at any time in American history since such statistics were first collected. And yet, growing alongside all this good is a harvest of evil. The pain, the darkness, the confusion and brokenness of this world seem to have reached new depths of despair. The disturbing news, according to Christ, is that things are going to get even more extreme.

How do we live in such a world as ours and know the right things to do? How could anyone know what direction to take, with all the conflicting voices and claims—even within the church? I have heard that some sociologists and economists believe that over half of all the new jobs in the next 25 years haven't even been invented yet. If this is true, then the questions, issues, complexities, and pressures of today demand an intelligence few people are striving to develop.

The Bible calls this intelligence "wisdom." The good news is that this wisdom is readily available to anyone who wants it. We can learn to properly handle the choices of our everyday lives and to take on the tougher issues of life.

Here is one of the many ways that Proverbs describes wisdom:

> *Get wisdom, get understanding; do not forget My words or swerve from them. Do not forsake wisdom, and she will protect you; love her, and she will watch over you. Wisdom is supreme; therefore get wisdom. Though it cost all you have, get understanding. Esteem her, and she will exalt you; embrace her, and she will honor you. She will set a garland of grace on your head and present you with a crown of splendor. ...When you walk, your steps will not be hampered; when you run, you will not stumble. Hold on to instruction, do not let it go; guard it well, for it is your life* (Proverbs 4:5-9; 12-13 NIV).

Smart people learn from their mistakes. Wise people learn from the mistakes and lessons of others. Take for example my friend Brad. I knew Brad from a church I used to attend. He was given one of the sharpest minds I have ever seen. The guy could cruise through classes like they were a child's board game. Not only did he graduate in the top 1 percent of his class, but he took on graduate school with the same effortless style. His life in corporate America blasted out of the gates. He was being groomed for one of the top spots. Then he met and fell in love with a beautiful, classy lady who had wit, intelligence, and a sense of humor that could match Brad's, laugh for laugh. They led Bible studies, took vacations across the eastern seaboard, and were soon blessed with three wonderful children.

Then one day, Brad's employer wanted to transfer him to another city. Brad thought it was a mistake. He figured that someone with his talents, track record, and MBA could talk them into sending a newer candidate instead of him. But the offer was not negotiable. Either transfer, they told him, or be let go.

Brad asked his Bible study what they thought. Most felt that staying with a huge, established company was worth a few years in another state. Besides, leaving the cold of the Midwest for the Florida sunshine didn't sound all that bad! However, Brad chose to turn down the offer and leave his job. He had mastered his product like few people in America. He knew he would be snatched up by one of a dozen competitors who had always dangled the carrot in front of him. In fact, he started to reflect on getting out of corporate America altogether. Wouldn't it be good to put more on his own table from what he produced by the labor of his own hands? Why knock himself out to make other people rich?

So, along with some friends from his college days, Brad launched into his own business venture. They knew most start-up companies failed because of a lack of capital, so they took out a large loan, using their houses as security. And before long...Brad was in serious trouble. His business never quite took off—but it didn't completely fail, either. He was landing a few clients here and there, but not enough to make the business a hit.

Like dying from a thousand paper cuts, this sad dilemma limped along for several years. Brad started borrowing from one person to pay another. Then he began borrowing in order to pay a few dollars on his increasing credit card bills. He was asking everyone he knew for money, always assuring them that the illusive "big sale" was just around the corner. He started losing friends. Every time he was with them they would counsel him that when you've hit rock bottom, you don't break out a shovel! But Brad kept digging himself deeper into the hole. His wife and kids began feeling the strain. An impenetrable, icy wall began to grow between them. Brad tried to reach out through the chill, but he could never give his worried family the time they needed to weather the storm.

Brad no longer teaches Bible classes. In fact, he openly says he is too angry with God to even mention His Name. Brad's marriage is near collapse. His wife is the only one really working. Brad just sits in front of the television, seemingly paralyzed with indecision about what to do. When he does make a little money or talks someone into loaning him more, he astonishingly spends it on a vacation, in order to try and drum up that old memory called "happiness." His debt right now is in the hundreds of thousand of dollars; much of the money loaned by family members, friends, and church folk.

What went wrong? How can someone with such a brilliant mind and a great family, who is healthy as a horse and has no substance abuse, become so enslaved to such bad choices? Brad is deeply bitter with life and with God.

Not to belittle someone else's pain, but Brad had been spared the truly huge losses many people experience. His anger and bitterness toward God are not from outside afflictions. He had been spared from ever being fired from a job, or from losing a loved one by death, or from life-threatening disease or illness. Yet, for the last ten years he has watched as his once-skyrocketing life of promise collapse into tragedy. How did Brad end up in such an emotional prison?

The problem isn't so much that Brad made a bad career decision and got off the road and into a ditch. The problem is, how could such a smart person continue driving deeper into the ditch when it was so obvious things were only getting worse?

The purpose of this book is not to examine missed potentials or one man's personal battles. But Brad's quagmire does highlight one of life's great mysteries, which this book is all about: Why do some people cruise through the storms of life, while others have their boats sunk? Some people seem to set their compass toward a distant shore, and in spite of headwinds and turbulent swells, they reach the island of their dreams. While others with similar gifts, talents, and energy, set their course only to find themselves adrift at sea, or reach their island only to find it to be more of a nightmare than a dream.

Is this all part of some divine plan, or is something deeper going on?

God's Wisdom

Compare Brad with another friend of mine. Jan had one of those storybook marriages to Bob. With his dark wavy hair and easy magnetism, he had been her college sweetheart, her one and only love. The day their infant son Robbie came home from the hospital was a joyous one. Jan's Air Force pilot husband and perfectly exquisite son radiated in her glow of happiness. Little Robbie cooed and smiled...while, unknown to them, he was growing weaker and weaker from a rare neuromuscular disorder.

Soon, Robbie died. Burying her face in his baby clothes and clinging to the fading scent of this precious nine-month-old, Jan railed at God and wept. Why had He taken her precious little Robbie away?

But soon, a new child was kicking inside of Jan and calling out for her attention. A confusing mixture of hope and apprehension churned within her as she patted her belly and whispered to her unborn baby. "Please Lord," Jan prayed, "let this baby be healthy."

The second that baby Lara made her grand entrance into the world, Jan was convinced her fears had been for naught! Lara was adorable and boisterous, kicking her tiny legs with a strength that Robbie never possessed. But then, as the months crawled by, it became all too painfully evident that Lara too had inherited the same neuromuscular disease that took little Robbie. Before her third birthday, Lara was also lifted from her mother's arms...and ushered into the presence of God in Heaven.

Jan subsequently raised and nurtured two more children, buried her only sister (who died in her thirties from heart problems), taught Sunday school, lived through a lengthy airline strike along with her husband, laughed much, prayed a lot, and loved many. Then one day at age 54, Bob was diagnosed with cancer. Jan prayed for healing, begging Jesus to save her beloved husband.

How vividly I remember watching Jan hold Bob's hand as I tried to remain composed. My dear friend Bob was barely recognizable. His salt and pepper hair had completely whitened in the few months since I'd seen him last, and his once robust physique was now a mere skeleton. Bob died two weeks later. He was barely 55. Why would God take such a great Christian husband and father so soon? I feared Jan could not continue to survive her storms. I thought she might give up on life, or possibly even her faith in a God who kept allowing such pain to visit this wonderful woman.

But Jan's response was different. Even though she went through all the appropriate responses of anger, rage, stunned disbelief, depression, and confusion, her life somehow bounced back. She kept on going—even *growing*. She started a ministry to widows, both young and older women, called "Jeremiah Gals." She is very involved with her two children and their spouses and grandkids, she travels the world on missions, and she is pushing forward with her life.

I'm sure there's not a day that goes by that Jan doesn't whisper her beloved husband's name. Yet, she has taken the hole in her heart and filled it with new purpose. She is taking her life in hand

and painting a beautiful and bright picture out of the pale, dark colors of tragedy and loss.

As a pilgrim through this bittersweet journey called life, and with the feelings of any normal person, I am driven to ask a question—one that will not tolerate the typical simplistic slogans, pat phrases, or Christian clichés we so lightly throw around. The question is this: *What is the difference between these two beloved people, Brad and Jan?* We all suffer trials and afflictions. Why is it that the friction of life seems to polish some people more into the image of Christ, while others simply become ground down?

In the Bible God lays out a clear and uncomplicated answer to that question. In the pages ahead, we will examine how you too can develop that internal wisdom, that grace and ability to weather life's storms, overcome its challenges, and deal well with the tougher issues we all face.

As you read these chapters, my prayer for you is that you will begin to realize that God has given us ways to discern the biblical answers and responses to virtually every problem we will encounter, and to sail through them no matter how stormy the waves that are crashing over you.

> *Therefore, since we have so great a cloud of witnesses surrounding us, let us also lay aside every encumbrance and the sin which so easily entangles us, and let us run with endurance the race that is set before us, fixing our eyes on Jesus, the author and perfecter of faith...* (Hebrews 12:1-2).
>
> *Run in such a way that you may win* (1 Corinthians 9:24c NASB).

CHAPTER 1

Spiritual Infancy

And so, brothers and sisters, I could not speak to you as spiritual people, but rather as people of the flesh, as infants in Christ. I fed you with milk, not solid food, for you were not ready for solid food. Even now you are still not ready (1 Corinthians 3:1-2).

With the loving but exasperated words in the passage above, Paul described the church at Corinth in the first century. It was a time when the decadent Roman Empire was sliding into new levels of darkness, yet the church was either avoiding the battle by retreating into petty interpersonal conflicts, or merely imitating the culture around them. Doesn't that sound like the American church of the 21st century?

The Corinthians were more than willing to study and accept the simple truths of the faith, but they resisted the thought of dealing with the tougher issues of life. Paul admonished them that although the Corinthians had the basics of their belief right, they were not growing in the Word. They had become stunted and were stuck in a state of spiritual infancy. The Corinthians wanted the feel-good, easy-to-digest teachings, such as God's love and forgiveness and the joy of going to Heaven, but they refused to go any deeper.

There are over 80 million Americans in the pews of churches every Sunday. That's more than the entire attendance of every professional football, basketball, baseball, and hockey arena *combined—for an entire year!* Yet sadly, this massive number of weekly churchgoers is almost irrelevant to our culture. The American church—the richest church in the world—is making as little impact on our society as at any time ever before in history. How can that be?

There are many reasons, but the primary one is that we live on a spiritual diet of "milk" when we should have long ago advanced to the protein—the "meat" of God's Word.

> *For though by this time you ought to be teachers, you need someone to teach you again the basic elements of the oracles of God. You need milk, not solid food; for everyone who lives on milk, being still an infant, is unskilled in the word of righteousness. But solid food is for the mature, for those whose faculties have been trained by practice to distinguish good from evil* (Hebrews 5:12-14).

A SPIRITUAL HIGH-PROTEIN DIET

Just as Americans are overweight because of poor diets and lack of exercise, so a *spiritual obesity* has afflicted the American church.

I love food. Who doesn't? What a marvelous gift of God. He could have created us to take in nutrients for our body in a bland and purely functional way. But the Lord, in His wonder, gave us tastes, smells, textures, and colors of food to enjoy. But too many of us patronize some food groups more than we should. It's a battle for many people.

I confessed to my congregation the other day that as I was driving by a Krispy Crème donut shop I prayed, "Lord, I am not going to have a donut. Unless You open up a parking space for me." And sure enough, on the seventh time around the block, I found one!

There is nothing wrong with carbohydrates. In fact, they are a necessary part of healthy eating. The trouble is, they are incomplete. We also need protein (even though proteins are more difficult to digest). We crave sugars because they taste good and are easier for the body to use, but the downside is that sugars metabolize into fat. When we eat only tasty, sweet foods, we create a lifestyle that greatly stresses the body, rather than strengthening it.

Unfortunately in the Body of Christ, we've created an entire religious industry of *spiritual cotton candy*. Yet Jesus called us to be the "salt" of the world, not the "sugar" of it (see Matthew 5:13). A snack here and there is fine, but to have sweet carbohydrates as our main source of sustenance stunts proper growth. Other downsides of an all-sugar diet are that we actually get hungrier faster after eating sugars and our bodies don't get the necessary nutrition for growth, disease resistance, healing, and strength.

The same thing occurs spiritually. The American church goes from sweet fad to fad, from the latest "Eight Easy Answers" to the next. Yet there is a deep hunger and spiritual void in the belly of most American Christians. So why do we have such a sweet "Get Rich and Prosper with Jesus" industry in Christianity today? Because life is so tough and we're all looking for a little joy in the storm.

One of the common responses many people have to the stresses and frustrations of life is to sit down with some "comfort" food and eat their troubles away. A sweet dessert or a bag of chips can bring a moment of satisfaction in a day filled with disappointments. Similarly, after a week of trying to survive and get ahead in this fast-paced world, the last thing we want is to sit down and study a Bible that seems filled with controversy. We'd rather curl up with a book on simple and easy nuggets to apply from God's Word. Don't misunderstand me, there's nothing wrong with that *at times*. In fact, it's necessary occasionally, in order to keep our spiritual energy up. But if candy is our main diet, then as the apostle Paul admonished the Corinthians, we're dooming ourselves to live lives of spiritual infants.

The church growth movement of the last 25 years has done many marvelous things for God's Kingdom. The primary benefit has been that the Gospel message is much more accessible to the average American. However, any strength carried to an extreme can become a weakness. The weakness is that many churches have tailored their message to the "seeker," the curious looky-loos who want a tasty handout that doesn't require more than a quick nibble before they run about their day, feeling, "Golly! I'm OK, you're OK!" This approach has unwittingly created mega-churches driven by "motivational speaker" types who appeal to the easy, no-effort-required road that avoids the truly difficult issues of life. There is a good reason why the American church is seen as irrelevant in the culture at large: we have tailored our message to the "least committed" when the times we are experiencing require the most committed to navigate through with intelligence and wisdom. We tend to keep our spiritual diet to the "Lite" things, we focus almost exclusively on *Find Happiness Now!* or *Success Made Easy!* or *Find Your Mate Today!*, rather than addressing tough or controversial matters that more deeply challenge one's spiritual growth.

Sadly, "church" in America has become more sweets and less meats.

> *For the time is coming when people will not put up with sound doctrine, but having itching ears, they will accumulate for themselves teachers to suit their own desires, and will turn away from listening to the truth and wander away to myths* (2 Timothy 4:3-4).

SPIRITUAL MEAT

Two thousand years ago, the apostle Paul recognized the lack of spiritual growth within the early church, and he implored the Corinthians to move beyond the elementary things to deeper spiritual lives. When you take a look at the list of what Paul thinks are elementary teachings, it's not hard to imagine how shocked he would have been at the level of commitment of the average American Christian. The writer of the Book of Hebrews admonished the readers to leave the elementary teachings about Christ and go on to maturity (see Hebrews 6:1).

So exactly how do you move on to spiritual maturity? How do you know, for example, exactly what God wants you to do in a particular situation? When there are many good options, which one should you pick? When all options are gone and every door slams shut, what should you do? What is the best way to ensure the most joy and love in your daily life? When your head and heart are in conflict, which one should you follow? How do we know which way the Lord is leading in certain relationships? How do we learn to tell the difference between the Lord's Voice and the voice of temptation?

This book is for spiritual meat-eaters and those who want to become one. It is the Christian's guide to spiritual intelligence in dealing with some of the toughest questions asked of me during the quarter of a century I have been leading churches. These are the difficult issues over which Christians are allowed to disagree—as long as the discussion is done with love, with respect, with the goal of glorifying God, and above all, using the Word of God as the final arbiter and last "Court of Appeals" in revealing His intention in how to deal wisely with life's toughest issues.

> *We must no longer be children, tossed to and fro and blown about by every wind of doctrine, by people's trickery, by their craftiness in deceitful scheming. But speaking the truth in love, we must grow up in every way into Him who is the head, into Christ...* (Ephesians 4:14-15).

CHAPTER 2

A Little Background

A RINGSIDE SEAT

I am a very privileged person. As a pastor I am allowed a rare glimpse into the inner lives of all sorts of men and women. Every Sunday for more than 25 years I have stood behind a pulpit and looked out over a sea of faces. Faces that on the outside look as if they have been smiled upon by fortune. But I know that just beneath the surface of those calm waters, storms are raging.

People give pastors entrée into their most closely guarded secrets. From these sacred times of sharing I have been struck with one haunting mystery: everybody gets knocked down, but the difference between the victor and the victim is *who gets back up!*

What forces conspire to help create a victor or a victim? Is it a question of inner strength? Is it environment? Are some people naturally tougher than others? Are life's survivors born with an internal wiring that enables them to handle the stress of life better than others?

I don't believe any of those are the answer. I think it's a matter of *intelligence.* After journeying with thousands of people and leading several large churches in America, I have noticed a pattern—some people are simply smarter in knowing *how to live life.* They are extremely intelligent men and women—but they possess a different kind of intelligence—a *spiritual* intelligence.

BEYOND IQ

The concept of IQ has become a large and controversial industry. We live in a culture that almost worships mental intelligence. Americans are fascinated with the subject. Our society has created mountains of information about mental intelligence. It's a hot topic in academic, political and business circles.

Decades ago an Intelligence Quotient (IQ) test was developed to determine a person's mental capabilities. Whether it's the grades we receive in our classes, or the results of standardized tests for college (such as the SATs or ACTs), trying to determine someone's IQ is a big business. But exactly what is "intelligence"?

One of the most successful formats of entertainment has always been the "who knows the most" contests. Whether it's Jeopardy, or Trivial Pursuit, or The Price is Right, testing peoples' knowledge of facts and trivia has always been entertaining. But is that intelligence? Being smart is a lot more than the usual stereotype of "intelligence." Being intelligent is even more than knowing how to solve complicated problems intellectually. True intelligence is a matter of the heart and head working in unison.

EVEN BEYOND EQ

Daniel Goleman's landmark book, *Emotional Intelligence*, has given wonderful insight into a second facet of intelligence, the emotional quotient. Through recent medical science discoveries, Goleman tried to answer the age-old problem of why we do the things we do. *Emotional Intelligence* revealed a complex relationship between the part of our brain that allows us to think, and the part that allows us to feel. His studies showed that the reason the smartest people often do the dumbest things is the result of the way certain chemical processes work in our brain.

Recent technological breakthroughs in advanced CAT scans and MRIs reveal that we are wired in a way no one expected. We actually have *two* "brains" residing in our skulls—we have a "thinking brain" and a "feeling brain" —which God has connected in a stunningly complex system. Technology is allowing us to actually observe the physical workings of this phenomenal creation of God called the brain. In many instances, science reveals, the complex physiology of

36

the human brain actually takes over against our will, and the "feeling" area of the brain often reacts *before* the "thinking" part of the brain receives the message. This is more than mere reflexes. It is *thinking*, but it's driven primarily by sensing or *feeling* thoughts, rather than by a calmer logic that first thinks things through.

The reason so many apparently smart people sometimes do such dumb things is the result of a chemical process in the brain that causes us to become "emotionally hijacked." Our feeling brain center can be a loose stallion running through our mind, taking our thinking brain for a wild ride. When something stressful occurs, the emotion part of the brain gets neurologically tripped. When these neurological switches are activated, the *feeling* center of the brain literally takes over the *logic* center. Once we *feel* something, it is quite a challenge to change direction (not to mention our opinion of the direction). Obviously it is possible to have our thinking overrule our feelings, but it is tremendously difficult. A great part of emotional intelligence pertains to our learning how to balance our two "minds"—the pragmatic, thinking brain and the emotional, feeling brain.

As great as these discoveries are, however, being emotionally balanced and healthy is not enough on its own to get us successfully through the journey of life. It is not enough to have just our head and heart working together; we need something more. Other factors come into play, requiring different sources of input and alternate methods of mitigating and solving life's challenges and conundrums. We need to develop the kind of knowledge, the kind of spiritual intelligence—an SQ—that is always ready to engage new realities and challenges. Merely attempting to memorize the latest volumes of facts and data—even with a positive "can do" attitude—will not suffice. We need to develop a mind and heart that can stand on the deck, stand up to the waves of life, see through the fog of today's voices, and chart the best course possible.

SQ

I've discovered time and time again that the people who successfully tackle the big issues of life are not always the ones blessed with great mental aptitude. They are not clever little Einsteins with super brains. Instead, these achievers possess something that is superior to sheer intellect. In fact, history is filled with women and men who were intellectually brilliant, but whose lives were a series of tragic missteps (proving that intellect alone, no matter how keen, does not guarantee a successful life). If you want to conduct an alarming study, look into the personal and family lives of history's geniuses.

Take Mozart, for example. He was an intellectual and artistic genius. Yet, the so-called "musical wonder of Europe" chose self-destructive paths that reduced his personal life to a melodramatic, emotional wreck of disastrous proportions. He made decisions on the basis of trying to please an impossible father, he suffered a stream of romantic failures, and he spent much more money than he made. Still, Mozart's musical accomplishments have astounded critics throughout the centuries. And yet, for all the outward happiness of this epic composer, "Mr. Sunshine" was actually a prisoner of appallingly bad choices.

Most of us have probably known such intellectual giants, who lurch through life from crisis to crisis, rarely encountering long stretches of tranquility along the way.

Getting ahead in life is about being smart. It always has been and it always will be. Life rewards intelligent people. The truly intelligent will be at the front of the pack every time.

I am not using the term "intelligent" in the common sense of the word. The intelligence I am referring to is something much deeper and more powerful than any written test can reveal. It is an intelligence that is different from all other kinds. The irony is that spiritual intelligence is available to *everyone*—yet only a handful of people ever take advantage of it!

KNOWING WHAT TO DO AND WHEN TO DO IT

It has been said that sometimes confidence is the feeling you have before you know what's really going on. We can be emotionally content while at the moment be making a wreck of things. Many people feel they have their emotional boat in order, but are completely unaware that they are about to go over the falls. It is more than tragic to work so hard to get to the top of the ladder, only to discover that the ladder is against the wrong wall.

Behaving intelligently is perhaps more of a challenge and dilemma today than at any time in history. The increasing velocity and complexity of life in America is literally grinding us down. Before 1800, the average person read the equivalent of the Sunday edition of the *New York Times* once—*in their entire life!* The explosion of knowledge, technological advances, and information that we must have and maintain in order to navigate everyday life is mind-boggling.

Ironically, at the same time that there is this unstoppable growth in information, there is also a frightening "dumbing down" of society in other areas. One reaction to this brave new world is a withdrawal into the escapist behavior of our media-driven culture. Information overload is forcing us to unplug our mind at a time when we need it the most. Sadly, more and more people are living by the credo, *They think for us so we don't have to.*

Yet, today more than ever, we need to be intelligent in order to make positive and constructive decisions every day in our lives. Some decisions are small and seemingly insignificant, while others are large and can determine our entire destiny. It's all a matter of knowing what to do and when to do it.

So how do we learn to discern our way through the myriad of social, emotional, and cultural situations we encounter every day? Situations such as:

- ◆ "Should I unplug a loved one from life support?"
- ◆ "Can a Christian divorce or remarry?"
- ◆ "How far can a Christian express sexuality outside of marriage?"
- ◆ "Is it all right for me to see movies depicting violence or sexual scenes?"
- ◆ "What about alcohol and smoking?"
- ◆ "How should I vote as a Christian?"
- ◆ "Is it better to execute murderers for justice, or to forgive them and try to rehabilitate them?"
- ◆ "Is it wrong to use stem cells from fertilized human eggs in order to heal the sick?"
- ◆ "Are Christians ever allowed to initiate war against other people?"

Questions, questions, questions! Is it even possible for spiritually savvy Christians to have all of the right answers? The better question is—would God leave us without the answers to the toughest issues of life?

The good news is—*no!* God didn't leave us without the answers.

This book is about how to make *spiritually intelligent choices.* My primary purpose is not to tell you what you should do on any issue (though I will share my convictions on them), but to show you *how* to discern the answers and make wise decisions when faced with the tough questions, so you can live a productive life that glorifies God.

> *Be strong, be courageous, and keep the charge of the Lord your God, walking in His ways and keeping His statutes, His commandments, His ordinances, and His testimonies, as it is written in the law of Moses, so that you may prosper in all that you do and wherever you turn* (1 Kings 2:2-3).

CHAPTER 3

The Four Sentinels of Spiritual Intelligence

A SLAVE OF THE MOMENT

Henry grabbed the kitchen tablecloth as he was thrown violently to the ground in the throes of another grand mal seizure. He was being subjected to the horrid episodes several times a day. Dr. William Pennfield had discovered the cause several days earlier—there was a tumor in Henry's brain. If it wasn't removed soon, he would die. But it was the 1960s and brain surgery of that magnitude had not yet been attempted. Still, Henry and Dr. Pennfield made the decision to go ahead and risk an operation.

Dr. Pennfield and his team managed to successfully remove the tumor. Henry never had another seizure. However, the surgery required Dr. Pennfield to remove part of Henry's brain tissue, the full impact of which was not understood at that time. As a result, Henry lost most of his long-term memory. He no longer remembered his childhood, no longer recalled any details about Toronto (his hometown), none of his time in the military, nothing about his career. Even more recent memories seemed to be fading in and out of Henry's mind.

In fact, after the surgery, Henry didn't even recognize Dr. Pennfield. Each week when they met, for Henry it was as if they were total strangers. What was even crueler was that Henry did retain a few select memories. For example, he had a favorite uncle who had died the previous year. Every time Henry asked about him, he was gently informed again of his uncle's death. And each time, Henry would grieve over the loss all over again as if for the first time. His past, which normally would have helped make sense of the present as well as offer hope for the future, was no longer accessible to him.

"Henry is a slave of the moment," Dr. Pennfield said in describing Henry's nightmare world.

Henry is not alone. Like Henry, many people make decisions solely on the basis of what *feels right* in the moment. As a culture, we are creating individuals who have lost the ability to either connect with their past or to dream and prepare for their future. The simple process of *learning* is slowly dissipating from us. This affliction, unlike Henry's loss, is not due to a terrible trauma society has received as a result of surgery. Rather, it is the effect of a systematic removal of our ability to make wise decisions that are rooted in an immutable, reliable anchor. Thus, we too are increasingly becoming prisoners of the moment. We as a culture and as individuals have forgotten how to learn from the past.

THE SOLUTION

We don't have to be ruled by the here and now. Every one of us can become wise and learn to make spiritually intelligent choices. We can instill into our thought process and mindset a mechanism that will safeguard us from being enslaved to the passions of the present and the habits of the past. God has given us powerful sentinels to *guarantee* such intelligence.

Historically, a sentinel was someone assigned to the oversight of the welfare of someone else. Whether it was the sentinels who stood guard on the walls of a city to warn of approaching danger, or the watchmen given charge of overseeing the Israelites in the wilderness, their purpose was to protect, to guide, and even to encourage. Likewise, God has given us four wise and powerful "sentinels" of wisdom, to guide us in making every decision in life, to assist us, and to stand watch over our choices. This is nothing new. These sentinels have always been used by intelligent people.

For example, Augustine (in A.D. 400 in Africa) would tell us to "love God and do as you please," because if you love God, what you do will be pleasing to Him. Aquinas (in A.D. 1200 in Italy) would teach that when you are confused, seek the *summa bonum*, or highest good. Luther (in A.D. 1500 in Germany) would encourage us to "live by faith alone." Yet all of these great men used, in different ways, the same four "sentinels" in making decisions in their life. John Wesley (in A.D. 1800 in England) would later use his own four "quadrilateral" decision-making guides. After studying these three men who possessed great minds and hearts for God, I was surprised to learn they each had four basic "corners" within which they framed their decision-making process. No matter how they approached various issues, they all combined these four cornerstone of decision making—four sentinels of spiritual intelligence, which are:

1. Scripture.

2. Reason.

3. Wise Counsel.

4. Inner Voice of the Holy Spirit.

The architecture of spiritual intelligence will always use these four pillars. Build your life on these cornerstones and you will become spiritually intelligent.

Practical, real-life wisdom knows *what* to do and *when* to do it. If we are going to make the right decisions, then we need to put all four sentinels into play simultaneously. They stand ready to counsel anyone who truly desires their guidance. Just like global positioning satellite (GPS) navigators in automobiles today, when we get off track, these four sentinels of spiritual intelligence kick in to "recalculate" our course and direct us back onto the right road.

The four sentinels of spiritual intelligence have been used instinctively by many men and women throughout the ages in making proper decisions and healthy choices. They stand as four shepherds, ready to guide us in this wild adventure called life.

At the busiest corner she [wisdom] *cries out; at the entrance of the city gates she speaks: "How long, O simple ones, will you love being simple? How long will scoffers delight in their scoffing and fools hate knowledge? ...those who*

43

listen to me will be secure and will live at ease, without dread of disaster" (Proverbs 1:21-22,33).

In the beautiful imagery of the passages above, wisdom stands as a sentinel, crying out to help anyone who will listen and heed.

Wisdom does not force herself upon any of us. Her gifts are available only to those who want them enough to work for their reward. These four sentinels, Scripture, Reason, Wise Counsel, and the Inner Voice of the Holy Spirit, create the Supreme Court of personal wisdom. They are not some kind of switchmen who automatically throw a lever on the track of your life when a potential wreck looms ahead of you. They are God's guides. They call to you, counsel you, encourage you, warn you. All the while, leaving the choice to act to your own will.

Let's take a closer look at each of these four sentinels of spiritual intelligence.

CHAPTER 4

The First Sentinel—Scripture

Indeed, the word of God is living and active, sharper than any two-edged sword, piercing until it divides soul from spirit, joints from marrow; it is able to judge the thoughts and intentions of the heart (Hebrews 4:12).

King David had not eaten or slept for days. The great king's child lay dying. The prophet Nathan had confronted David over his terrible sin of adultery with Bathsheba and his subsequent murder of her husband Uriah, a top commander in King David's army and one of his mighty 30 warriors (see 2 Samuel 12:9; 23:39).

The sordid affair was reaping terrible consequences. David was well aware that his sin had wronged at least two lives; now this precious, innocent little boy lay at death's door. David wanted his child to live and had been in unapproachable agony with the baby sick. David cried out to the Lord with all his heart for days. He could do nothing to change the past. All he could do now was await God's response.

In the early hours, David's closest counselors heard the news…the child had died. How gut-wrenching the king's response would be!

David heard the somber whispering of his counselors outside his door. "Is the child dead?" he called out.

45

"Yes, my lord," they responded timidly. "The child is now gone."

What David did next has been discussed for the last 3,000 years. He changed his clothes, went to the kitchen, got something to eat, and (to loosely paraphrase him) said, "Well, we have a busy day ahead of us, men. Let's get going."

His royal guards and counsel must have stood in stunned disbelief. *Let's get going?* What happened to all the mourning and wailing and tears? What a bizarre reaction to the most feared outcome David had been praying against! Didn't this guy feel anything? Was David just suppressing his feelings? Was he a "Mr. Ice in the Veins" who felt nothing?

Hardly. Nobody in all of history was more emotionally open with his feelings than was King David of Israel. In fact, read David's psalms if you want to experience the heights and depths of joy and despair to which a person can travel.

With some of the greatest spiritual intelligence in history, the king explained, "My prayers were that God would heal the child. I prayed and interceded as intensely as humanly possible. But God chose to take the child to Himself, as He had said through Nathan. Nothing in the entire world is going to change the situation. The Lord has spoken. I will see my boy someday" (see 2 Samuel 12:15-23).

We have a Book that speaks to us through the Spirit of God. King David was also guided by God's Word as given to him through the prophets Samuel and Nathan. Today we have God's written Word, in Scripture, which is the first sentinel of spiritual intelligence. God's Word took David by the hand and firmly pulled him to higher ground. He analyzed the situation, embraced the feelings he had, and responded with wisdom. Rather than be a captive to seeing the world only through the eyes of personal loss, he integrated the higher truth of God's Word.

Self-loathing, self-pity, or even holding a grudge against God would not bring the child back. David had a life to live and a mission to accomplish. Allowing himself to push on past the event was not only permissible, it was the only reasonable thing to do, according to God's Word. God had spoken, and David was believing it and pushing forward.

WHAT DOES GOD SAY?

A question we must train ourselves to ask when trying to seek the correct response to any problem or issue is, "What does God's Word say about this?"

In my 25 years as a senior pastor, one unchanging truth I have observed is the striking difference between people who actually use God's Word in life's decisions, and those who merely go on instinct—basically making "holy guesses" about "what the Lord would want."

God is not some far off deity who plays hide-and-seek with His creation. As King David said from personal experience in Psalm 23:1, "The Lord is my Shepherd." The Lord walks behind us to forgive us and to redeem our past. He walks in front of us with dreams, plans, and a path already prepared. And He walks beside us to comfort, strengthen, and guide us.

As Christians, we do not worship a book; we worship the risen Christ. Yet the trustworthy witness to this Living Word of Christ is the Written Word of the Bible.

No other book in the world is as unique as the Bible. It is not a book that suddenly one day fell to us from Heaven. It is a library of God's plan and a picture of His heart. Written by more than 40 authors over a span of 1,500 years, it is an infallible testimony of God's hand moving throughout history. It is a historical record of real people who were witnesses to actual events. Inspired by God, these people told exactly what happened and what was spoken in events that amount to the story of God invading history through His people Israel, and culminating in the Person and work of Jesus Christ. In the Bible, no one writer felt any compulsion to agree with any other writer, except to say "Thus says the Lord." Yet the unity, the verifiable documented events, and the interconnection of the Bible is unique in all the world's religious books.

The Bible is our infallible Guide. When we use it along with the other three sentinels of spiritual intelligence to direct our life, it simply *cannot* lead us down the wrong path or incite us to do wrong.

USING SCRIPTURE TO MAKE DECISIONS

As the man left the gravesite of his beloved wife, he felt utterly broken over her death and nearly paralyzed with emptiness. She was the only thing that made the pressure of his monotonous job bearable. And now…she was gone. What would he do?

The year was 1038. The man was King Henry III of Germany, and the relentless pressures of leading the country were sucking the life out of him. Henry knew instantly what he would do. He had always loved the Lord and wanted to serve Him for the rest of his days. Now, with his wife gone, he would become a monk, and sing and write and serve the poor until he died.

So one day as autumn raked its vibrant colors through the German countryside, the king mounted his horse and rode to the monastery. Poor Richard, head of the order, bowed as Henry strode into the stone sanctuary and proclaimed, "I have come to take the vows of a monk and to spend the rest of my days serving my Lord Jesus the Christ."

Richard knew Henry's heart was sincere. Over the years he had often observed the king's response to his great love for Christ. But he was in a quandary. Accepting the king of Germany into the order would deprive the nation of her monarch. "Do you know, lord king," Richard asked Henry, "that to join this monastery and become a postulant of our holy order requires that you accept and adhere to all of the vows—including vows of absolute obedience, which require that you do whatever I instruct?"

King Henry replied, "Yes, I do. I accept that, and I am prepared to give my complete obedience."

The two men then prayed together and shared a simple meal of bread, soup, and some wine. That night, Poor Richard paced the monastery, unsure as to what he should do with this newest member of the order. What do you assign the king of all Germany as his first duty? Richard earnestly sought the Lord and opened the Scriptures…and a particular passage seemed to jump off the page at him. Poor Richard had his answer.

The next morning, Richard asked Henry if he was prepared to receive his first orders.

"I am more ready than I have been my entire life," the king proclaimed and knelt in submission to whatever the Lord was about to ask of him through Poor Richard.

"Then here is my command," Richard responded. "Go. Return to your throne. You are ordered to serve the risen Christ with all your heart in that place of need. You are no more merely Henry the Third. You are now a servant of Christ Jesus and a member of this order. Serve Christ in all you do where God Almighty has placed you. Serve the Lord as your King, in the same way that you would serve Him here in caring for the poor."

King Henry went back to the throne, and soon met a wonderful woman named Agnes, whom he married in 1043. In 1046 he became Emperor of the entire Holy Roman Empire. By the time of his death in 1053, he had appointed four popes and had dramatically transformed much of Europe for the good. Engraved over his tomb are the simple words, *He learned to rule by obedience to God.*

We alone determine whether we want a large spiritual capacity by which God can guide us throughout our life, or a limited capacity. Allow the Spirit to pour a lot of Biblical language into your life, and He can speak into different areas of your life all the more. However, give the Spirit only a few limited verses, and He can only lead you so far.

APPLYING GOD'S WORD

As we will see in the chapters ahead, there are times when God's written Word is very clear in helping us make specific decisions. God's love for us, His call to mercy and justice, His desire for our sexual purity, for humbleness and for caring for the poor, are just a few issues where God's Word is abundantly clear in displaying His will for our Christian walk.

There are times, however, when the Scriptures don't seem to address a specific problem or situation at all. There was no specific passage precisely instructing Poor Richard to tell King Henry III to return to the throne, so how did he know it was the Lord telling him to do so? The answer is simple: Through spiritual intelligence and the gift of Scripture.

There are three guidelines to help us understand the Scriptures in our decision-making processes:

1. **Knowing what God said and why He said it.**

    The more we know what God *has said*, the more we can know what He *is saying*. The first rule when we come to a particular passage is to ascertain what it meant to the *first hearers*. All verses have context in that they had specific reference and meaning when they were first written. The first hearers didn't hear the message from whomever was speaking and say, "What in the world was *that* all about?" They knew what it was referring to. They may not have understood everything right then and there, but they had a pretty good idea what it was dealing with.

    The more you and I ask, "What did it mean when it was first spoken?" the more we can know what God is saying to us today. Knowing about the times, the setting, the culture, and even the language of the first hearers of God's Word gives us more ability in applying the same truths to us today.

2. **Interpretation and application.**

    While there is only one accurate *interpretation* of a passage, there can be many *applications* of the same passage. A particular verse, in its original setting and time, can be accurately interpreted only one way. However, the Holy Spirit may apply the interpretation in different ways for different situations. That's why it's important that we don't skip over tough passages, but that we attempt to interpret them in light of the whole counsel of God. This is because the Lord will often reveal something new to us by a verse we've read a hundred times before.

    The written Word is alive and active because of the fact that the living Word (the risen Christ) is alive to apply it to us.

3. **Open your heart.**

    We get out of the Bible what we bring to it. One of the greatest gifts the Holy Spirit gives in rightly discerning the Scriptures is that of *removing pride*. Very often our problem is not that the Bible may appear to contradict *it-self*, but that it contradicts *us*—what *we* want it to say to support what we want to do. Asking the Lord to give us an open heart is the wisest way to eliminate pride when reading His Word.

The Bible is not a spiritual fortune-telling magic book. It often takes the hard work of study to release the Bible's wisdom. Lots of people have smatterings of the Bible in them here and there, but are unwilling to really open up the Bible and *study* it—to let it teach them.

A pastor friend of mine was sitting on a plane one day preparing his sermon for the coming Sunday. The person next to him was observing his hard work. The man inquired, "You seem to be working hard. What is it?"

"It's for my sermon this Sunday," the pastor replied.

"Oh," the man said. "Organized religion. I believe in the Golden Rule. I don't need the rest. That's religion to me."

"What do you do?" the pastor asked him.

"I'm an astronomer over at the university," the man answered.

"Oh," the pastor replied. "Organized science. I don't believe in all that. Twinkle twinkle little star. That's astronomy to me."

The Bible was written for people with a brain. It enables us to study and to search out wisdom that applies to us today. It can be a tough Book to apply at times, too. For instance, what in the world do all the bizarre rules and regulations of the Book of Leviticus have to do with us today? After all, weren't they written to a bunch of former slaves in the desert 3,500 years ago? How do we understand what the sentinel of Scripture is trying to tell us in reference to them today? In other words, how do we *read* the Bible? The answer rests in learning to pull out the eternal truths that apply to us today from the times, settings, and cultures during which the different books of the Bible were written.

The more we let the sentinel of Scripture lead us, the more blessed our lives will be. In the example of King Henry III, an entire continent was transformed by a simple passage of Scripture leading the right person—who was prepared to listen and to heed—in the right time.

The Scriptures are literally the primary language of the Holy Spirit. The more we know of God's *written* Word, the more we can be led by His *living* Word, Jesus Christ.

The Scriptures in themselves are intrinsically connected to the second sentinel of spiritual intelligence, which is Reason.

CHAPTER 5

The Second Sentinel—Reason

"Come now, and let us reason together," says the Lord... (Isaiah 1:18 NKJV).

I once heard that when Lawrence of Arabia took some of his Bedouin warriors to a hotel for the first time, they stood in awe of one thing in particular: *water*, as it flowed out of the wall through a shiny, metal faucet. When they left to return to their home after traveling the desert, Lawrence discovered that some of them had hidden the faucets from the walls in their bags. The Bedouins reasoned that they could have water whenever they wanted by merely turning the faucets they had stolen!

The flaw in their thinking was that they did not understand that removing the faucet from the pipes also removed them from access to the water.

Likewise, many people have removed wise decision-making from their fixtures of sound thinking and have created barren deserts in their life instead of colorful gardens. Learning to use the gift of *reason* is the second step in gaining spiritual intelligence. No matter how much Bible someone knows, a person will never develop spiritual intelligence if they refuse to listen to the call of reason.

The first question many of us ask when we find ourselves at a crossroads in life is something like, "What should I do?" Instead we should be asking, "Is my thinking process reasonable as I decide what I should do?" Can I "hear" what I'm thinking and feeling?

As a pastor, I often deal with people who make the most unreasonable decision, only to later become angry or depressed at the outcome of their own decision.

God is not a God of chaos. He has given order to His universe. He has set patterns and laws that never change. He has also given us perhaps the greatest marvel of all—the mind, with which, when trained properly, we can successfully navigate this world and arrive at fairly predictable outcomes.

When confronted with a problem in this beautiful (and often precarious) journey of life, the mind's ability to analyze a situation, figure out a solution, and make a choice for our long-term welfare is incredible.

REASON VS. DESIRE

Two centuries ago the great scientist-philosopher Pascal observed how desire too often runs our lives right at the moment when we think we're being rational. He said, "Reason is the blind, lame man who rode upon the shoulders of the dumb brute called desire." In other words, we may perceive that we are being logical and clear-thinking in our decisions, when in reality it is the "brute" of desire taking us along for a ride. Pascal observed that people make up justifications for the hungers we try to please.

I recently experienced a situation where my feeling brain overruled my thinking brain. My college-age children convinced me to ride on one of the scariest thrill rides in America, at a recreational theme park called Six Flags Magic Mountain. At this park there is a scream ride called Extreme. It takes you up 18 stories lying on your back, rolls you over face down, and then pushes you in a freefall for several seconds with the ground screaming up at you. Then this metal horror starts turning you every-which-way-but-loose on an inverted roller coaster. For this we *paid money!*

What fascinated me was that I intellectually knew there was no way I was going to fall out of the metal harness, which had collars and restraints that could secure a Mack truck. Besides, as I stood in line, I watched scores of people safely ride the contraption (though none were my age, I might add!). Nevertheless, when I was strapped in, lying on my back, riding slowly to the top of what I increasingly felt was my impending doom, I became convinced that I was about to pass out. My heart was racing, my hands were sweating, my face was contorted. My wife, who was riding next to me, was beyond amused at my fearful dilemma. I tried to convince myself during the eternity of three minutes I rode that infernal ride that I was *not*, by God, going to meet Jesus on *that* particular afternoon!

Why couldn't I calm myself down? What was going on in my mind? Medical science today would ask, "Which mind?" The sentinel of Reason uses both the "thinking brain" of the cortex and the "feeling brain" of the lower brain centers. This is why it is imperative that we listen in on the mental words and self-talk we use to analyze situations. It is easy to believe that we are being completely rational about someone or something, only to later reflect that it was emotional reasoning all along. Emotions tend to fool us with reasoning that goes something like this: "I feel something therefore it must be true." Pascal's "dumb brute called desire" can lead us into making decisions that at the moment seem totally rational, yet we later scratch our head and say, "What on earth was I thinking?" The answer is that too many of us think with our emotional center, rather than the logic center. How often have we done something to only later realize we were trying to get back at someone or to "prove" ourselves, but in the moment we *thought* we were being motivated by noble desires?

Now it is possible—and vital—that we train ourselves to switch our emotional brains over to *Slow Down*. The impulses and passions of life are good—passion and spontaneity can deepen our experiences—as long as they are guided by a measure of reason, which doesn't diminish our ability to feel *la dolce vita*—the sweet life!

Reasoning, or logic, is neither good nor bad in itself. But it does need a little emotional *spice*. Likewise, feelings and emotions are neither good nor bad in themselves—they are the spice that helps us experience the highs and lows of life.

Emotions were also given by God as a way to react quickly, for survival. God has wired us in a way we can react emotionally before our thinking brain has kicked in. That's called *reflexes*. They can be very fast, but are often fairly sloppy in that we react before we've thought the situation through. Both *reasoning* and *feeling* are gifts from God, to be used together to compliment each other within problem solving contexts.

However, the sentinel of Reason does have its limitations. The downside of reason is that it's useless without some kind of factual input. A person cannot be reasonable or logical if they lack reliable information to work with. Take away valid information and facts from reason and it becomes blind and helpless. That is why true spiritual intelligence uses not only our reasoning mind, but also Scriptures to guide and lead our thinking.

But even these two sentinels together are not sufficient to get us successfully through life. Even with Scripture and Reason we can still come up with some pretty bizarre and wild conclusions—even about the Bible. And that's why God gave a third sentinel: Wise Friends.

CHAPTER 6

The Third Sentinel—Wise Friends

Sometimes there is a fine line between faith and foolishness. Letting Tim talk me into learning how to technical rock climb up Boulder Canyon was the latter. But how could I go wrong with a guide like Tim? He was a remarkable athlete. He had won All-Conference in football and was on the varsity team in other sports. Not only that, but Tim was brilliant. Phi Beta Kappa and a member of five honor societies. He had graduated from seminary with his doctorate in family counseling and never received a grade below an "A" in any class.

When Tim gracefully and powerfully moved his muscular frame across the rocks, flashing his impish smile and laughing all the while, you knew you were with someone whom life could not scratch. I could trust this guy. Besides, he was my younger brother and there was no way I was going to let him show me up!

Within an hour I was frozen in sheer terror, clinging to a rock hundreds of feet above a torrential river. I had been following Tim's lead as we climbed the face. I saw no way forward. There was no way I could go back down. I still vividly remember Tim fluidly proceeding back down to my position, smiling, making a joke to ease my fear, and pointing out a route that even I could climb. Brilliant!

It was one of those precious memories I will cherish forever. The smell of the pine trees, the roar of the river below, the bright sun as it turned our faces cherry red. We had climbed our mountain together as if we had just won the Olympics. We laughed and shouted out a *WHOOP* from the thrill of our success.

When Tim was 36, as I stood over his casket I was racked with grief at the sight of his silent, marbleized face. His strong, handsome features were fixed forever. His mouth, once so quick to erupt in contagious laughter, and his eyes, once so inquisitive as they soaked in the world, were now tightly shut. Loneliness enveloped me like a musky fog. I felt compelled to touch his hands as they lay draped across his chest. They were cold and hard. How could this be? Tim was the pastor of a large church. He was a husband. A father. A brother and son. *Why*, I cried out to God, *is my brother gone in his prime?*

Death was no stranger to me. I had felt its cold breath on my neck many times before. I'd stood over the bodies of other precious loved ones. Some, like Tim, also gone in their prime. But Tim's death was an impossible one for me to get a grip on. What was so different about his passing was that he had taken his own life.

I tried and tried to make sense of my younger brother's suicide. Tim was an overcomer who had experienced trials and had climbed back from them all...nearly all. The oldest of his three children was severely retarded. By the time of his death he had survived numerous surgeries, raised a severely retarded child, had his leg amputated from a train accident, and seemed to be moving his life victoriously forward. He experienced ministry success, enjoyed a great lifestyle, had good looks, intelligence, and a loving family.

He was "Fearless Tim" and he helped me climb a mountain one summer day in the Rocky Mountains a long time ago. But his own mountain proved to be more than he could summit. I miss him still.

It is not the purpose of this book to try and address the deeply complex and emotional issue of suicide, nor my own dear brother's wonderful life and tragic death. However, one thing that I am convinced aggravated and contributed to Tim being pulled under was this—he lacked close, wise friends. He had a loving family and a couple of high school friends who had walked with him through life's trials, but what he didn't have was enough of them.

The Bible all by itself is not always sufficient to deal with tough issues we are trying to sort through. There are countless brilliant people who have memorized the entire Bible and still make the worst choices for their own lives. There are times when we can have a clear and educated mind, coupled with the Bible in our hand, and still not know the proper thing to do. God knew we needed another guide. True spiritual intelligence calls out to the third sentinel of wisdom: wise friends.

INTIMATE FRIENDS WHO KNOW US WELL

A wise man will hear and increase learning, and a man of understanding will attain wise counsel (Proverbs 1:5 NKJV).

It is said that you can tell a person's character by the close friends they keep. And it's true. One of the key indicators that a person possesses spiritual intelligence is the quality of the people in their closest circle of friends. Biblical spirituality is a relational skill. In fact, our primary relationships can determine our entire future.

As a pastor and just another person in today's world, I know how lonely life can be. Everyone experiences loneliness. It's one of the many results of the Fall in the Garden of Eden. People naturally keep away from each other because of sin. We all know that if you let people too close, they will hurt you. Besides, many of us don't want to be around some people because they're so much work! But it is impossible to gain spiritual intelligence without having wise friends to share with.

Who do you think you will be in ten years? Not your job title or how much you will have accomplished, but who do you think you'll be as a *person*? Knowing just two specific things about you, I can give you a fairly accurate profile of your future. Tell me the books you are reading and planning to read, and tell me about the people you're going to spend significant time with. From that information I can paint a pretty clear picture of who you really are—and the person you will become in the next ten years.

Other than Jesus of Nazareth, King Solomon was the wisest person who ever lived. He was smart enough to know he needed other people. And not just anybody; he needed close friends, "counselors," as he put it in Proverbs 11:14 and 24:6.

Close friends will possess three very important qualities:

1. They will know who you are.

59

2. They will want the best for you.

3. They will be wise.

The Latin word *intimus* (the root of the word *intimate*) means the "inner room." It is a beautiful word that describes the inner closet found in each of our lives. This inner room is where we keep our most precious and vulnerable treasures. Our dreams, our fears, our fantasies, our memories, and the deepest longings of our heart are all safely hidden there. If we have no one in our life close enough to us that we feel safe to share these things with them, then life is little more than a complex facade of closeness.

It may seem that life is easier to live by keeping people at a "safe" distance, but in reality that can be a danger to us.

I once read the story of a princess of China's Ming Dynasty. This princess was deeply beloved by all of her subjects. It had long been a law at that time, under penalty of death, that the people were never to come near or touch the princess. This law probably came about as a measure of security to ensure her physical safety, as well as keeping her on a "higher plane" as a royal.

One day as she was boating in one of the beautiful canals of the city, this protective law cost the princess her life. It was warm and sunny, and all the people had gathered on the banks to see and greet their beloved princess. She stood up to wave, and to their horror she tumbled into the water! She could not swim, and those around knew the royal "do not approach or touch" law so no one reached out to help her, and she drowned right there in front of the entire horrified and helpless throng. All because of a misguided royal law enacted for her protection but which ultimately, and sadly, served her demise.

There are many intellectually smart people who are drowning in their own lives from failure to let others touch them. By letting no one close to us because we think people may harm us, we may actually be dooming ourselves to lives of loneliness and limited productivity for God.

TRUE FRIENDSHIP

The more you develop close, honest, caring friends, the greater your spiritual intelligence will become. Notice I said "develop." Healthy friendships no more just *happen* than healthy physical bodies just happen. It takes work. But, oh, how it's worth the effort!

The process of friendship is a journey of *shared experiences*. All friendships require give and take—and abundant patience. There are things that you know about yourself that no one else on earth knows. And there are things about you that others know and see but which you have no clue about. However, one of the great joys of life is to "know and be known." It is life-affirming to have someone hold those precious dreams, failures and memories with you and to know that you are not judged. What a sweet experience when someone returns the compliment and opens their heart to you. These are the wise friends who hold us accountable, yet love us unconditionally.

When we're headed down the wrong path, a true friend will tell us. When we're discouraged and making decisions out of fear rather than through God's urging, a true friend will come alongside us. When our faith is weak, a wise friend will let us lean on theirs. In short, you will know a real friend by their *fruit* (see Matthew 7:20).

A FRIEND IS ONE HEART THAT FILLS TWO LIVES—EVEN FROM THE PAST

In addition to our own wise friends, there are other people we will never meet in this life from whom we can also learn.

The saying, "A friend is one heart that fills two lives," is attributed to Plato. There is a kinship that bonds two people into one, almost like one soul filling two different bodies. The Moari tribes of New Zealand greet each other by the traditional "hongi," a touching of their noses twice. They believe when the life breath touches twice then you can be a friend.

What is fantastic is that we can "touch noses" with people who lived before us. The saying "friends from the past" means that we can experience bonding with like-minded men and women from other centuries. For example, Solomon, writer of most of the Proverbs, was much like you and me. In Proverbs 18:24 (NASB), he said, "There is a friend who sticks closer than a brother." Such a friend may have already left this world, but they have left their counsel and insight from which we can learn. Spiritual intelligence listens to and learns from "lives lived well," whether they journeyed in another time or in our own.

One of the great mysteries to me is how many Christians actually think that the Holy Spirit came 2,000 years ago at Pentecost but has been on some sort of an extended vacation ever since. These unfortunate people refuse to even try to find out what those in other times learned or thought or experienced. Incredibly, they think that anything connected with the past doesn't apply to today.

However, I have not met one spiritually intelligent person who has not learned the secret of listening to the past. Having a high SQ means that we have the wisdom to invite wise friends from history speak into our current lives. History speaks to us all the time. There is a continuing presence of the past among us today. Even from hundreds or thousands of years ago, people's words and actions still stand as wise "friends" and "counselors."

One clear cause of today's puzzling spiritual ignorance is a disconnect from the wisdom of the ages. If we will make the effort to seek out past sages, we will discover some astounding examples of wise men and women who kept close friends with others who had gone before them.

NOTHING IS REALLY NEW

Is there a thing of which it is said, "See, this is new"? It has already been, in the ages before us (Ecclesiastes 1:10).

If you want to be ignorant (the original word for which means "not to know") then walk through life deluding yourself into thinking that the issues of our culture have never been faced before. They have! Again and again. Maybe not the technology or the exact same settings, but the key questions of living life have been addressed again and again by brilliant friends who went before us.

When making a decision, an important question to ask yourself is, "What have other wise people in history thought about this?" Many other people have already wrestled through many of the hard choices, complicated decisions and other tough issues of life that you are dealing with today. You'd be surprised how similar their lives were to ours. There are oceans of knowledge, insight, and wisdom already available to us *if* we will take the time and make the effort to embrace them.

Spiritually intelligent people understand that they don't need to reinvent the wheel. You don't need to run yourself through many of life's mine fields over and over. We can learn through the experiences and earned wisdom of people who've already proven the answers to what you're struggling with.

One of life's delicious treats and great miracles is the power of time travel—through *reading*. Isn't it a marvelous mystery how opening a book and reading the words, the thoughts, the experiences of wise people throughout the ages is like having them in your own front room?

But remember, wise "friends" who are already in Heaven can answer our questions only to the extent that we do our homework in recalling their spoken words and the example they lived, and in searching out their written words. When we have to "chin ourselves up" by our own wrestling and searching out wisdom, the Spirit seems to teach us on a whole new level! Even Jesus Himself worked at growing in wisdom, as Luke tells us: "And Jesus increased in wisdom and stature…" (Luke 2:52 NKJV).

A person with a high SQ will always possess three things:

1. A knowledge and love for the Bible.
2. An intelligent faith from a sound thinking process.
3. A cadre of wise friends in their life to share with and listen to.

But there are times when neither the Scriptures, nor our understandings, nor even the wisest friends we know or who have ever lived can lead us. God has given a fourth and powerful voice into our lives, a fourth and final sentinel of spiritual intelligence: the Inner Voice of the Holy Spirit.

CHAPTER 7

The Fourth Sentinel—The Inner Voice of the Holy Spirit

As I stood over her hospital bed, my heart was breaking in two. This beautiful woman in her mid-forties was lying there on life support. I had been called in to pray with the family before they were to unhook her. I knew this painful drill; I'd been through it before. You go in, you say a prayer for God's peace, and you pray for the comfort of the Resurrection to sustain them in the days ahead.

A few days earlier, Susan had been playing golf with her beloved husband when she felt an excruciating pain in her forehead. She suffered a severe stroke and collapsed in a coma. In the coming days, the family was called in to say their final goodbyes. They were still waiting for one child to fly in from Arizona before they would then disconnect her life support equipment…and tell her goodbye.

Then something so strange took place that I hesitate to even share it. As I took the hands of the family around her bed, I sensed the Lord saying to me, "*I want you to pray for her healing—and pray for it **now**.*" Now, you need to know that I am a Presbyterian, and Presbyterians just don't do things like that! When a Presbyterian gets really excited we say something like, "…Indeed."

I do not believe that I have the gift of healing—though I absolutely do believe in healing. Just not necessarily through me. So I ignored the voice or thought or whatever it was in my head, and I continued to pray for everyone's comfort. And again I sensed the inner urging to pray audibly for her healing *right then!* I whispered to myself, "Lord, if that is You, You had better make it real clear to me, because I am about to embarrass myself, I am about to embarrass the family, and I don't want to embarrass You. So if You don't want this to take place, then get ready to shut my mouth, because I'm about to do this, Lord."

And I went ahead and prayed out loud, "I pray in the Name of Jesus the Risen Lord for Susan's healing. I ask by the power of the Holy Spirit that she be restored, healed, empowered, and that her body be renewed to wholeness and life. In the Matchless Name of Christ I pray, Amen."

I opened my eyes, and saw nothing but bewildered, gape-mouthed Presbyterian family members staring at me, and Susan laying there motionless while the machine breathed for her. I awkwardly hugged each of them as they stood speechless at my brazen display, and I kicked myself all the way out to my car.

As I drove, I tested different excuses in my mind as to the best way to explain to them why God had not healed their beloved Susan. Not to mention why I, their pastor, had prayed to the contrary. *Why did I give in to that nutty voice and make a sad situation worse?* I groaned to myself in the afternoon traffic.

The next morning I went to see the family. I knew I had a lot to explain. When I entered the room I almost fell over. There was Susan, *sitting up in the bed—brushing her hair!* She was supposed to be hooked up to life support and near death! I asked one of the doctors who was checking her vitals if I might have a word with him in the hall. We stepped out and I asked what happened.

He said he didn't know exactly, but conjectured, "Maybe she had another stroke or something, and it kind of reset the switches in her brain."

"Oh really," I responded, and then added—admittedly with a tiny hint of sarcasm, "That happens a lot, does it, Doc?"

"No," he said. "But we need to release her in the next few days so we can make room for others."

No problem!

I believe that what happened that afternoon at St. Joseph's Hospital in Denver was nothing less than the Holy Spirit speaking to me. It was that blessed "Inner Voice of the Holy Spirit," the sentinel of spiritual intelligence, the head of the "Supreme Court of Wisdom."

The problem is, we have so many "voices" speaking to us all the time. How do we tell God's Voice from all the others?

SPIRITUAL CALLER ID—WHO IS REALLY ON THE OTHER END?

I saw a T-shirt the other day on which was printed, "You're just jealous because the voices don't speak to you!" Outside of auditory hallucinations, the truth is there *are* voices that speak to us. The ultimate challenge in developing spiritual intelligence is in learning, as First John 4:1 (NASB) says, to "test the spirits to see whether they are from God." The reason this is so crucial is that no matter how flawless our reasoning, no matter how much Scripture we bathe our minds in, no matter how wise our friends are, the ultimate urging is the direct leading of the Holy Spirit. True, we should be using the other three sentinels constantly, but when we earnestly want God's will, then we need to tell the Lord, as the prophet Samuel did, "Speak, for Your servant is listening" (see 1 Samuel 3:10).

There are three ways to know that the voice we're hearing and listening to is really God's:

1. ***We recognize the voice by spending time with the person.***

   The more time we spend with the Lord, the more we learn to recognize His voice. Everyone can recognize a family member's voice, even in the middle of a crowded lobby. Mothers are astounding in how they can pick out their baby's cry from among those of a hundred screaming kids.

   The first way we learn to discern and recognize the "still, small voice" is by spending time in prayer alone with God. I know many people who say they have audibly heard the Voice of the Lord—and I believe them. I just never have personally heard Him *audibly*. For me, when the Lord speaks, it is almost *supralinguistic*—beyond mere words.

Thinking is done almost exclusively in language and words. Words cover our raw thoughts like clothes. It's nearly impossible to think of anything of substance without words (other than in images). Words are molds that shape and direct our thinking process. But when the Lord speaks, it's almost as if we struggle for our words to catch up with what He is impressing in us and perfectly communicating to us. In other words, in our spirit we have received a direct touch of what the Lord wants, and then we flesh it out with language. Only through time with Him can we learn to distinguish His Voice from among the din of mental noise and the clutter of the world around us.

2. *The other three sentinels of spiritual wisdom will harmonize with the inner leading of the Spirit.*

When all four sentinels are in agreement, we can have confidence that we are in God's place of direction. Many times, the four sentinels will not be exactly on the same "note," but they will be in harmony with one another. Scripture, Reason, Wise Friends, and the Inner Spirit may not be singing precisely the same note, but they will be humming the same tune, so to speak.

Just following the inner leading is powerful, but can also be powerfully misleading. One of the favorite ploys of a particular false religion is to ask the intended convert to "pray and see if the Spirit bears witness" to the thoughts and ideas being presented. Such an innocent-sounding request seems very open, verifiable, and led by God, doesn't it? The trouble comes when you tell the person, "Nope. Sorry. Didn't hear the Spirit of the Lord confirming your teaching there, buddy." These people generally react by assailing you with an onslaught of semantics and coercive mind games about your apparent "inability to hear the Spirit."

The first century church experienced a similar problem in Galatia. The apostle Paul learned that a teaching was going around that "real spirituality" was beyond Jesus. All you really need to do, these false teachers were telling people, is to obey the law and listen deep inside your heart.

Paul responded, "if we or an angel from heaven should proclaim to you a gospel contrary to what we proclaimed to you, let that one be accursed!" (Gal. 1:8). The spiritual intelligence of Paul would never let someone get away with saying "it must be true because the Lord told me." Yes, we must have the courage to listen internally for God's voice, but such leading *must* pass through the grid of reason, Scripture, and outside wise counsel.

Long ago, as Martin Luther stood trial before the church court, subjected to unyielding scrutiny and intense pressure to recant his thesis on how the church had gone way off the theological track, he cried out, "Here I stand by Scripture and reason. I can do nothing else!" Because we are so easily led astray and can even deceive ourselves, we need all of the checks and balances of Scripture, reason, wise counsel and the Holy Spirit, working in unison in order to keep our inner convictions accountable.

3. ***We know we've heard and responded to God's voice because, when we're in His will, He releases the fruit of the Spirit.***

God will release the fruit of peace when we're walking in the right direction. This doesn't mean we won't have questions. It means there will be a sense of calm that "passes all understanding."

Inner leading calls for some advance work. This type of leading requires that we spend time in the Scriptures, that we become keenly aware of our own needs and issues, and that we develop long-term, wise, and accountable friendships. Then we can begin to trust our listening skills, and our decisions will be verified by the peace and the fruit of the Holy Spirit.

Every one of us experiences times of confusion—which can only be clarified in the crucible of prayer. I have, on many occasions, been completely split on some decision I was faced with making. The more I wrote out the pros and cons, the more confusing the choices became! There were Scripture verses that seemed to indicate that I should push ahead, and others that seemed to indicate that I should stop and wait on the Lord. I spoke to my trusted counselors, and they too were undecided. I needed to make a decision, and soon. The final tipping point came from spending time on my knees. From that point on, the more I prayed and envisioned one direction over the other, the more I felt a sense of peace, and even joy.

FAITH IN HEARING

Once we learn to discern God's voice within, He gives us that internal assurance as a response to our faith that He is the One communicating to us.

How did the people of the Bible know when it was truly God speaking? The answer is *faith*. They may have encountered external walls or internal leadings, but either way, they had the faith to believe that what they had heard was from the Lord.

Faith is the ultimate trump card in every decision. When we release the power of faith into our choices, we delegate the outcome to the Lord. It is not like magic, and it's not like we're forcing God to do our bidding. In fact, faith is just the opposite. Faith is when we release the outcome to the Lord, knowing that His answers are always better than our requests. And if we are off base, the Lord will show us. He knows we are weak and that we are prone to being spiritually hard of hearing.

Faith means we are open to whatever He wants done, and knowing that He has heard us, we can then bank on His sovereign hand to accomplish everything accordingly.

PUTTING ALL THE PIECES TOGETHER

People who enjoy jigsaw puzzles know that the fastest way to complete the daunting task of connecting thousands of apparently meaningless shapes and colors into a sensible order is to first find and assemble the corners. Once the corners are together and connected, the interior contours guide the image as the picture gradually becomes visible. In the same way, unveiling the pattern of God's call on each of our lives—and His direction in various challenging issues we face—is best discovered when these four corners are first set into place:

1. Scripture: Verify what the Bible has to say about the issue at hand.

2. Reason: Make sure our thinking process uses both the thinking and the emotional dimensions of our mind and heart.

3. Wise Counsel: Invite input from our wise and trusted friends in making important decisions.

4. The Inner Voice of the Holy Spirit: Pray and invite the leading of the Spirit's voice within us.

The great adventure of the Christian life can be gloriously enriched when we increase and enhance our spiritual quotient—our SQ—by learning to listen to the fourfold voice of spiritual intelligence.

Too many Christians are surrendering to the forces of blind, short-sighted philosophies. Even though we are experiencing some of the most difficult days in all of world history, we can weather the challenges and live a blessed life *if* we will submit to the wisdom of God. Life can be a tremendous journey *if* we develop the spiritual intelligence to think and to choose wisely.

The great news is that God is raising up a new movement of spiritually intelligent followers of Christ, and you can be one of them! With the foundation of spiritual intelligence laid, let's examine some of life's toughest issues, and see how contemporary Christians should respond to them.

PART II

20 Tough Issues and How to Respond With Spiritual Intelligence

Introduction

This part of the book is for those of us who are wrestling with some of life's toughest issues—issues that sometimes even divide Christians. There are many helpful books out there with the "Three Easy Answers" to life's questions, or "Seven Simple Secrets" to spiritual success.

This book is *not* about quick solutions, and it's not about the easy-to-answer problems. It's about addressing the areas that many Christian leaders shy away from because they are so controversial. The reason they're controversial is because godly, Bible-believing, intelligent, and caring men and women are deeply divided over how to deal with them.

Now, the manner in which we deal with those differences is another issue altogether. There are some of us who, sadly, as in every church, have never been taught how to dialogue and discuss. So many in our culture today sit entrenched in the warring camps, warming themselves by the fires of their own chants and slogans. The media has taught us that you debate by lining up pundits and shouting at each other, winning points by having the loudest or most aggressive and mean-spirited speech.

But then there are those who are touched by God's grace and love, and who respond, in turn, with grace and love to others.

How we handle these issues is of vital importance. The eternal principles involved in decision-making and the skills necessary for working together are critical to building Christ's Church. We cannot ignore these issues and hope to be effective in furthering Christ's Kingdom. We must face these issues head-on and continue to grow as a body despite our differences.

Though tough issues will always involve areas of disagreement, we can live boldly and confidently if we implement the four sentinels of spiritual intelligence in our lives, which we discussed in Part I—Scripture, Reason, Wise Counsel, and the Inner Voice of the Holy Spirit.

As the apostle Paul told the church in conflict at Corinth, "Now these three abide, faith, hope, and love. But the greatest of these is love," (1 Cor. 13:13). We may disagree on matters of *faith*, and we might have differing opinions about what we *hope* Christ will do in our individual lives. But if we always agree that God's *love* for us, and our love for God is the basic clarion call of life, we will honor God in all our choices. And if we always strive to love others as ourselves, then we will make it through the storms that we encounter during our brief time here on earth.

THE ANCIENT MORAL COMPASS

The moral compass of Western culture has its roots in the teachings of the Bible. For example, in Luke 6:31 Christ summed up His ethic of love as doing to others as you would want them to do to you. This "Golden Rule" principle is generally valued in Western culture. Another example is the Ten Commandments, which Moses handed down to the Israelites at Mount Sinai. Anyone familiar with the Ten Commandments realizes that many of them permeate the laws of our land.

The first four Commandments in Exodus 20 represent the "vertical" instructions, the "dos and don'ts" with regard to our relationship with God:

1. No Other Gods (God is the center of life)

    You shall have no other gods before Me (Exodus 20:3).

2. No Idols (God cannot be controlled or replicated)

    You shall not make for yourself an idol, whether in the form of anything that is in heaven above, or that is on the

earth beneath, or that is in the water under the earth
(Exodus 20:4).

3. No Taking God's Name in Vain (God's reputation and
   covenants are to be honored)

   *You shall not make wrongful use of the name of the Lord
   your God, for the Lord will not acquit anyone who mis-
   uses His Name* (Exodus 20:7).

4. Honor the Sabbath (God is the God of our time and
   schedules, and we need rest)

   Remember the sabbath day, and keep it holy (Exodus
   20:8).

After God set the priority on our relationship with Him, He then
gave the remaining six Commandments, which are instructions on how
to handle our "horizontal" relationships—in other words, how we are to
deal with each other and how we are to live among other people, including family members, neighbors, friends, and even enemies.

God sums up these issues succinctly:

5. Honor Your Parents (The priority of family life for society)

   Honor your father and your mother (Exodus 20:12).

6. No Taking Life (You shall not harm your neighbor's
   physical life)

   You shall not murder (Exodus 20:13).

7. No Committing Adultery (You shall not harm your
   neighbor's relational life)

   You shall not commit adultery (Exodus 20:14).

8. No Stealing (You shall not harm your neighbor's economic life)

   You shall not steal (Exodus 20:15).

9. No Slandering or Lying (You shall not harm your neighbor's social life)

   You shall not bear false witness against your neighbor (Exodus 20:16).

10. No Coveting (You shall trust God in your life and in your neighbors' lives)

> *You shall not covet your neighbor's house; you shall not covet your neighbor's wife, or male or female slave, or ox, or donkey, or anything that belongs to your neighbor* (Exodus 20:17).

The Ten Commandments are actually ten responses to God's love. In Exodus 20:2, when God said, "I am the Lord your God, who brought you out of the land of Egypt, out of the house of slavery," He was saying, "I loved you before there was anything lovable about you. Therefore, here is how you are to respond to My act of deliverance and grace-filled love."

The Ten Commandments aren't intended to give us instructions for every single detail of life; God didn't hand us down an examination of life's minutia. Instead, they are more like primary colors on a palette, which we then use ourselves to paint on the canvas of our lives. They are like surgical tools that the Great Physician intends for us to use in the right ways—to treat, to heal, and to restore life as He ordained.

And they, like all Scripture, must be used and applied properly in solving life's tough issues.

SECTION A

*Life Intervention Issues—Do
No Harm, and Allow No Harm*

ISSUE ONE: **Mercy Killing**
ISSUE TWO: **Abortion**
ISSUE THREE: **Justified War**

Introduction

I could tell something terrible had happened the moment Annie came into my office.

Annie was one of those pleasant-looking, frail girls with a heart and smile that won you over in a heartbeat. She was also a severe diabetic who had never really been on a date in her 28 years. And then one day she met Mike at the hospital where they were both receiving dialysis treatments. They were thrilled when they found out they were both Christians…and soon, they fell in love.

I was privileged to perform their wedding less than a year before she entered my office on that fateful day. Mike had to keep his beeper on during the wedding because there was a chance he might have to leave, as he was on the list for a kidney transplant.

Life was going grand when Annie received news that she was pregnant. Normally such news would be reason to celebrate, but this devastated Annie. Her doctor had been very clear: if Annie were to become pregnant in her frail condition, she would not survive and if the baby lived, the child would suffer lifelong medical complications. Yet in spite of their precautions, Annie conceived. If she did not lose the pregnancy, she would lose her life.

"Pastor," she sobbed, tears streaming down her cheeks, "should I lose my baby? What does God want me to do?" She went on, frantically searching for calm through her gut-wrenching pain. "I've had some friends tell me that if there is one chance in a million that the baby might survive, then I have to trust God and take that chance. I've had other Christian friends tell me that to continue on and possibly die and leave Mike is not to trust God but to tempt Him. What should I do?"

What would *you* do? For me, it is a given that abortion is the taking of a life and that the use of abortion as mass birth avoidance is a profound sin. The tougher underlying issue is this: is the taking of life ever justified? If homicide is sometimes justified, then is there *ever* justified feticide? Should we never harm the unborn, even at the expense of the mother? Should children be created as a result of rape and incest? Should such babies be allowed to live, or is that transferring the consequences of the perpetrator onto the mother/victim?

Why do we hold funerals for stillborn infants and not for miscarried ones? Should we always allow birth, even with the severely handicapped? What about the use of stem cell research, and fertilized frozen embryos?

THE TWO DIMENSIONS OF LOVE

When the Pharisaic lawyer in Matthew 22 asked Jesus what the greatest Commandment was, Jesus answered, "'You shall love the Lord your God with all your heart, and with all your soul, and with all your mind.' This is the greatest and first commandment. And the second is like it: 'You shall love your neighbor as yourself'" (Matt.. 22:37-39). Thus, the great command of the Bible is love.

Historically, from this driving purpose of life, the Church established two dimensions of love:

1. Do no harm to others: "You shall not murder" (Exodus 20:13).

2. Allow no harm to come to others:

If you hold back from rescuing those taken away to death, those who go staggering to the slaughter; if you say, "Look, we did not know this"—does not He who weighs the heart perceive it? Does not He who keeps watch over your soul know it? And will He not repay all according to their deeds? (Proverbs 24:11-12).

Or as James sums it up, "to him who knows what is right to do, and fails to do it, to him it is sin" (James 4:17).

These two dimensions of love seem logical enough. However, if you think it through, there's a built-in dilemma. Why? Because it's a paradox. The first half of the ethic of love (do no harm to others) at times conflicts with the second half (allow no harm to come to others.)

For instance, is war ever justified? If the law of love is to allow no harm to come to others, how can we be pacifists who refuse to intervene in protecting other life? Yet if the law of love is also to do no harm to others, how can we engage in warfare when we know that innocents will be harmed and perish? What about capital punishment? Does taking the life of a criminal defend justice or merely feed personal retribution?

Life support is another tricky area. Is it ever justified to unhook someone, knowing that will bring about or hasten their death? Technology has forced choices upon us that the writers of Scripture could never have imagined! Is there a difference between mercy *killing* and mercy *dying*? How can we tell if we are actually prolonging a life, or merely prolonging the dying process?

The question of whether or not to intervene in someone else's life is tough indeed. Sometimes love means we dare not stick our noses into the lives of others; life is holy, and it is not ours to cavalierly mess around with. Yet there are other times when we dare not refuse to become involved, or else we have broken the "law of love" for God and for others.

And then there are those horrible times when protecting and helping one person means that we have to intervene, and in the process possibly harm another human being.

How is a Christian to reconcile these seemingly conflicting halves of the ethic of love? How can we do no harm and still allow no harm, when oftentimes abiding by one of these commands necessitates breaking the other? This is what makes life intervention issues so tough, particularly since different Christians reconcile these halves of the ethic of love in different ways.

THE CHRISTIAN "RELIGION"

"When you say that you are a Christian, what exactly do you mean?"

That wasn't an unusual question, but the setting was. I had been invited by the University of Judaism in Los Angeles to discuss with a leading Jewish Rabbi, a Muslim Imam, and a Buddhist Monk the basics of our respective religions. What followed was a delightful and intense evening of dialogue and questions from the audience.

Answering this question is something almost every believer has tried to do. What do we mean when we say we are followers of Christ? How are we to think? How are we to live? How does the world view us?

Francis of Assisi used the phrase "living the gospel," only he said it in Latin: *vita evangelica*. For Assisi, in the year A.D. 1220, it meant giving away earthly possessions, making peace, and caring for the poor.

What about us today? Living out the Gospel is much more than ideals we try to pursue. It's being "religious" in a Jesus way. Religion (which comes from the Latin word *religare* meaning "to bind") is the way we organize our lives. What are the driving values and beliefs in our lives that we bind ourselves to? What does it mean to "live the Christian Gospel" today?

For Christians of any era, "religion" means that we put our hope and faith in the person and work of Jesus Christ. We are bound to Christ and not just to a new set of rules. We believe the risen Christ is alive to empower us, to lead us, and to transform us.

Just how did Jesus sum up life? Like this: "You shall love the Lord your God with all your heart, all your strength, all your soul, and all your mind. And you shall love your neighbor as yourself" (see Luke 10:27; Mark 12:30-31). We are to live a life of love for God first, and then of love for others, and finally of love for ourselves. Ultimately, this is what determines how we will handle the tough issues of life intervention.

CHRISTIAN ETHIC OF LOVE

If you believe in Darwinism and the "survival of the fittest" theory, then when someone dies you say, "That's life. The toughest survive. That's the way it is. It's an impersonal universe. You're born, nobody knows why, and then you die. So just enjoy it while you're here."

If you're into Determinism, then you believe that God (or the "forces" behind the universe) made everything go the way it is and there is no fighting it or figuring it out. So just go with it.

If you follow Hinduism or Buddhism, then you believe that when someone dies, they are reincarnated to continue working through a thousand different lives. This is often as payment for sin in a past life. In other words, your sin will find you out in some future life.

If you follow Islam, then you believe that no matter what happens, ultimately it is the will of Allah.

But what about a follower of Jesus? First, Christians are called to know that life is sacred in itself.

In Genesis 9:1–7, Noah and his family came off of the ark, and God initiated a new covenant:

> *God blessed Noah and his sons, and said to them, "Be fruitful and multiply, and fill the earth. The fear and dread of you shall rest on every animal of the earth, and on every bird of the air, on everything that creeps on the ground, and on all the fish of the sea; into your hand they are delivered. Every moving thing that lives shall be food for you; and just as I gave you the green plants, I give you everything. Only, you shall not eat flesh with its life, that is, its blood. For your own lifeblood I will surely require a reckoning: from every animal I will require it and from human beings, each one for the blood of another, I will require a reckoning for human life. Whoever sheds the blood of a human, by a human shall that person's blood be shed; for in his own image God made humankind. And you, be fruitful and multiply, abound on the earth and multiply in it"* (Genesis 9:1–7).

God stated this covenant, and then He hung the rainbow as a sign in the sky, sort of like hanging a warrior's bow on the wall. And He said, in effect, "I'm not at war with you anymore; I will not destroy the world by a flood again." But notice that He said that you and I have value. Not just because we're alive but because we humans are made in *His* image, indicating that *He* is the ultimate source of value.

The value is that God is first. The "vertical relationship" with God should flow into our "horizontal relationships" with each other. This includes justice, mercy, and the lives of all who are made in His image.

You and I are called to support the humane and to resist the inhumane and inhuman.

Just because you're upset with or disagree with somebody does not mean you can take that person's life. You cannot say, "If this person were out of here, my life would be better. It's in my self-interest to grease them!" To that, God says, "No! Because of your relationship with Me. Life is sacred because *I made it*. Not just because you like it or because you're nice, but because I made it." God brings us back to the ethics of love: *do* no harm to others.

Buddha (as well as many Rabbis) said, "Do not do to others what you don't want done to you." That's a good point, but even a tree stump can do that! A rock doesn't do anything wrong to others. Jesus took it one step farther. He said, in Matthew 7:12 and Luke 6:31, "*Do to others as you would have them do to you.*" It's not just avoiding what is wrong; it's a proactive *doing* of what is right.

When we get into tough situations, it's very easy to want to live for ourselves and say, "Hey, I can't take care of everybody, so I'm gonna just take care of myself and my own."

It's like the old joke about the two guys who went camping and heard a bear crashing through the woods behind them. One guy cried out, "It's a grizzly!"

The other guy started putting on his running shoes, and the first guy said, "Are you crazy? You can't outrun a grizzly!"

"I don't have to outrun the grizzly!" the other yelled. "I just have to outrun you!"

People do that same thing financially and relationally. They get to a place where they say, "Hey, I just need to take care of myself." God's response to that is, "It's not *everyone for themselves* here."

Jesus says that if you save your own life, if you hoard things up, you lose. But if you give your life to others, then you gain (see Matthew 16:25; Mark 8:35; Luke 9:24 and 17:33).

Every great man or woman who has ever lived has pointed to the life of love as the highest and greatest way to live life. But to love in the way Jesus loves goes beyond the common understanding of kindness in society (Luke 6:31). In other words, simply *not* harming others isn't enough; you must actively will and work *on their behalf.*

And that raises the first dilemma: requiring enough spiritual intelligence to *discern* when to "let live" and when to bring about death in order to protect another.

SORTING IT ALL OUT

The tough issues we will address in this section deal with the extreme spectrums of life itself—birth and death. A generation ago, the question of when life began and when it ended was fairly clear-cut. But today, God has allowed us to have a frightening array of technologies that can do great good—or cause great harm.

Exactly when conception takes place, birth, and even death have become increasingly less defined. We have to grapple with the crushing choice of quality of life versus quantity of life. Also, living in these times of "wars and rumors of wars" requires each of us to get into the discussion of how Christians should respond to aggression, evil, and destructiveness in places of power.

But all is not bleak and confusing. The great comfort and thrill of being alive is the power of God's love to save and to redeem, even in the toughest of situations. He is the Master of bringing good out of evil.

THE RIGHT CAUSE, OR THE RIGHT PERSON?

For us as Christians, the question arises, "When, if ever, do we have the freedom to intervene and interfere in somebody's life?" Since every person is made in the image of God, regardless of who he or she is, every person has intrinsic value—not for what they do or produce, but simply for *who they are*. When, if ever, do we dare to intervene and stop that life?

The issue of life-taking is a tough one—one that demands our attention and consideration. In this section, we are going to look at just three life-taking issues occurring at the end of life, at the beginning of life, and in the middle:

Issue 1:   Mercy Killing

Issue 2:   Abortion

Issue 3:   Justified War

Each one of these issues has invaded my life. And no doubt, if they haven't already, one or more of them will enter into your life as well.

Issues of the taking of life all boil down to this: either you follow what you feel is the right *cause* in determining a life or death issue, or else you follow the words, ways, and decrees of the right *person*. The *only* right person is Jesus, and His Word is the final authority on these urgent issues of life intervention.

CHAPTER 8

Issue One—Mercy Killing

Can a Christian Help Someone Die?

Are we ever allowed to make a decision that would result in hastening somebody's death?

What does the average person in society think about mercy killing? Here is a sampling of actual responses from typical people we interviewed in a shopping mall:

"I just think that's something that should be in God's hands, not man's hands."

"That's just sad, really. I mean, there is no excuse for it."

"I believe that if a person wants to go that way, then that's all right."

"I still believe that God determines when it's time to go, but it would be a decision that would be tough to make."

"We all have to realize that we are made from one spirit, the Spirit of God, and we are all here to share each other. So killing is the wrong way to go."

"Say right now if I wanted popcorn, I could just go down and get popcorn. I don't have to have someone tell me I can't. And if I decided I wanted to die right now, I could die. It's my choice as a person."

That last response should resonate deeply with us. I've done three funerals for suicides of children 13 and younger. We live in a culture of death. Many people honestly believe that if they want to take their life, it's their own choice.

But what about helping *others* take their life?

The Book of First Samuel records the first mercy killing in Scripture. In this passage, King Saul is surrounded by the Philistines. He has rebelled against God and has attempted several times to murder David, who Samuel anointed as the king of Israel. In a classic pincher maneuver, the Philistines have driven Saul into a corner. He is badly wounded. He knows, by the way that the Canaanites and the Philistines have dealt with the royalty and commanders of their enemies, that they intend to skin him alive before they kill him and drag him through town and then mount his head on a pole—and he definitely doesn't want to die that way!

The Philistines have the Israelites on the run, who are fleeing before them on Mount Gilboa. The Philistines overtake Saul's army, and his sons—Jonathan, Abinidab, and Malki-Shua—are killed. With the battle pressing hard upon him, Saul is trapped by the archers and severely wounded. First Samuel 31 picks up the riveting story:

> *Now the Philistines fought against Israel; the Israelites fled before them, and many fell slain on Mount Gilboa. The Philistines pressed hard after Saul and his sons, and they killed his sons Jonathan, Abinadab and Malki-Shua. The fighting grew fierce around Saul, and when the archers overtook him, they wounded him critically. Saul said to his armor-bearer, "Draw your sword and run me through, or these uncircumcised fellows will come and run me through and abuse me." But his armor-bearer was terrified and would not do it; so Saul took his own sword and fell on it. When the armor-bearer saw that Saul was dead, he too fell on his sword and died with him. So Saul and his three sons and his armor-bearer and all his men died together that same day* (1 Samuel 31:1–6).

Here you have Saul, who is gravely wounded, has taken arrows, and knows he's going to die. He does not want to be captured alive and tortured and humiliated before being killed, so he says to his armor-bearer, "Kill me." His armor-bearer won't do it, so Saul takes his own sword and falls upon it. And his armor-bearer does the same.

My Personal Experiences with Suicide and Mercy Killing

Now, this is an issue that I do not come to lightly. Not only did my own younger brother commit suicide, but as my older brother lay dying of leukemia, he begged for more morphine to ease his suffering and end his life.

Often with leukemia you can medicate and eliminate much of the pain. Generally death comes from a massive bleed. But he was not bleeding, just agonizing in and out of consciousness in horrific, unbearable pain.

I was alone with him in the room that last night. We knew that he was dying. I clutched his hand and assured him, "I will stay with you—I won't leave you." I asked the nurse to give him more morphine.

"No," she answered. "I can't give him anymore."

"Why?" I asked her. "Look at him—he needs it."

"It'll kill him, and I cannot kill him," she said.

"He's going to die soon anyway!" I pressed her, emotion choking in my throat.

Again she responded, "No—*I can't*. I can't do that!" The catch in her voice and her pained expression betrayed her struggle between compassion and the Hippocratic Oath.

I confess to you—I was tempted to put a pillow on my brother's face and absorb his pain away. But I did not—and within four hours, as I held him there in that bed, he breathed his last.

He had a very terrible death. More morphine would have eased his final painful hours of life on earth…and eliminated them.

This is a tough issue for which there are no simple answers. The challenge is that much of what goes on under the name of euthanasia today is simply assisted suicide. I believe that is wrong in many situations. Life is precious.

Still, I made such decisions for my grandmother, and I helped others unhook loved ones from life support. The question is, when can we as Christians do that? Where do we draw the line?

MERCY KILLING VS. MERCY DYING

Keep in mind that there is a difference between *mercy killing* and *mercy dying*. Mercy killing is where you *initiate* death. Mercy dying is where you let death take its process. There's a difference between prolonging life—which we must—and prolonging the death experience—which we don't always have to do.

I believe the biblical worldview demands that we be allowed to medicate and to help people. That's the wonder of today's medicinal advancements. There are some great drugs out there that can soothe and stop pain. Still, physicians wrestle with this issue all the time. How much do you medicate if such medication will ease the pain but hasten the death?

It's a tough distinction to make, but the ultimate question is, "Am I prolonging life or am I prolonging the dying experience?" Technology today has given us the ability to keep the body alive almost indefinitely. But is that the most loving thing to do? Or are we just wrestling with an inability to let our loved ones go? It is a tough issue, indeed.

As Christians, we are not allowed to push Grandma off the bed to end her life. But there may be times when we are allowed, if not even compelled by love, to just "release her balloon" to let her spirit go home to be with the Lord. We should pray and work hard for every precious moment of life for any human. But we can't be afraid of death. As Christians, we know that death is not the end.

For the Christian, death is simply the transition from this world into Christ's presence. That's why Christ said, "I am the resurrection and the life. Those who believe in me, even though they die, will live" (John 11:25).

I believe that refusing intravenous nutrition when death is inevitable is not ending life so much as it is allowing the dying process. It is reassuring to know today's medications and pain relief can give great comfort and help in the last stages of life. The love of life and the knowledge of Christ's presence for eternity can be brought together in an act of faith to either continue lifesaving attempts, or to sometimes let our loved ones go home to be with the Lord.

SUICIDE

At my younger brother's funeral someone asked, "Will he be saved?" They were unsure, since he took his own life, if he would make it to Heaven.

Obviously, to take your own life is an insane act. Even though we all tire of the battle of life, the heart has been wired by God to want to live. It is a crazed kind of thinking that leads someone to say, "I will make my life better by ending it." However, God is compassionate to the mentally broken, and I believe that God is compassionate to the suicidal.

I have often heard people say that suicide is the ultimate act of selfishness. I disagree. *Homicide* is the ultimate act of selfishness. Taking someone else's life because you deem it unworthy or because you wanted something they had is selfish. Now, don't misunderstand me. There are plenty of self-absorbed people who live like that all the way up to their self-absorbed suicides. But the people I have counseled, helped check in to hospitals, and spoken with after suicide attempts were not all selfish people. Some of them simply wrestled with dark waves of depression.

Still, suicide is the last thing anyone should ever do. To stand before the Lord after taking the life He gave you would probably be more shocking than the effects of the suicide itself.

Paul told the Corinthians that if a man destroys his body, God will destroy him (see 1 Corinthians 3:16-17). Of course in the context, he was talking about somebody who was *destroying the body of the church of Corinth.* (Remember the principle of the first hearer!)

Scripture repeatedly teaches us that salvation is an unearned gift, and God doesn't yank His gifts back and forth based on our day-to-day behavior. Remember it's not what people accept and believe, it's more about what they reject that denies them salvation. Reject God and His Son, and you reject salvation.

You cannot repent of being merely human. What we repent of is the stubborn rebellion in our hearts called *sin.* To render every suicide as evidence that the person rejected the grace of Christ for their lives paints too narrow a view of grace and salvation. I firmly believe, with my brother Tim, for example, that he accepted the grace of

Christ given to him and that I will see him in Heaven. And that's not just because he was my brother. It's on the biblical teaching of God's mercy. This is not the case with every suicide, of course. It points out the old conundrum: "If you're not good enough to earn your salvation, can you be bad enough to lose it?"

Only God knows the answer to each precious life lived, but He makes it clear that the grace of Christ is sufficient for *every* kind of sin.

If a person is truly saved, then when that person stands before the Lord, His grace will say, "Come in," not on the basis that they committed suicide, but on the basis of the work that Christ did on the Cross and in that person having accepted and embraced that gift.

But I also feel that, in that moment when they look down and see the life that God had planned for them, the amazing path He had in store for them to circumvent their dire circumstances, rise victorious, and lead an incredible life as they trusted and followed Him (as I think may have happened with my brother once he arrived in Heaven), then that person would think, "What in the world was I doing?!"

Trust Him! God has great plans for those who do. Our call in this life is not to judge the salvation of anyone. To warn? Yes. To tell of God's salvation? Of course. Our call is to help each other and to carry one another's burdens so we can fulfill the law of Christ, just as it says in Galatians 6:2.

CARRY EACH OTHER

What do you want the Lord to say when you look into His eyes? That's the million-dollar question. When He looks at you, will He speak the words, "Well done, good and faithful servant. ...Enter into the joy of your Lord" (Matt. 25:21 NKJV)? Or will He say with sorrow, "I never knew you; depart from Me" (Matt. 7:23 NKJV)?

I heard a story about a Christian missionary in the late 1800s who was walking with a Hindu businessman in the mountains of northern India. In that high country, when snowstorms blow in, they can easily kill people who are exposed to the elements. So between some of the mountain passes, the villagers had constructed small huts, about a day's walk apart, so that travelers could be protected from the storms.

As the missionary and the businessman were walking along, sure enough a storm blew up. They pressed onward through the sleet and the snow when suddenly they heard someone crying off to the side of the ravine. They looked down, and there was a man with a broken leg.

The Hindu man said, "We must keep going. We cannot help him."

"I am a Christian," the missionary responded. "I cannot just leave him. I have to help him."

To which the Hindu businessman replied, "We all die anyway. This is because of his Karma. It is something between him and life now, not us. We have to go on."

"You go on," the missionary said through the blowing wind and storm. "I'm going to stay." And he went down and helped the man out of the ravine and put him on his back. As he stumbled along, with the burden of the man on his back and the feel of the man's hot breath on his neck, he kept praying, "Lord, please help me get farther, just help me get a little farther." Finally, looking down about a hundred yards away, there was the light of the traveler's hut!

He got excited and started to go faster with his new friend on his back, and suddenly he tripped and they fell in the middle of the road. As they lay sprawled in the snow, they could make out a shape on the ground in front of them—the frozen body of the business-man who had gone on alone! What prevented the missionary from also freezing to death was the warmth of the body of the man he had been carrying.

There are going to be people in your life who will be more than a pain to deal with. They're going to be an unbelievable burden for you to carry. But trust me, if you're a follower of Jesus, you are called to carry them. Not to enable them, not to constantly rescue them, not to make it so that they don't feel responsible. But to come next to them. To walk beside them in life. To help shoulder their burdens.

Life is precious. Therefore, the answer to the question of whether to take life or not comes from God Himself:

> *You shall love the Lord your God with all your heart, and with all your soul, and with all your might* (Deuteronomy 6:5).

You shall not take vengeance or bear a grudge against any of your people, but you shall love your neighbor as yourself (Leviticus 19:18).

As we bear one another's burdens, and as we prayerfully seek God's wisdom in discerning which actions prolong life and which actually prolong the dying process, He will guide us in knowing when to "let live" and when to "let die."

CHAPTER 9

Issue Two—Abortion

Can a Christian Ever Stop a Pregnancy?

What about the issue of the beginning of life? Is abortion ever justifiable?

The previous story about Annie and her life-threatening pregnancy was one of those terrible dilemmas. "Annie," I counseled her, "I know this baby is precious to the Lord, but I think you need to lose this pregnancy, because the life you have takes precedence over the life that's on its way."

Annie prayed about it with her husband, and ultimately they decided to terminate the pregnancy. I cannot even begin to tell you the number of vicious hate letters I got from the congregation on sharing that story. Yet I believe that the ethic of love—of allowing no harm to come to others—dictated that it would have been harmful to allow the mother to die on the chance that her child might live. I have also counseled many women not to have abortions, and they went on to have beautiful, incredible babies who have changed their lives.

Let's go back to the streets and get a sampling of actual responses from people we interviewed to see whether or not the "average Joe" thinks abortion is ever permissible.

"You ought to be put in jail. It's murder."

"I'm totally in favor it. I mean, especially in extreme circumstances like rape. I mean, if you didn't want the baby, you shouldn't have to have it. And I also think that for a lot of people, if their child is going to be raised in a bad situation, it's better that it not be raised at all."

"It's not a good resort, but probably sometimes it's necessary."

"Abortion should be the right of the individual. That's my feeling there."

"I don't think it's personally right, but it's up to each person, their own individual opinion and the consequences they suffer afterward."

"I think it's worse to tell somebody what they can and can't do with their own body."

"I believe it's a woman's right to choose."

"Life is sacred. My daughter had one, and we looked at the baby through—what is that picture they take?—and once you see that little critter in there, you know it's alive."

Those are some fairly typical responses to this issue in today's culture. It's life, it's holy—but whose right is it to decide that? Is there ever allowable feticide? I believe at times there are, but it's even more rare than justifiable homicide. The questions is, when is it a life, and when is it just cells that are "holy"?

As a pastor, I have done funerals for stillborn babies. But interestingly enough, we do not do funerals for miscarriages (which can often be only weeks apart in age difference from stillborns). Why is that? Because a funeral is a statement that a life (which is eternal) is passing from this world and on into eternity.

Even though there is the same pastoral caring and love with the terrible loss and sorrow that comes with losing a pregnancy, the Christian community as a whole does not usually respond to miscarriages in the same way as the death of an individual. The rationale is based on the fetus not yet being at the stage of having a spirit. But just because the "bundle of cells" may not have a spirit yet in the first few weeks does not mean it is just a bundle of cells. They are cells that will become an eternal person *if* the process were to continue. Therefore, while they may not be a viable human, they are holy.[1]

In Ecclesiastes 11, Solomon said a fascinating thing, which people tend to skip over:

> *God's ways are as mysterious as the pathway of the wind and as the manner in which a human spirit is infused into the little body of a baby while it is yet in its mother's womb* (Ecclesiastes 11:5 TLB).

Solomon is saying that, at some point inside of a mother, the child is given a spirit that is eternal. How or when, no one knows (I happen to think it has to do with the development of the central nervous system, but God alone knows). But there is a point when it is not…and then it is.

A DIFFERENT STANDARD?

The Book of Numbers says that if a man accidentally killed a person (like if he accidentally put his chariot in reverse and ran over your mother), then he could go to one of six towns of refuge, which were set apart for those who had killed someone accidentally so that they wouldn't be killed by avengers prior to standing trial before the assembly (see Numbers 35:11–13). The person who perpetrated the killing would have to stay in the town of refuge until the High Priest died. Only after that would the accused be free to go back home without reprisal.

That's all about "life for life." Even if you *accidentally* killed somebody, it was still a life taken, so you still had to wait until another life was given.

But here's the odd incongruity to that rule. If I bumped into a woman and caused her to miscarry, the Book of Exodus says that I wouldn't go hide out in a city of refuge. I would only pay a fine.

> *When people who are fighting injure a pregnant woman so that there is a miscarriage, and yet no further harm follows, the one responsible shall be fined what the woman's husband demands, paying as much as the judges determine* (Exodus 21:22).

Is there a different standard going on here? Not at all. The issue is about *threshold of life*. Just because something is not eternal doesn't mean that it's not holy. A miscarried child, for example, may not be an entity in Heaven, but it is still something created by God—and therefore holy. Some people do believe there are miscarried babies in Heaven. (We'll just have to wait and see.)

However, interfering with this process isn't something to be taken lightly. Just because a fetus may not yet be "eternal" doesn't mean it is valueless and therefore expendable. In Psalm 139, the psalmist talks about how God saw his *unformed body* while he was still in his mother's womb:

> *Your eyes beheld my unformed substance. In your book were written all the days that were formed for me, when none of them as yet existed* (Psalm 139:16).

Note that it is not "an" unformed body, but "*my*" unformed body, indicating that the fetus is a viable human in the making. Before there are toes, before there are fingers, before there is even the beginning of a heartbeat, God is knitting together each precious life.

EVER JUSTIFIABLE?

However, I do believe there is justifiable feticide in *some* instances, such as when the birth would place the mother's life in grave danger, or in a situation involving rape or incest. Why rape or incest? Because the pregnancy was forced upon the person.

I have a dear pastor friend who was the birth of a rape. His mother was brutally raped, she kept the pregnancy, and he has been a blessing to the world ever since. Yet I think it is the decision of the baby's mother, for the highest good.

RESPONDING WITH LOVE AND GRACE

I have never heard, in any counseling sessions in my office, any woman who said about having an abortion, "I'll just go ahead and lose this one. It would be such an inconvenience to have this child." I'm sure that probably takes place, but I've never encountered a woman so glib about such a character-defining decision. In my experience, it is always an excruciatingly difficult decision for every woman.

Even when we disagree with what a woman has done, we need to show the love and the grace of God for them. Even when we think that what they've done was absolutely wrong. God forgives when we ask for His mercy, so we should give grace as well.

No matter how sincere a person is about their belief on this issue, standing outside of abortion clinics and yelling at people is plain dumb. It's not effective in any way whatsoever. We, as the Church, should stand in union and truly love these moms and love these kids and take care of them. Just as there is enough food, water, and space on this planet for everyone, there is also enough love, including for the woman who aborts, as well as the child brought to full term.

We can be positionally right and behaviorally wrong in how we deal with this issue. To those of us who have wrestled with this question and have gone through it, we have learned that God's grace and mercy combine perfectly with His truth: do no harm to others, and allow no harm to occur to others. We've seen how it lives out in the end and beginning of life, but what about life taking in the middle of life?

ENDNOTE

1. There is, in today's culture, a loss of understanding of the concept of "holiness," which dismisses it as a criterion for decision-making. This is why it may be difficult for some to understand how I can be against abortion, even when I don't consider a child as "eternal" until a later point in the pregnancy.

CHAPTER 10

Issue Three—Justified War

Can a Christian Go to War?

I once did a funeral for a young man who stepped on a landmine in Iraq. I had prayed with him and his mother for his safety before he left for the conflict. And then I received an e-mail from a chaplain in Afghanistan, telling me they had just lost another one of their boys in a firefight.

The issue of Christians deliberately taking the life of someone who maybe never even attacked them directly (as in shooting at combatants from a distance), or someone they might never have even seen as they killed them (as in dropping bombs from thousands of feet in the air), is a crucial discussion today.

Is there ever "justified war"? Here are a few responses from regular people on the street, representing a wide cross-section of society:

"Um, no war is good."

"I think it's stupid to fight. Even though I do it anyway. I think it's kind of dumb to like, just kill people for no reason."

"There is always such a thing as a just war, but it rarely happens."

"I believe that there are causes that need to be fought for."

"No, I don't believe so. To apply the word *just* to the word *war* is like, you know, saying, *a properly killed person*. So, it doesn't fit."

"I don't know. I kind of stand on both sides of the fence. I kind of understand the need to defend yourself. But on the other hand, I think it's wrong to kill somebody as well. So, I don't know, man. That's a good question. I think everyone needs to make up their mind for themselves on that."

Is war *ever* right? What should a Christian do? Many Christians believe that it is not only permitted but actually mandated. If you see the innocent suffering you must intervene. Even unbelievers often believe this.

There are times when you come to a paradox, where a lethal response is required in order to stop a lethal attack. We give our police lethal force authority. Citizens are legally allowed to respond to an attack with equal force or with force enough to stop the attack and defend themselves and others. But the taking of life in defense should be used ever so carefully and only as a last resort. It's never to be done in anger or because you're upset. Taking life is only because you're protecting the lives of those who are in imminent danger.

I have wonderful brothers and sisters, who likewise love the Lord and know His Word, yet disagree with this stance. They would say that the test when somebody does wrong is to ask, "What was Christ's response to evil?" He turned the other cheek; He went to the Cross peacefully, without calling down a legion of mighty angels on His own murderers.

Some people even say, "Christians are not to be the ones pulling the triggers or dropping the bombs, since it's hard to tell someone about the Lord when you're shooting at them from a quarter-mile away or bombing them from three miles up in the sky." Or they say something like, "The devil will always find those who are willing to do the killing."

Indeed, some people quote the following Scriptures in support of the position that Christians are not supposed to engage in war. Though these passages mostly address the issue of interpersonal vengeance, they can be used to make a good case against any form of conflict:

> *Vengeance is Mine, and recompense; their foot shall slip in due time; for the day of their calamity is at hand, and the things to come hasten upon them* (Deuteronomy 32:35 NKJV).

Seek peace and pursue it (Psalms 34:14b NKJV).

Better a patient man than a warrior, a man who controls his temper than one who takes a city (Proverbs 16:32 NIV).

If your enemies are hungry, give them bread to eat; and if they are thirsty, give them water to drink (Proverbs 25:21).

Do not say, "I'll do to him as he has done to me; I'll pay that man back for what he did" (Proverbs 24:29 NIV).

But I say to you, "Do not resist an evildoer. But if anyone strikes you on the right cheek, turn the other also" (Matthew 5:39).

Love your enemies, do good...Your reward will be great, and you will be children of the Most High; for he is kind to the ungrateful and the wicked (Luke 6:35).

Love your enemies, do good to those who hate you, bless those who curse you, pray for those who abuse you. If anyone strikes you on the cheek, offer the other also; and from anyone who takes away your coat do not withhold even your shirt (Luke 6:27–29).

Bless those who persecute you; bless and do not curse them (Romans 12:14).

If it is possible, so far as it depends on you, live peaceably with all. Beloved, never avenge yourselves, but leave room for the wrath of God; for it is written, "Vengeance is mine, I will repay, says the Lord." No, "if your enemies are hungry, feed them; if they are thirsty, give them something to drink; for by doing this you will heap burning coals on their heads." Do not be overcome by evil, but overcome evil with good (Romans 12:18–21).

We do not wage war according to human standards; for the weapons of our warfare are not merely human, but they have divine power to destroy strongholds (2 Corinthians 10:3b–4).

Do not repay evil for evil or abuse for abuse; but, on the contrary, repay with a blessing. It is for this that you were called—that you might inherit a blessing (1 Peter 3:9).

See that none of you repays evil for evil, but always seek to do good to one another and to all (1 Thessalonians 5:15).

People who quote these passages feel that we are called to simply bear what evil is out there in the world, in the same way that Christ bore what the world did to Him. I honor that position, although I disagree with it, because there is Scripture that clearly tells us to protect those in danger, such as:

> *Rescue those being led away to death; hold back those staggering toward slaughter* (Proverbs 24:11 NIV).

DEFEND THE DEFENSELESS

I believe that there comes a time, as our Declaration of Independence asserts, when the shackles of tyranny must be broken. There is a legitimate use of force, even lethally, against oppressors in this fallen, broken world. But I am reminded that as General Sherman marched through the South during the Civil War, he had great insight, and was partially right, when he said, "War is hell." I say he was "partially right" because hell is actually a lot worse than war. Of course Sherman said that because he was experiencing the hellishness of what war creates.

Historically, the Church has defended a limited use of war to defend the innocent. Killing during times of war is not considered the same as the taking of a life as in murder, because the soldier does not operate with personal malice or from hopes of personally gaining from the conflict. Armies in the past tended to consist of professional soldiers or mercenaries, and not men drafted from the public.

Many church leaders throughout the centuries saw war as a way of obeying the scripture to "honor the king" Peter stated in First Peter 2:17. It wasn't so much the question of war, but of whether the king or queen or emperors were advancing peace and Kingdom values.

In the 12th century, Thomas Aquinas built upon Augustine's doctrine of "justified war." He had three basic criteria for waging a just war:

1. Is the end noble?
2. Are the innocent protected?
3. Is the war winnable?

The last point is interesting. He was not against someone laying down their life for a just cause, even if they could not win (like martyrdom for Christ or helping the enslaved). What Aquinas was addressing was the "last option" of war. In other words, make sure you've tried everything else first and thoughtfully analyzed the possible outcomes. If war would still not change anything, then Aquinas was saying that the war should not be waged.

THE CHRISTIAN RESPONSE TO WAR

I thank the Lord that I missed the Vietnam War by about six weeks with my draft number. I've never had to go to war or face its horrors firsthand. So I'm speaking as a man who has not been in that situation. Could I pull the trigger on another man, who might even be a fellow Christian, a fellow father, a man whom I don't even know, but whom my commanding officer told me is my enemy and whose life I must take, or else forfeit my life and the welfare of others? I hope I'm never in a situation where I have to find out. I have such admiration and gratitude for the men and women who have found themselves in that situation. Many a Christian has fulfilled their obligation to country and not negated their obligation to Christ. God, in His power and His grace, is able to be in every situation.

When should we intervene and when should we not? The human race only recently emerged from the most violent century in history. During the 20th century, conservative estimates say that over 70 million people were killed in wars—16 million alone in World War II.

In centuries past, kings and emperors had private armies or captured slaves whom they sent to war. Then, when the nation-states rose up, it became possible to mobilize an entire population with new technology of unimaginable destructiveness. How in the world do Christians respond to such insane carnage? We respond any way possible that stops and prevents war.

If only we realized how many wars are initiated and fought due to ego or pride or greed or real estate—then we might stop and reconsider.

A little girl once asked her parents, "Why did World War I start?"

"Well, because there was an assassination, honey," her father answered.

"No, Dear," her mother retorted, "it was actually due to economic factors."

"No, really," the father said firmly, "it was because of an *assassination*."

107

"Oh, you don't know anything," the mother shot back. "It was over the deteriorating *economy*!"

"If you had ever done your homework," the father yelled, "you would know it was—"

"Never mind, never mind," the little girl cut in. "I think I understand how they start."

We live in a nation that has unparalleled power. At the end of 1800s, there were five great nations. After World War II, there were two superpowers. Now, there's one: the United States of America.[1] Not since the Roman Empire has one nation had so much power—economically, politically, and militarily. How do you and I as American Christians handle all that power? I believe there are times when we need to intervene, even knowing how violent and deadly war is. When the innocent are being harmed, or the oppressors are enslaving the masses, the use of force can be justified.

One of the elders in a church I once led was an older gentleman who served in the Nixon administration and was involved in the talks with the Soviet Union about disarmament. He quoted a Soviet general as saying, "I want to remind you that it's always better for old men to lose their temper across the negotiating table, than for young men to lose their lives on the battlefield." As a nation, we must ask if our "national interests" are also the interests of God. As Christians in this society, we must be the prophetic voice that asks if we are using our military for God-honoring ends, or is it our pride, greed, or even a vengeful spirit, which can lead many a nation to unnecessary wars.

Nevertheless, it seems in life there also comes a time when turning the other cheek is actually unloving. Might does not make right, but weakness can encourage wrong. If we try to appease the radical extremists of Islam that Osama Bin Laden represents, will that save lives? Will they befriend us? Of course not. They're willing to kill innocent bystanders with TNT strapped to themselves to try make us understand one thing—they want us to convert to Islam or die. Period. If we all turn the other check, many innocent people will suffer.

WAR FOR PEACE

One of the central purposes of war is to stop war, to incapacitate a hostile enemy, and to protect the innocent. When the enemy is incapacitated, you don't kill them. You cease hostilities and instill peace. If winning the war and losing the peace is as common as history teaches us, then we must use violent conflict rarely, as the very last response and in the most limited means possible.

War is a horrible thing. At times I believe it is justified, yet we must seek to bring it to an end as quickly as possible and to make every effort to protect the innocent. The best way to honor the men and women who serve our country is to do all we can to keep them from harm's way, to hold them in our prayers, to provide for their mission, and to make sure they have political leaders who are wise and prudent.

And for us as the Church, we must "wage peace" boldly out of love for God and for all of His creation. In most of life, we must have an extreme bias toward God's "shalom" or full peacefulness.

Blessed are the peace makers, for they shall be called the children of God (Matthew 5:9).

ENDNOTE

1. It must be noted, however, that China has a substantial nuclear arsenal and has a standing army that is up to ten times the size of that of America's. However, in her modern history China has not used nuclear weapons and has not launched a preemptive military strike at an enemy outside her own borders.

SECTION B

*Life and Relationships—What
Glorifies God Most?*

ISSUE FOUR: **Divorce and Remarriage**

ISSUE FIVE: **Homosexuality**

ISSUE SIX: **Sexuality Outside of Marriage**

Introduction

Spirituality Is a Relational Skill

It is easy to agree with the cynical statement, "I love humanity—it's people I can't stand!" It's one thing to be loving and caring in the bigger questions of life support or justified wars. It requires a whole different level of love to live in relationship with others. If I cannot love the person in my own little word of relationships, then it is a spiritual farce to believe that it's important to love those in the greater world outside. If any dimension of life required the four sentinels of spiritual intelligence (Scripture, Reason, Wise Counsel, and the Inner Leading of the Spirit) it is definitely in learning how to love others personally.

Some wise counsel comes from the spiritual and intellectual leadership of England in the 1600s. The Westminster Shorter Catechism sums up the purpose of life wonderfully: "What is the chief end of man? To glorify God and to enjoy Him forever." What a delicious summary of why each of us is alive. We are here to glorify God.

In the Greek, this is called *doxia*, which means "to reflect God's glory back to Him." Glorifying God always ends up in our enjoying life and its Creator to the maximum. God has made all things to reflect His glory and goodness. When a flower blooms, or a bird sings, or a child laughs, or a sunset paints the sky, the glory of the Creator is exhibited for all to see. Yet the greatest reflection of God's image was when He made man and woman and ordained them to live together.

Life is a relational existence, because the triune God who created it all is a relational God. The Father loved the Son before the first drop of water was in the Pacific Ocean. If fact, our salvation is being caught up in this love affair with the Trinity, when the Son will someday present us as a flawless gift back to the Father, who so loved us by the power of the Spirit of God Himself.

It's easy to see that spirituality truly is a relational skill. When we relate to others with love, we are glorifying God. Yet we must always be careful *who* we love first, God or humankind? Anytime we put something or someone before God, we are giving in to the constant temptation of idolatry. The double edge of idolatry is that ultimately it destroys both the worshiper as well as the idol. It is not fair to others to let them take the place of God in our life. So we love others not because they are so lovable, but because we love the Lord of life first. The good news is that God wants eagerly to love them *through* us as much as He first loved us.

GLORIFYING GOD MOST WITH RELATIONSHIPS

If life is the vertical (our relationship with God) flowing down into the horizontal (our lives with each other), then what exactly is the best way to glorify God? What happens when two people are daily wounding each other or are estranged from one another? How does that glorify God?

The spiritual intelligence for living relationally today raises many tough issues. Is it more glorifying to God to live life single or in marriage? What about when the marriage dies? And how far can I act out my sexuality as a woman or a man and still glorify God? What about those who love the Lord but are only attracted to the same sex?

At the heart of answering these tough issues is developing the spiritual intelligence to have not merely spirit-filled individuals but also spirit-filled relationships. God loves to reflect His nature and glory in the midst of broken people. Having Christ, the Great Physician, actually dwelling between the spaces that our relationships inhabit is to touch God's redemptive power at its purest.

Jesus Himself said, "If you love those who love you, what credit is that to you? For even sinners love those who love them" (Luke 6:32). Learning to love the unlovely sometimes takes us to conclusions we are not ready for. It is here that we grow.

In this section, we'll examine four key issues that relate to life and relationships.

DIVORCE AND REMARRIAGE

If, as in Malachi 2:16, God states that He hates divorce, then why is divorce not prohibited in the Ten Commandments? Is there ever a justifiable reason to end a marriage? When do we know if we're merely dragging the dead corpse of a past relationship around that needs to be buried, or prematurely burying and ending a living, breathing relationship?

If I am divorced, how do I know if I can remarry? Are there ways to tell if the "relational virus" that killed the first marriage is still infecting me?

What about those who have been married and then widowed or divorced? If getting married punishes me financially, is it permissible to do a private ceremony before God but not before the state? Can we be both holy *and* sexual beings?

HOMOSEXUALITY

Homosexuality—hottest topic in the church today. How is sexual orientation developed? Does God really mandate heterosexuality, or is the biblical injunction more about fidelity? If sex is covenant-making between a man and woman with God, then in the lifelong commitment of marriage, what do I do if I'm not formally, legally married? Why would God care if two men or two women who truly love and care for each other (and also love Christ) want to act it out sexually?

SEXUALITY OUTSIDE OF MARRIAGE

Sex is a mysterious bonding event. Like tape used over and over, a powerful "stickiness" is lost when we misuse this phenomenal creation. How are we to use sex?

How far can we go with another person if we don't go "all the way"? Does the Lord really think we should never kiss someone until our wedding day? How can we know if we're compatible with someone if we've never been physically intimate with them?

And what about adultery? "No adultery" means much more than just controlling one's sexual urges. It is about a fundamental reverence for the power of sexual bonding. This raises the tough issues of sexuality within oneself, outside of marriage, and after marriage.

Just as the sixth Commandment ("You shall not murder") demands respect and value for someone's physical life, so too does the seventh Commandment ("You shall not commit adultery") demand respect for my neighbor's relational life.

We'll take a look at each of these tough issues in the following chapters.

CHAPTER 11

Issue Four—Divorce and Remarriage

One of the few times I ever saw my mother cry was when I was in high school, after my father left our family, and the ministry, for the church secretary. I remember that morning, I just held my mother as she wept.

The issue of marriage and divorce is an area that has touched my life in a very personal way. My older brother and too many friends of mine have also gone through the agony of divorce. My wife's parents divorced, as did some of her siblings. This is not a distant theoretical issue. The pain touches me deeply.

In my first pastorate I once preached on divorce, and after the service a divorced woman went home, took her life, and left a note saying that because of what I had said, she felt she could never really be married again. I sat at her funeral, next to her two sons, and vowed that I would never preach on the subject again. I have, and I will. But I do not do it lightly.

MARRIAGE AND DIVORCE

I read recently of a surgeon who was involved in a team that separated conjoined twins. The difficulty they faced was in deciding whether they should separate these two precious little boys since they shared the same heart and lungs. The challenge was how to separate them and still have them both live. Chances seemed good that one of them would die. How do you make that kind of a decision?

It's the same with divorce. Divorce is much, much more than merely a partnership breaking up. Some people say that the marriage separation "surgery" is so radical that you never truly "live" again afterward. Others say that, in unusual situations, since the death of the marriage is already really taking place while the couple is still together, it is almost more honoring to the relationship to end it before things become even worse.

What does God's Word say about marriage and divorce? How can we respond to a devastating wave that has threatened this nation perhaps more than any other area? What is the witness in Scripture? What does God say about divorce? Let's take a look at:

1. What's clear in Scripture?

2. What's not clear in Scripture?

3. How we as followers of Christ are supposed to respond to this issue.

WHAT'S CLEAR IN SCRIPTURE?

The Bible doesn't get hung up so much on the death of a marriage, but focuses more on the glory and the wonder of two people becoming one. The bottom line is that *God loves marriage.* If you think you're high on getting married, you should see how high God is! He invented it, He created it. And He loves it. It reflects the very *Imago Dei* (Latin for "the image of God"), the triune God Himself.

Have you ever tried to explain the Trinity? You can't, because God is not *exactly* reproduced in anything in all of His creation. God is not in any one single series of events. He is Father with Son with Holy Spirit. They're One, yet they're also distinct, individual Persons. There are no great analogies, but "one" comes closer (at least according to God in Genesis 1:26). When a man and woman come together in a healthy marriage, it's much the same way. They're not fused together so that their identities are lost; they're still male and female. Yet they are blended together in God in a new light, as one. It's a mystery. And God loves it.

It is very clear in Scripture that God *hates* divorce. Divorce is the violent death of a living relationship, and God views the death of a marital relationship almost on a par with the death of an individual. God detests divorce because He deeply loves the people who are going through it.

Sometime around 400 b.c., the prophet Malachi addressed the Israelites about how they had been handling marriage:

> ...*The Lord is acting as the witness between you and the wife of your youth, because you have broken faith with her, though she is your partner, the wife of your marriage covenant. Has not the Lord made them one? In flesh and spirit they are His. And why one? Because He was seeking godly offspring. So guard yourself in your spirit, and do not break faith with the wife of your youth. "I hate divorce," says the Lord God of Israel, "and I hate a man's covering himself with violence as well as with his garment," says the Lord Almighty. So guard yourself in your spirit, and do not break faith* (Malachi 2:14-16 NIV).

In the eyes of God, a relationship is a living, breathing entity. It is as holy to Him as the persons of flesh and blood who make up that relationship. So when a relationship is killed (when it is "murdered"), God takes that almost as seriously as murdering another person. We belong to a relational God. He cares about relationships because He cares about the people who are in them.

The Romans were very creative people. One Roman governor was particularly creative in meting out punishment. If a person committed murder, for example, the penalty was for the murderer to have the body of the victim tied to him, and he then had to drag around the rotting, decomposing corpse of the victim for a prescribed period of time before it was buried. And then the killer was executed.

Do you know how many people have killed relationships and are dragging them along like that? There are things that may kill a relationship first, before divorce occurs, such as adultery. But many people have this mixed-up notion that anything short of divorce is OK and glorifying to God. They drag around this horribly rotten corpse of a marriage, and yet they boast to God, "At least we're not divorced!"

What is very clear in Scripture is that God loves marriage and God hates divorce.

WHAT'S NOT CLEAR IN SCRIPTURE?

It's interesting, but there is actually no direct prohibition in the Ten Commandments or other biblical life codes against divorce. "Thou shalt not steal…Thou shalt not murder…Thou shalt not commit adultery…." God could have said, "Thou shalt not divorce." But He didn't. Instead, all He said is, "I hate divorce." Why? Could it be that God tolerated it? He *hated* it…and yet He tolerated it?

Throughout the Old Testament, God tolerated polygamy. There's not a statement in Scripture that God was against Abraham, Isaac, Jacob, Solomon or any of the other great leaders, kings, and prophets, for taking more than one wife. (We won't go into the questionable wisdom of having all those wives.) David was severely punished for adultery and premeditated murder, but not for having many wives at the same time. Does that mean God was in *favor* of polygamy?

No, He wasn't. In fact, in Genesis 2:24 (NIV), God said, "For this reason a man will leave his father and mother and be united to his wife, and they will become one flesh." This verse doesn't say "wives." It doesn't say "many fleshes." And yet, although it wasn't the God-ordained way, it does seem that He tolerated polygamy at one time.

When Mark Twain first met some Mormons, they asked him, "What do you think about polygamy?"

"It's not biblical," he responded.

They asked him, "Where does the Bible say that?"

"No man can serve two masters," Twain shot back.

All joking aside, the fact remains that the Bible nowhere comes out and explicitly says, "Do not divorce." Yet, we clearly know that divorce is not pleasing to God and that He hates it.

I was in Egypt the summer of 2007. We were working with a pastor there who deals with a different question: Some of the men who are quietly converting from Islam to Christianity have up to four wives—what should they do? How do they care for these women, and their children, and yet honor the biblical model of one man and one woman? (The only good news in this messy situation is that some of those wives would love to be set free from their husbands!)

THE NEW TESTAMENT WITNESS

Believe it or not, in the first century, divorce was more prevalent than it is today. There were rabbis who were teaching that if your wife embarrassed you, that was grounds enough for divorce! Divorce was so widespread that the great rabbinical teaching schools of Hillel and Shimei debated what were valid grounds for divorce.

In traditional Orthodox Judaism, in order to divorce someone you had to get a notice from the rabbi and then say to your spouse, "I divorce you, I divorce you, I divorce you," three times. If you did that, then the divorce was complete and the marriage was over.

In Matthew 19:3, the Pharisees, in trying to trip up Jesus so they could denounce Him, asked Him, "Is it lawful for a man to divorce his wife for any cause?" Jesus' response was that once you get married, you stay married.

> *They said to Him, "Why then did Moses command to give a certificate of divorce, and to put her away?" He said to them, "Moses, because of the hardness of your hearts, permitted you to divorce your wives, but from the beginning it was not so. And I say to you, whoever divorces his wife, except for sexual immorality, and marries another, commits adultery; and whoever marries her who is divorced commits adultery"* (Matthew 19:7–9 NKJV).

Did you catch that one key word in the passage above? Jesus said that Moses *permitted* divorce. He didn't preach it or celebrate it or encourage it or require it. He simply permitted it. It was a necessary evil because of the hardness of their hearts.

When two people join hearts, spirits, and bodies, an ontological reality takes place—something you can't physically see. What Jesus is basically saying here is, "Guys, I can't talk to you about divorce, because you don't even understand marriage." Jesus wasn't there to set a new rule. He was there to talk about the wonder of two people becoming one. He said, in effect, "Marriage is a great creation of my Father. But because of the hardness of the hearts of many humans, and the state of this broken and fallen world, Moses allowed divorce as the lesser of evils" (sort of the flipside of Thomas Aquinas' *what is the highest good*).

God gives us guidance in First Corinthians, which was a letter the apostle Paul wrote to the church in Corinth. Corinth was a big, rich city, somewhat like Las Vegas. Paul had started a church there, in an area similar to the Strip in Vegas. In addressing the issue of marriage, he wrote:

> *Now concerning the matters about which you wrote: "It is well for a man not to touch a woman." But because of cases of sexual immorality, each man should have his own wife and each woman her own husband* (1 Corinthians 7:1-2).

In other words, Paul reiterated that marriage is a good thing. The super asceticism of many Greek sects at that time taught that if you were really brilliant, you didn't need physical pleasure. They felt that the physical pleasure derived from sex (and even from food) was wrong. Paul said, essentially, "Nonsense! God made all of it to be enjoyed in His way."

> *The husband should give to his wife her conjugal rights, and likewise the wife to her husband. For the wife does not have authority over her own body, but the husband does; likewise the husband does not have authority over his own body, but the wife does. Do not deprive one another except perhaps by agreement for a set time, to devote yourselves to prayer, and then come together again, so that satan may not tempt you because of your lack of self-control. This I say by way of concession, not of command. I wish that all were as I myself am. But each has a particular gift from God, one having one kind and another a different kind* (1 Corinthians 7:3-7).

After I've done a wedding, the husband doesn't own his body anymore, and the wife doesn't own her body. They own each others.

For going on three decades, my body has not been mine own; it belongs to my wife. I say, "Praise the Lord!" She says, "Pray for me!"

Interestingly, Paul also said that it's actually better to remain single:

> *To the unmarried and the widows I say that it is well for them to remain unmarried as I am. But if they are not*

practicing self-control, they should marry. For it is better to marry than to be aflame with passion (1 Corinthians 7:8–9).

Paul is basically saying that rather than walk around drooling at the opposite sex, *get married*. That sounds very *functional*. And it is; with good reason. The Bible presents marriage as something mystical and amazing, and yet very practical as well.

But for Paul, the issue wasn't whether you were having sex or not, or whether you should have children and a white picket fence and a cute home. His position was that there is a Lord, who is our Savior. Singleness is not our lord, neither is marriage. The risen Lord is our Lord! That is to be our main focus. So many times we obsess on this one facet of life and forget that Christ is our Lord. It's neither our singleness nor our marriage.

Paul goes on to give more guidance about marriage relationships:

> *To the rest I say—I and not the Lord—that if any believer has a wife who is an unbeliever, and she consents to live with him, he should not divorce her. And if any woman has a husband who is an unbeliever, and he consents to live with her, she should not divorce him. For the unbelieving husband is made holy through his wife, and the unbelieving wife is made holy through her husband. Otherwise, your children would be unclean, but as it is, they are holy* (1 Corinthians 7:12-14).

What a passage! For families where one spouse is non-believing, the Christian sanctifies the whole family just by their walk with Christ. That's an amazing thought. And then Paul adds:

> *But if the unbelieving partner separates, let it be so; in such a case the brother or sister is not bound. It is to peace that God has called you* (1 Corinthians 7:15).

In other words, if the non-believing spouse wants to leave the marriage, the believer shouldn't try to force them to stay. And if they leave, then you are free to remarry someone else. However, if you divorce someone for another person just because the other person is more fun or better-looking or richer or whatever, God cannot bless that new marriage.

A woman once went to her pastor and said, "I'm leaving my husband."

The pastor responded, "You can't. You took him for better or for worse."

"I know," the woman said. "But he's worse than what I took him for!"

Many people come to me and say, "I married *this*?" But God says, "This is not a mission project for you. Your husband or wife is not a fixer-upper or a charity case. This marriage is a place for My grace to come in. It's *My* project."

THE CLEAR CALL: OUR RESPONSE

So how do we, as Christians, respond to the tough issue of divorce? First, we realize that marriage is a wonderful, unique creation: two people becoming one. One physically, one emotionally, one financially, one spiritually. Two people becoming one. What an amazing thing. And it's never easy. It's tough a lot of times. That toughness is not to grind us down, but to polish us into people who bear the image of Christ. It's worth it, too. And God is gracious to make it work when we are willing to follow His instructions and guidance and humble ourselves in submission to our spouse.

Another New Testament passage sheds some light on this subject. Once again, the teachers of the Law were trying to "trip up" Jesus:

> *Some Sadducees, who say there is no resurrection, came to Him and asked Him a question, saying, "Teacher, Moses wrote for us that if a man's brother dies, leaving a wife but no child, the man shall marry the widow and raise up children for his brother. There were seven brothers; the first married and, when he died, left no children; and the second married her and died, leaving no children; and the third likewise; none of the seven left children. Last of all the woman herself died. In the resurrection whose wife will she be? For the seven had married her." Jesus said to them, "Is not this the reason you are wrong, that you know neither the Scriptures nor the power of God? For when they rise from the dead, they neither marry nor are given in marriage, but are like angels in Heaven. And as for the dead being raised, have you not read in the book of Moses, in the story about the bush, how God said to him, 'I am the God of Abraham, the God of Isaac, and the God of Jacob'? He is God not of the dead, but of the living; you are quite wrong"* (Mark 12:18-27).

Once again, the Sadducees were out to trap Jesus. But Jesus turned the tables on them and showed them how foolish their question was. They were all caught up in the details of marriage and who was going to be married to whom in Heaven, and Jesus came right out and said, "You've got it all wrong. There won't be marriage in Heaven." The intimacy and closeness couples experience in the best marriages on earth won't be anywhere near as close as all of us will be in eternity. The angels have a closeness that makes our marriages seem like e-mail spam by comparison.

When I was young, I had a fiancée who died, and my children once asked me, "Daddy, when you get to Heaven, are you going to be married to Judy or to Mom?" My eldest responded, "I'm sure when we get to Heaven, Mom will say, 'Hi, Judy. He's all yours. Good luck to you!'"

Again, the bottom line is that the intimacy we'll experience in Heaven will make the greatest love on earth look like mere pen pals. There will be no jealousy, no anger, no grudge, no sorrow, no insecurity. Can you imagine a relationship with no sin? With all the creativity, the surprises, the joy, the adventure, the different ways to share. We will have an intimate relationship that shames the best and closest heterosexual marriages here on earth.

If you say, "Lord, show me how to come alongside and be committed," He will show you how. This is why we need to get marriage in perspective. God loves marriage. But it's only one part of His incredible universe.

HEALING AFTER DIVORCE

What about those who have been through divorce? Is there healing?

Yes, yes, and yes! God wants to forgive, heal, and restore. But He can't forgive excuses—only sins. In every divorce I've ever witnessed, I have yet to meet an innocent party—though there are certainly many situations where one party may own a greater share of responsibility and culpability for their negative actions. Each spouse contributed to the wounds of the marriage in their own way. Acknowledge where you've gone wrong, confess it, and get ready for God's healing in your life.

God can't heal extenuating circumstances, but He can heal broken lives. So be willing to be humble and be ready to confess. If you've failed, don't hide it. God can only heal you once you've laid it at His feet…and once you have, leave it there—and oh, how He can heal!

If you find yourself divorced, be prudent. God may glorify Himself best by having you married again, but be spiritually intelligent. The virus that "killed off" the first relationship might still be in you. Whatever is in you that came from, or contributed to, the breakup, take time and let the healing process of Christ work it out of you. Go slow. Don't rush into another marriage. Take the time to live your life healed by your walk with God, before you walk with someone else.

If you're currently single, find wholeness in Christ. As the saying goes, there is only one thing worse than being single, and that's being miserably married. Develop an attitude of, "Lord, I'm here to serve You first." Make that your priority—and *keep* it your priority, so when marriage presents itself in the future, your heart will be ready for a healthy relationship.

If you're currently married, then be married, stay married, and enjoy it.

> To the married I give this command—not I but the Lord—that the wife should not separate from her husband (but if she does separate, let her remain unmarried or else be reconciled to her husband), and that the husband should not divorce his wife.…Are you bound to a wife? Do not seek to be free. Are you free from a wife? Do not seek a wife (1 Corinthians 7:10-11,27).

Perfect Love: A Picture

In 1977, an Australian journalist named John Everingham fell in love with a Cambodian girl named Kyo Cherishhon. The horror of those days in Cambodia was tremendous. Millions were killed by their own people in the Communist takeover. When Vietnam collapsed and Pol Pot began the killing fields, John was thrown out of the country, but Kyo was locked up.

Just to get to the prison camp required the crossing of a wide, deep river. The Cambodians didn't worry about people escaping by water; it was just too far.

But before he left, John told Kyo, "I will come back for you." He returned to Australia, and for six solid months, he practiced swimming and holding his breath. He then took every dollar he could scrape together, wrapped it in plastic, and on an August night in 1977, went back to Cambodia to swim that deep, dark river.

He thought his lungs would burst. His legs got caught in barbed wire. He broke his ankle and lacerated his calf pulling his foot free. Finally, he made it to shore. He approached a guard and offered him all of his money if the man would just bring out Kyo. The guard looked at him like he was crazy. John didn't know if he was going to be shot or what. But the guard brought her out and said, "Go. Get out of here!"

John carried her away—even with his broken ankle. He loved her so much, he said later, "Her weight on my back was the sweetest feeling I ever had."

There is only one love story I know that is greater than that one. It is the love story about when we were imprisoned by this fallen world. It is the story of God saying, "Somebody must rescue them," and His Son answering, "I will do it." And Jesus didn't just hold His breath and swim a mile in the dark to rescue us. He emptied Himself out and put on flesh and lived among us.

He has been here. He knows what life is like. He who filled the cosmos forever and ever was in that body then and is in His spiritual body now. He didn't just lacerate His leg as they hung Him on the Cross; His body was broken, and He poured out all of His blood. And every time Jesus holds us and we try to go running back to the prisons of this sinful world, He keeps coming back to rescue us.

That is true love. If He can love us that deeply, surely we can love our spouse enough to refuse to allow our marriage to drift away.

Never forget—love is a verb!

CHAPTER 12

Issue Five—Homosexuality

I'd like to address an issue now that gets a lot of attention in our culture today: *homosexuality*. Both inside and outside of the church, this is a hot topic.

I have never received so many books, articles, and even preemptive angry e-mails on any sermon as when I preach on the subject of homosexuality. Some people just get ahead of the crowd and start blasting away at me!

I have done my research. I've read over a dozen serious books on the topic and have even researched the so-called "Christian" gay Websites out there. One book I read was titled *Living in Sin? A Bishop Rethinks Human Sexuality*, by John Spong. This book argues that commandments against homosexuality in the Bible were *cultural edicts* that don't apply to us anymore. In other words, we're free to practice and celebrate homosexuality because it's not a sexual covenant issue. Is that really true?

Let's see what the Bible has to say about that.

GOD'S WORD ON HOMOSEXUALITY

Someone once asked me, "How do you want the homosexuals who attend your church to feel?" Well, I want them to feel love, first of all. I don't want them to feel judged. If they're Christians, I want them to feel like brothers and sisters in Christ. And I want them to feel holy, which means *living according to God's standards*. And according to God's standards, there are to be no sexual relationships outside of a *man and a woman in marriage*.

But more than "feeling" all of these things, I want them to live them—in a life of holiness, obedience, and love—toward God, His Word, and other people.

Let's look at a few Scripture passages that stand clearly against homosexuality. As God was leading the Israelites into their Promised Land and setting down the Ten Commandments, He told the people through Moses that they must not do as the Egyptians did and that they must not follow the practices of the Canaanites (see Leviticus 18:3). And then He added, very clearly:

> *Do not lie with a man as one lies with a woman; that is detestable...If a man lies with a man as one lies with a woman, both of them have done what is detestable* (Leviticus 18:22; 20:13a NIV).

The teachings in the Book of Leviticus often seem so strange to us today; and yet they help us delineate what is cultural and what is eternal. Throughout the Book of Leviticus, in fact throughout all of Scripture, God reminds His people that they are different from the cultures they live in:

> *The Lord said to Moses, "Speak to the Israelites and say to them: 'I am the Lord your God. You must not do as they do in Egypt, where you used to live, and you must not do as they do in the land of Canaan, where I am bringing you. Do not follow their practices. You must obey My laws and be careful to follow My decrees. I am the Lord your God. Keep My decrees and laws, for the man who obeys them will live by them. I am the Lord'"* (Leviticus 18:1-5 NIV).

As these passages indicate, God is very clear on this topic. These passages leave no "wiggle room" for cultural adjustments over the centuries in different times and various societies. Some Christians (who I admire and respect) take these passages in Scripture to be bound to a "pre-Christ" understanding. One problem with that way of interpreting Scripture is that it leaves no place for a cross-cultural truth or perspective on anything.

Beginning with Leviticus 18:6, God talks about sexual purity, clearly outlining those things that are not permitted. He reminds the Israelites that they are different from the Canaanites and different from the Egyptians, and that they are therefore to behave differently. These human-to-human sexual purity statutes culminate with verse 22:

Do not lie with a man as one lies with a woman; that is detestable (Leviticus 18:22 NIV).

God is very serious about this issue. Many people think God's guidelines concerning homosexuality are in the Old Testament only. But the New Testament amply covers the prohibitions against homosexuality as well. In the Book of Romans, the apostle Paul wrote to the Roman Christians during a time when the Greeks thought homosexuality was a higher form of love than heterosexual love:

Therefore God gave them over in the sinful desires of their hearts to sexual impurity for the degrading of their bodies with one another. They exchanged the truth of God for a lie, and worshiped and served created things rather than the Creator—who is forever praised. Amen. Because of this, God gave them over to shameful lusts. Even their women exchanged natural relations for unnatural ones. In the same way the men also abandoned natural relations with women and were inflamed with lust for one another. Men committed indecent acts with other men, and received in themselves the due penalty for their perversion (Romans 1:24-27 NIV).

Paul said that these people did not acknowledge God and that they worshiped the creature rather than the Creator (see Romans 1:25,28). They lost their identity and their very crime became their punishment, since they "received in themselves the due penalty for their perversion" (verse 27 NIV). When you reject God, He lets you fall in on yourself. When sin entered into this world, we lost our identity. We lost who we really are as God's creations. Some people say that the term used for homosexuality back in Paul's time actually meant prostitution-related homosexuality. But there is no evidence indicating that how the word was used then (the Greek word *pornea*) was related to merely prostitution. It meant then what it means today. Simply put, it is the "misuse of sex." This applies to heterosexual as well as homosexual acts.

131

As Paul said in these verses, we are all slaves to sin since we exchanged the truth for a lie. We are all in danger of not inheriting the Kingdom of God when we turn from His truths and His ways.

> *Do you not know that the unrighteous will not inherit the kingdom of God? Do not be deceived. Neither fornicators, nor idolaters, nor adulterers, nor homosexuals, nor sodomites* (1 Corinthians 6:9 NKJV).

What Paul is talking about in this verse is not just the act of practicing homosexuality; he's talking about a heart issue, about those who say, "My will, my body, my choice to do what I want with it."

For those people who say, "I know my desires and I want my desires or nothing," that's exactly how hell will be—people who are saying they want it their way and not God's way. But the Lord says, "I'm the Source of a deeper desire inside of you that's also warning you."

The gay agenda is no different than the heterosexual agenda. We heterosexuals have as much to repent of as the homosexuals do from this "me" mindset. All of us are broken and deeply in need of Christ's love.

These are just a few of the many passages that speak against homosexuality. And now, let's examine the Scriptures that speak in favor of it—*none*. From Genesis to Revelation, there is not one single verse that condones homosexuality. This is not because God is a harsh God or because this is merely a cultural issue; it's because this is not God's way, despite what the fallen world would have you believe.

According to the sentinel of Scripture, homosexuality was not a part of God's *creative* purposes, it was not His design for relationships, and it was not part of his *redemptive* purposes. God's Word does not change; it's the same now as it was in the beginning. Even today in Christ there is no embracing of sexual relationships between the same sex.

In the area of sexuality, Scripture is unified. It speaks against sexual promiscuity from the Old Testament all the way through the New.

REAL-LIFE EXAMPLES

I want you to know that I don't speak of homosexuality lightly or as some callous outside observer. I have stood over the gravesites of many lovely people who died of AIDS. (And I do realize that not all AIDS victims are gay.) I have counseled countless individuals struggling with homosexuality. I even witnessed my closest friend in high school, who is now living with his partner in San Francisco, come out about his homosexuality. There are hundreds of gay and lesbian individuals who attend my church every week. (At our church in Los Angeles, over half of our members work in the entertainment industry. So many in our congregation are, or bring to the services, gays and lesbians.) I have gone to many gay Bible studies and have many gay friends. So when I talk about homosexuality, I can see real faces and real friends.[1]

I preach what I preach on this topic for two reasons: because it is God's Word; and because I care about those I talk to and want them to know that God's Word is the best way for them, and His Word says that homosexuality is wrong to engage in.

HOW SELF-DETERMINED IS OUR ORIENTATION?

One thing I encounter time and again when talking with those who practice homosexuality is that they feel "helpless" against their homosexual urges. Even if they want to live differently, they feel they can't.

I was once asked by a gentleman in my church to basically officiate a gay wedding. He wanted me to perform a "committal service" for him and his partner, both of whom had given their life to the Lord. I said, "No. I can't do that. You know what I believe and preach."

He responded, "Well, I know what you *say*, but...," insinuating that maybe I preach one thing but turn a blind eye of compassion to its practice by those in my church.

"And I *mean* what I say," I told him. I care about this brother very much, so I was honest with him. "If you marry," I admonished him, "marry a *woman*."

"Pastor," he responded. "I have tried. I've tried so hard, so many times, to step across, and I just can't."

How do we respond to something like that? How do we deal with homosexuality in light of such testimonials? Do we accept that it's beyond a person's control, and therefore condone it? And is it beyond their control? What would the world today say? Here's another interview sampling of what the average American thinks about homosexuality in the year 2007:

"I don't knock it. I say, different strokes for different folks."

"I'm for whatever the person is into: I don't knock it. I'm not biased or anything."

"To each his own."

"Whatever floats your boat."

"That's a very individual thing. It's a private issue. It's not my business what anybody else does in the privacy of their own home."

"I mean, if they want to do that in their personal lives, that's fine with me."

"It's all right with me. My friend and I enjoy it."

"I don't go that way; I don't like homosexuality. That's their own thing, though. If that's what they are, that's what they are. That's up to them."

The underlying thought in each of these opinions is that a person doesn't *choose* to be homosexual—it just is. Well, if that's the case, then how do we get our sexuality?

A SCIENTIFIC LOOK

A quick biology review: a sperm and an egg come together to form a zygote. If there are 46 XX chromosomes, you've got a little girl; if there are 46 XY chromosomes, you've got a little boy. Other than that, at birth there's very little difference between little boys and little girls. Aside from the genitals, they're practically identical.

They grow up. Boys naturally hang around boys, and they find out that girls have cooties. Girls naturally hang around girls, and they find out that boys are stupid. Until something happens at puberty. The secondary pituitary endocrine complex in the body starts pumping out something called trophic hormones. These things make heroine seem like decaf coffee!

All of a sudden, wild changes take place. Boys now start to talk in deeper voices, they start looking at girls, and they begin to realize that girls don't have cooties after all. Girls change too. They start looking at boys and realizing that they're not dumb after all—or at least they look good while they're being dumb.

But what about the little boys or girls where these changes take place physically, but when they grow up they're still not attracted to the opposite sex and find themselves wanting to be romantic with the same sex? How do we explain all that? Is it choice? Or is it some "pre wiring" from our genetic code? Both the worlds of psychology as well as biological genetics try to explain.

According to classic Freudian psychology, that anomaly is attributable to conflicted parenting. Freud based his theory on his experiences in dealing with many homosexual men in Vienna. Freud said that if you have a domineering mother and a weak present father, there is a reaction formation in the son so that he identifies with, bonds with, and empathizes with the weak father. Although he may be close to his mother, he develops a general dislike for women, because every woman he gets close to reminds him in some way of his domineering mother.[2]

I know many gay males who would say, "That's not true in my life," and many others who would say, "Yeah, maybe." But nine times out of ten, it seems that homosexual individuals were exposed to at least one of the major "perfect storm" factors in their upbringing that are most likely to produce an adult with homosexual tendencies. Sometimes it is parental influences, or at times sexual abuse, or peer or friend dynamics. There is no one "blueprint" of how someone finds herself or himself being strongly pulled to being gay or lesbian. With the other 10 percent, it is possible that it is simply an individual's choice to practice homosexuality for a certain time period in their life.

Behavioral psychology has a similar conclusion. Behaviorists in the 1970s such as the late B.F. Skinner say that homosexuality is the result of environmental factors in one's upbringing. They say that we're pretty much born as empty sheets of paper, and through conditioning and response to a very complex set of specific stimuli, some people end up homosexual.

Psychology rubs against genetic physiology with many today who say there is such a thing as a "gay gene." However, genetic studies indicate that there simply is no genetic evidence for homosexuality, and the science to date shows that there is no physiological cause for homosexuality. There are some MRIs and brain mappings that could *possibly* show that the limbic system (the feeling brain, the amygdale, and the hippocampus) *might* be firing a little differently. It's all still unproven theory, and there's nothing to say such misfiring didn't begin *after* the initial decision to engage in homosexual acts. (Ironically, what's sad is that the political pressure **not** to do research is quite strong from the gay lobby. They fear "typing" or "tagging" homosexuality as anything physiological would be to equate it with something that they are doing that is wrong or bad. Until 1972, the American Psychological Association listed homosexuality as a pathology to be cured.)

Homosexuality seems to be much more a result of a complex weaving of environmental influences in the important, foundation-laying, formative years. Many people, sadly, have been victims of some form of abuse. But what of those who never had any of the "storms" that possibly released or created or added to a person's propensity toward desire for sexual activity with the same sex? First, we unconditionally love them, no matter what. And second, we try to understand the current existing scientific information pertaining to the topic.

Scientific studies dealing with identical twins shed some interesting light on the whole "gay gene" theory. It is scientific fact that identical twins have an identical genome, and yet there have been instances where twins who were either raised in separate households or who had different experiences within the same household developed different sexual orientations. If there were such a thing as a "gay gene" (as some would have us believe), then *both identical twins would have the same sexual orientation* (either homosexual or heterosexual), and neither would have a choice in the matter.

In short, there are no studies or other incontrovertible evidence that genetics play a role in causing a person to have homosexual tendencies. Even if we say there could be possible "physiological tendencies" toward homosexuality, that still does not change the creative and redemptive purposes of God. Scripture declares sexuality is between a man and a woman in a lifelong relationship called marriage. No Christian wants to open the floodgates to people attempting to excuse other behavior by reason of physiology. Help explain, yes. Excuse, no. It is true that our compassion and understanding uses science to help us "know a person's burden" about things that others don't know or understand.

But our burdens are known to God. No one but Christ knows the pressures and burdens others carry due to no fault of their own. However, it is also true that while we may "treat pathologies" we have to "repent of sin." It's not a sin to have an illness. It is a sin to stubbornly say in my heart, "I am not going to change." That's why the issue of the spirit and the heart requires repentance, turning first to our loving, accepting Heavenly Father. Then we can go get the help and treatment to restore us, whatever the challenge may be.

The bottom line—to be spiritually intelligent, means that we listen to the sentinel of Scripture, even when it seems to us to be harsh. Behavior identified in God's Word as being against God's will is ultimately destructive for Christians to engage in, no matter what the cause of the behavior.

THE CHURCH'S TWIN FALLACY

Let's put science and reason and Scripture aside for a minute, for the sake of argument, and suppose that there *is* a gay gene. Even if a person does not choose their orientation, they *do* have to choose how they will handle their orientation. Just because they feel drawn toward homosexual behavior doesn't mean they are *slaves* to it. This is where the Lord comes in, with His grace and His mercy—the same grace and mercy that the church needs to demonstrate to those struggling with homosexuality.

Those of us who do not practice or condone homosexuality need to repent of how we have treated people who do. So often we've just stood there, immutable as stone, demanding of homosexuals, "You need to repent!" Yet we haven't come alongside them to love and guide them. Judgment is not a safe environment to induce growth and change, especially when we represent a God of grace and forgiveness.

I once read a wonderful book by Dallas Willard called *Renovation of the Heart*. It said that in sinful relationships, we either attack or we withdraw. When we are on the throne of our lives instead of Christ, everyone around us is just somebody to be "used" in a subtle way. We either attack them if they don't give us what we want, or we withdraw from them until they do.

THE RIGHT RESPONSE

Unfortunately, we in the evangelical church community have been prime examples of this, simultaneously attacking and withdrawing from those struggling with their sexual identity. We need to realize that these are people who have dreams and hopes and fears, just like the rest of us. They're not Martians; they too are God's beloved children. We need to love them and support them and help them toward change—graciously, patiently, and lovingly, as God does with us. If we truly love them, we will want their highest welfare and will help to make it happen in the most loving and caring ways that glorify God.

If you don't wrestle with the area of homosexuality, thank God for that. If you don't wrestle with issues of sexuality at all—if you don't have an overactive libido or a sexual need—that is not weird. Praise God for it; you're like the few freed ones of the world! If you're not tempted in sexual ways that go against the Word of God, it's not necessarily because you're so righteous, but celebrate the fact that you don't have that as this issue to deal with, and be available to help those who wrestle with it.

Regardless of sexual orientation, any time you deal with somebody who does not have Christ on the throne of their life, you are talking to two people within the same body. One is a scarred, scared person who wants God in their life so much. The other is a selfish, rebellious person who wants God out of their life if He gets in their way. This is true for every human being because of something we all carry within us—*sin*.

Only Jesus was grace and truth blended perfectly. We all need to work better at showing the same grace to others that He extends to us.

WHERE THE WORLD WENT WRONG

Don't misunderstand me. I'm not saying that the church is the only one with blame on her hands. The truth is, the world needs to repent for saying that homosexuality is a "lifestyle" to be "celebrated." Unfortunately, it has gotten to the point in the world that if you are tempted homosexually, it's no longer strange or abnormal. We have so lost our identity as God's creation that sometimes even Christians no longer bat an eye at this deviation from God's perfect norm. In fact, it's becoming less and less unusual to find situations within the church where homosexuality is tolerated and actually celebrated.

My ordination vow contained the words, "Fidelity in marriage between a man and a woman, and chastity in singleness." Period. And that's not just for our church leaders—it's for the laity as well. We are *all* called to sexual purity. You can be sexual without sexually acting out. You can be intimate with other people—you can love them, hug them, share with them—all without having to *sexually* act on it.

ALL THE SAME

It's easy to see how the gay rights agenda in this country is really just the stepchild of the heterosexual rights agenda. In the "sexual revolution" of the 1960s, we started to hear people say, "It's my body. I'll do what I want with it. Pleasure is what life's all about." That's why, on the other side of the hill from my church in Southern California's San Fernando Valley, there's a pornography industry that pours billions of dollars worth of pornographic trash into the world every year. The dehumanizing of people into mere objects and the encouragement of sexual addiction is big business. This is one of the reasons why the Taliban, extremist Muslims, and al-Qaeda hate America—not so much because of our Christianity but because America has become the cultural cesspool of the modern world, through our domination of the media.[3]

As a side note, I had to quit calling it the "porn" industry because of an elderly lady who visited our church one day when I was talking about the porn industry. I went on and on about the porn industry in the valley and how much damage porn was causing and how awful it is. After my sermon, the old woman tottered up to me and asked, "What's the problem with the corn industry here, young man?" That's a true story. The corn industry is fine, by the way.

This is a free society, and they can make all the adult films they want. This is a free society, and I can also muster everything I can to stop it. But in this free society, the fact remains that we are sawing the moral limbs off the tree we're perched in.

Powerful nations aren't generally overthrown; a collapse of morals is what overtakes a nation. When morals decline, totalitarianism takes hold. The Roman Republic became Imperial Rome after wealth and licentiousness took over. No nation can survive incessant, increasing debauchery—which is what destroyed the mighty, 500-year-old Roman Empire.

We shouldn't be surprised that sexuality in any form no longer bothers our culture the way it once did. When we treat any sexual deviation from God's perfect standards as "OK," it's just a matter of time before we start accepting all sexual sin as OK.

THE CONFESSING GAME

If you're homosexual and you truly want to be free of that lifestyle and walk in God's ways, what should you do? Here's my suggestion: don't repress it and think it's not true, but don't express it and celebrate it, either. Simply confess and say, "I've got this challenge."

It's not a bigger sin than any other. In fact, if there were such a thing as a "sin scale," this one would possibly rank lower than other sins. It doesn't show up in God's Ten Commandments, and Jesus Himself never specifically addressed the subject, possibly because it didn't work Him up as much as other sins.

Let me be clear: Jesus *never* agreed with it or condoned it. But it was the sins of the spirit that really got to Him, like gossip, idolatry, unforgiveness, legalism (thinking that we can earn God's salvation), and the like. Those were the sins that Jesus spoke out against the most. It seems that while He was here He was more concerned with addressing the "sins of the heart" than of the flesh.

Jesus ministered to the world on behalf of the Father. That's our model. He wasn't here just to set the public agenda. He was here to set a godly example for us to follow. In fact, He said to the people, "I'm not here to do My own will, but My Father's" (see John 6:38).

> *For I did not speak of My own accord, but the Father who sent Me commanded Me what to say and how to say it* (John 12:49 NIV).

His ministry was for the Father because He knows the Father loves us. And we are to minister to the world on behalf of Jesus. Jesus Himself is the One who set the agenda of loving the gay community and reaching out to them.

MOVING FORWARD

What do you do once you've acknowledged your struggle and confessed it? Get in a support group that can help you along the way. Find fellow Christians who will come alongside you and give you strength, encouragement, and prayer as you deal with this issue in your life. A solid support network is vital.

I have a friend who gave his life to Christ. He said that was the most liberating thing in his life. He said the second most liberating thing was the first time he went to a gay bar, because he had wrestled with homosexuality all his life and grew up in the church as a closet homosexual. He said, "Just to see other men celebrating who I am was so liberating."

So what do I do? Do I cut off my friendship with him? Of course not. I still see him. Do I love him with all of my heart? Yes. And I tell him that he can be very close to the same sex, but *he cannot sexually act it out!* Sex is covenant-making between a man and a woman and God, and it's to be reserved for a lifelong marriage relationship between a man and a woman. This isn't just a sex thing; it's an entire identity thing. And it's a tough issue in our society.

That is why, if you wrestle with this issue in your life, it's so important to get some support. Surround yourself with other Christians who understand and who aren't put off by the subject. Find some friends who, when you're tempted sexually, won't say to you, "Uh, man, you're weird." Get some real, quality, honest, loving help. You may even need to get some professional help from a Christian counselor or therapist.

I also encourage homosexuals who really want to move forward to set guidelines in their lives that they will adhere to. Commit to them, and make it a priority to act them out. Men, you can be close to men as friends, but you cannot sexually act it out. Ladies, the same thing— you can be close to women as friends, but you are not allowed to sexually act it out. With the help of your support network, figure out what you need to do so that you can stick to these guidelines.

There are pro-homosexual Christian groups out there comprised of men and women who believe that homosexuality is to be permitted and actually celebrated. These aren't the folks I'm talking about. I'm not talking about Christians who jump around from gay bar to gay bar. I'm talking to the men and women who love Christ, who want to try to follow the Lord, and who genuinely want to know, "What do I do? How should I deal with this?"

A RESPONSE OF GRACE AND LOVE

If you don't struggle with these sexual issues in your life but you know someone who does, then help them. Tell that person, "Hey, let me pray for you about that situation." And then offer to be there when they need to talk, or when they need a distraction to avoid temptation.

We who are heterosexuals need to repent, because we have tended to categorize the particular sin of homosexuality as some extraordinarily evil bizarreness. And we've done so little to try to understand, help, and support those involved.

The gay lifestyle is hardly one of happiness and fulfillment, but we heterosexuals don't exactly have all the answers either. In one way or another, we're all twisted or unhappy or tweaked because of sin. We each need God's grace and need to embrace a life of repentance.

Everyone alive is tempted in one way or another. And with God, sin is sin. Period.

For whoever keeps the whole law and yet stumbles at just one point is guilty of breaking all of it (James 2:10 NIV).

THE BOTTOM LINE

Wherever you are, whether you're struggling with sexual issues yourself or offering support to a friend, always, in every case, make a beeline to the Cross! Get right to Jesus and to what He says. Getting advice from others is good, but first and foremost, get to the person of Christ.

God's grace is here for us all. He wants us to understand what sexuality is all about. He wants us to be close to people of the same sex, as well as with the opposite sex. He wants us free from this *worship of the body* nonsense of the world. Life is more than the physical.

Some of us need to repent. Our hearts have so hated the gay community and the lesbian community. We get so mad and we think that there's something so insidious about that particular sin over others.

Where did we get that idea? Instead, we need to love and we need to change our attitude.

How? Jesus told us exactly how:

"Love the Lord your God with all your heart and with all your soul and with all your mind." This is the first and greatest commandment. And the second is like it: "Love your neighbor as yourself" (Matthew 22:37-39 NIV).

ENDNOTES

1. I am not saying that I closely and regularly associate with people who openly profess to practice homosexuality, as we are admonished against doing in First Corinthians 5:11: "I am writing to you not to associate with anyone who bears the name of brother or sister [that is, men or women who call themselves Christians] who is sexually immoral."

2. Freud didn't address lesbianism in such detail, so the question of developmental issues with lesbians is more recent and not as extensive as with male homosexuality.

3. While America may seem to be sexually what the Greeks were in the first century, other Western democracies are actually worse than the U.S. Sexually suggestive billboards depicting topless women dot the roadsides and leer over cities including Rome, Athens, and others, and peer out from ads in the pages of even the most mundane magazines.

CHAPTER 13

Issue Six—Sexuality Outside of Marriage

SEXUALITY: A PRIMER

Probably one of the toughest issues in our culture today is that of sex and sexuality. Unless you're a hermit, you're more likely than not bombarded with sexual images and messages day-in and day-out, whether you're watching television, reading a magazine, surfing the Internet, or even just passing billboards as you drive down the highway. In today's society, sex is a hot topic, in more ways than one.

How's a Christian to handle this tough issue? Should we take the free-for-all, no-holds-barred, no-consequences approach of Hollywood? Should we simply tolerate it as a necessary evil required for procreation? Or is there a balance somewhere in between? What about singles? Just how far can they go with sexual expression?

First, let's take a look at the purpose of God's gift of sexuality. Here is another smattering of responses we received when we talked with people in an average shopping mall about what they think concerning the purpose of sex:

"Um...to show that you love someone."

"To satisfy the mind."

"It's not an experience of the physical, though it's so physical—yet, it's so spiritual."

145

"Enjoyment. To feel good. And to make someone feel good."

"To be free."

"For me, I like to have sex. It's fun, you know. It's real good exercise. And it's fun."

"Oh, it's great. It's a gift from God."

"Well, I'm too old. I don't know anymore."

I want to draw your attention to something that quite frankly might blow a lot of minds. Did you ever stop to consider the fact that God created sex? He didn't look down at all the people making love and say to the angels, "What the heck are they doing down there now?" He's the One who thought up sexual intercourse. Sex was God's idea in the first place, and He's the one who determined its purpose.

IN THE GARDEN

So what does God say about the purpose for sex? Why did He create sex and give us our sexuality? The answer is found in examining the very first human love story, the story of Adam and Eve.

But first, there's an old story about God talking to Adam right after He made Eve and presented her to Adam. "Well, what do you think?" God asked Adam.

"She's really great, Lord," Adam replied. "But I have a couple of questions."

"Sure," God said. "What do you want to know?"

"Well, why did you make her so pretty?"

"So you'd be attracted to her," God replied.

"And why did you make her so soft?"

"So you would be *attracted* to her, Adam."

"Then why did you make her so...dumb?"

God hesitated and then answered, "So she'd be attracted to *you*, Adam."

Joking aside, the creation account we find in Genesis is truly amazing. A beautiful picture of how God lovingly formed this world and pieced it together so it would work just right. He truly did shape Adam and Eve uniquely to complement each other.

It all started in Genesis 1, where God looked at His creation thus far and said, "This is very good. But now I'm going to make My highest creation—something in My very image." And God went on to form Adam in His very own image.

> *Then God said, "Let Us make man in Our image, in Our likeness, and let them rule over the fish of the sea and the birds of the air, over the livestock, over all the earth, and over all the creatures that move along the ground." So God created man in His own image, in the image of God He created him; male and female He created them* (Genesis 1:26-27 NIV).

Why did He make "male and female"? Because in chapter 2 of Genesis, we see that Adam felt alone. He had no helper, no companion.

> *The Lord God said, "It is not good for the man to be alone. I will make a helper suitable for him." Now the Lord God had formed out of the ground all the beasts of the field and all the birds of the air. He brought them to the man to see what he would name them; and whatever the man called each living creature, that was its name. So the man gave names to all the livestock, the birds of the air and all the beasts of the field. But for Adam no suitable helper was found* (Genesis 2:18-20 NIV).

And so God, like a great anesthesiologist, put Adam into a deep sleep, took his rib, and fashioned a woman from that rib—a companion for Adam:

> *So the Lord God caused the man to fall into a deep sleep; and while he was sleeping, He took one of the man's ribs and closed up the place with flesh. Then the Lord God made a woman from the rib He had taken out of the man, and He brought her to the man* (Genesis 2:21-22 NIV).

Even the name given to the woman reflected the miracle that had just taken place. In Hebrew, the word for man is *ish*. The word for woman is *ishah*, which was formed from the word for man (just as the woman herself was formed from the man's side). It's an incredible and beautiful account of how God made humankind, both man and woman, in His image.

The most beautiful part is that their existence was sinless. There was no jealousy, no anger, no embarrassment, no guilt. Adam and Eve were both naked, and yet they had no shame; they celebrated and enjoyed each other fully.

In fact, the very first words Adam said, the very first words spoken by any human being ever, were essentially a love poem. He said, basically, "Wow, God. Good job! This is bone of my bones and flesh of my flesh" (see Genesis 2:23). Right away, they were different sexes, and yet of the same heart. They were totally naked, totally transparent, and yet there was no guilt, no shame. Just utter delight as they shared in this new creation.

> The man said, "This is now bone of my bones and flesh of my flesh; she shall be called 'woman,' for she was taken out of man" (Genesis 2:23 NIV).

SEX IS LIKE TAPE

The Genesis account then goes on to tell us that this is a model for all marriages. Just as Adam and Eve were united as "one flesh," so too should all husbands and wives be. In fact, a husband and wife should "cling" together:

> Therefore a man leaves his father and his mother and clings to his wife, and they become one flesh (Genesis 2:24).

This is where we get our first glimpse in the Bible of the God-given purpose for sex. You see, sex isn't just for *pro*creation (although it *is* the mechanism God has also chosen in order to keep the species going). And sex isn't just for *re*creation either (although sex *is* lot of fun). While both of these are legitimate purposes for sex, the ultimate and highest purpose of sex is *unification*. Sex is intended to unify a man and a woman in a lifelong relationship called marriage, and in this way it is intended to reflect the very image of the triune God.

Social scientists (or bio-psychologists) tell us they're at a loss as to why sexual intercourse is so psychologically and emotionally bonding, although they've managed to come up with quite a few theories. Currently there is some evidence of a "bonding" hormone that is released during intercourse.[1] God's Word is way ahead of the studies. He tells us precisely why: sex is covenant-making between a man and a woman and their Creator. It is powerful and it is bonding. Sort of like tape for relational bonding.

Just as tape has a stickiness to it, so with sex a bonding takes place that holds couples together. But when you use the same piece of tape over and over in different places, after awhile it loses its stickiness. The same thing happens with people who change sex partners over and over. The bonding aspect no longer works as intended.

The reason some people doom themselves to a lifetime of loneliness is that they've lost that intimate adhesiveness. When you sleep with a bunch of different people, you literally reduce your ability to emotionally and spiritually bond with others.

So often in counseling sessions, I talk to men and women who have been going from bed to bed over the years, thinking they were in love. Now they don't understand why they can't seem to feel close or attach to people anymore. It's a natural consequence of the way God wired us. We were made to bond with one person within the confines of marriage—that's the way sex works best.

PROBLEMS IN PARADISE

Back to Adam and Eve. They're in the Garden together. Everything's perfect, pure, sinless, carefree, joyful, fulfilling. They don't have a care in the world, because there are no cares to have.

Enter the serpent. Now, a lot of people think that satan brought sin into the world. But the truth is, he only brought the temptation. When Adam and Eve gave into temptation, that's when sin entered the world.

What was the temptation? A tree. It all came down to a tree and its fruit. God had given Adam and Eve all of Eden to enjoy—except for one tree. You think the couple would have been satisfied. But no, *nearly* everything wasn't enough for Adam and Eve. They had everything but one silly tree, yet they listened to the serpent and began to believe that they just *had* to try that forbidden fruit.

> *Now the serpent was more crafty than any other wild animal that the Lord God had made. He said to the woman, "Did God say, 'You shall not eat from any tree in the garden'?"* (Genesis 3:1).

Remember, the serpent didn't bring sin into the world. He brought temptation. Sin came when mankind chose to disbelieve God and the same holds true today. Sin, in essence, is whenever we choose to disbelieve God. Whether we lie, gossip, murder, steal, or commit fornication, we are actually *disbelieving*. We disbelieve that God knows what He is talking about, that His way is best. So we go ahead and disobey Him by doing our own thing.

That's exactly what happened to Adam and Eve that day in the Garden. The serpent slithered in and planted the thought in their minds that what they had wasn't enough. He said to Eve, "You're not eating from that one tree over there. How come?"

Eve answered, "Well, we can eat of all of these other trees and everything else. But not that one. God says we can't touch it. Or else we'll die."

"What?" the serpent spewed. "God said that? He's lying to you! You're not gonna die, dummy."

Eve gave in. She bought into satan's temptation to disbelieve God, and right then *bam*! Sin entered the world through humans.

I have to say, in Eve's defense, that at least she put up a discussion with the serpent about the matter.

But not Adam. He bought into it in an instant. He came cruising up and asked, "What's up, Eve?"

"Eating forbidden fruit," she said. And she sold the forbidden fruit idea to Adam.

"Why not," he responded and took it. He didn't even discuss God's prohibition like Eve did.

From there, it just got uglier. Adam felt guilt (which, up until that point, was a completely foreign feeling) and he actually hid from God. He'd never even heard of hiding before that day.

> But the Lord God called to the man, "Where are you?" He answered, "I heard you in the garden, and I was afraid because I was naked; so I hid" (Genesis 3:9-10 NIV).

And then, one of the most painful words in all of Scripture:

> And He said, "Who told you that you were naked? Have you eaten from the tree that I commanded you not to eat from?" (Genesis 3:11 NIV).

God was saying, essentially, "Do you know what you have done?" He was already visualizing in His mind the aftereffects of the act, what it was going to cost to redeem us back to Himself. From the get-go, sin took off in the world because Adam immediately pointed the finger at his precious wife...and the blame game began:

> *The man said, "The woman whom You gave to be with me,*
> **she** *gave me fruit from the tree"* (Genesis 3:12).

"*She* did it!" Adam whined to God. "*That woman* was the one who gave it to me!" Then Adam took it one step further and actually blamed God:

> *The man said, "The woman You put here"* (Genesis 3:12 NIV).

Then Eve jumped on the bandwagon:

> *The woman said, "The* **serpent** *tricked me"* (Genesis 3:13b).

"The *serpent*!" she screamed. "The *serpent* pulled a fast one on me!" And all of a sudden, in the Order of the Fall, blame and shame came gushing into the world.

INTRODUCTION TO THE LOWER LAWS

We live in a culture that is obsessed with the physical. Stop for a minute and consider how many times each day you think about how your body looks, feels, or smells. How many times each day do you check your hair in the mirror? How many times do you weigh yourself each week? How many anti-aging, wrinkle-erasing creams and lotions and potions do you have in your medicine cabinet?

For many of us, it has truly become an obsession. Is this an American obsession? No—it's a *spiritual* thing. When Adam and Eve sinned in the Garden, the Lower Laws entered the world. When Adam and Eve chose to reject the Higher Laws (God's laws) they became slaves to these Lower Laws.

Think about it this way: When a plane flies, does it break the law of gravity? No, it simply becomes governed by a higher law (the law of aerodynamics and lift) instead of the lower law of gravity. If the higher laws of aerodynamics cease, the plane becomes a slave of the lower law of gravity, and down it comes.

In the case of Adam and Eve, they learned that we are always free to choose, but never free of the consequences of our choices. They had been governed by the Higher Laws of God, but as soon as they sinned the Lower Laws took effect, and they were now enslaved to those Lower Laws, and no longer able to "fly" in a sense. And right away, from the very beginning, a struggle began. Why? Because Adam and Eve had disbelieved God, rejected His authority, and ultimately set themselves up as their own "gods."

Understand this: If the Lord is not your God, then you are living by the Lower Laws and trying to be the god of your own life. If you think you are doing a 100 percent great job at it, then carry on. But if you can't say you're doing a perfect job of being your own god, that's because there is only one God who does a 100 percent perfect job of being God. The reason things don't feel "right" whenever the Lord is not our God is because that's not the way it's supposed to be. We were made by Him Who made the Higher Laws that we are to live by, not the Lower Laws with their disharmony, fighting, guilt, and blame.

WHO'S ON THE THRONE?

No matter what any commercial, movie, or television show might tell you, being your own god doesn't feel good. The moment God is not at the center of your life, the moment you take over, then you start to feel it. You know it. It's not a fulfilling feeling. It's emptiness at its worst.

Anyone who tries to live life outside of Christ, whether they are religious goodie two-shoes trying to earn God's favor, or rebellious boys and girls who are into drugs, rock and roll, and sex, they will never live a full life. The supposed "life" they live will always be a corruption of the true life that God intended. The result is lost identities, feelings of emptiness, and tremendous loneliness. This isn't what God intended for us. Instead God says, "Come. Replace these things with Me. I alone can fill your needs."

THE BODY PARADOX

A strange thing happens when you worship the body. You start to hate it. We always resent the idols we put in our lives.

The ancient Greeks were a perfect example. Anyone who has ever studied Greek culture knows that the Greeks worshiped and idolized the body. It was the subject of much of their artwork and sculptures. And yet, despite this love for the body, they were also body-haters. In fact, when Paul came to Athens and told some of the Greeks about the resurrection, a handful of them actually responded, "Who'd want their body back?" Particularly one growing old.

> *When they heard about the resurrection of the dead, some of them sneered* (Acts 17:32a NIV).

When I was in Ireland, I was told that as an aging old Robin Hood lay dying in his bedroom, Little John asked him where he would like to be buried. The great old warrior said, "Get me my bow!" Little John brought Robin Hood his bow, and Robin Hood said, "Bring me an arrow!" So Little John gave Robin Hood an arrow. Then Robin Hood said, "Open the shutters." Little John did that. Finally Robin Hood said, "When I shoot this arrow, bury me wherever it lands in the forest." So the great Robin Hood stretched back his bow with all his might and let loose the arrow...and they buried him there. On his dresser.

That is why the ancient Greeks, Americans today, and anyone else who has ever tried to worship the body has ended up hating it—because it ultimately fails! It ages. It decays. It dies. It reminds us that we are mortal. Despite all our attempts to be "god" of our own lives, someday we will be six feet under, just like the next person. Why do you think this culture so hates wrinkles and fat? It's not just because they're unattractive. It's because they reveal the impotence of the "self-god." We're dying, and there's nothing we can do about it. We're not as much "in control" as we thought we were.

The Greek word for sin is *hamartia*, which means "to miss the mark." I don't care how good we think we are. You can have the best aim, the strongest arm, the steadiest hand, but you're going to miss the mark. Just like Robin Hood, we're going to fall short in our lives. Next to God's standards, we already have fallen short.

SIN AND SEX

Today, because of the Fall, sex has become all about taking care of one's self. It was initially designed as a covenant, as an opportunity to

153

give to another person and enjoy togetherness as a result. The initial purpose of sex was captured in the question, "How can I give myself to my spouse?"

But today it has become all about "me"—the big M-E. Now the question is no longer "How can I give?" but "What can I get?" It has become all about taking and using instead of giving and nurturing. We live in a world that is awash in open, rampant sexuality, and people are clueless as to what its original intent was really all about. The delight over giving, over sex as a pleasurable covenant, is gone—replaced instead with whatever people can get for themselves.

The raw truth is that you can only find satisfaction and joy in life when you have the attitude of giving. That's what *making love* versus *having sex* is about. Although humankind's misunderstanding of the purpose of sex can be traced back to Adam's and Eve's sin in the Garden, sex has been devalued and cheapened over the years even more.

Consider the big sexual revolution of the 1960s. I was in school at the time, and I remember hearing that the pill was going to save us from pregnancy. We were going to be able to do whatever we wanted, whenever we wanted, and not have to pay for it. And then we heard that penicillin was going to be able to save us from the two big venereal diseases of that day, gonorrhea and syphilis.

Yeah, right. Within the past 40 years of that so-called sexual revolution, over 120 different sexually transmitted diseases have now surfaced or been identified. Some of them make syphilis look like a bad case of the flu.

Then came the king of all transmittable infectious diseases—AIDS.

According to the Center for Disease Control and Prevention, one of the fastest-growing populations contracting AIDS is the new population of people over 50. Viagra has allowed what is now called the "Condo Casanovas." In Florida, it is reaching epidemic levels. They don't know what to do about it. (I would surmise that they possibly slept with prostitutes and then went back and started sleeping around.) We now have elderly people infected with AIDS.

If we as a culture are going to have the morality of the barnyard, then we're going to have the diseases of the barnyard. The number of unwed pregnancies are through the roof. Teen pregnancies are epidemic. Why? It's all a natural consequence of not using God's gift of sexuality the way He intended it to be used.

A DIFFERENT PEOPLE

The world may not understand how to use sex but we, as God's children, can. God has called us to be different, and with His help we can be.

As God says in the Book of Leviticus, we, His children, His followers, are not to behave as the world around us behaves. We are to be holy, sanctified, and living in accordance with His laws, commandments, and statutes.

After the great Fall and sin entered and marred the creation, God said to His people, "I will not leave you alone." He was talking about how He would redeem us. And you and I know that on the other side of the Cross is the order of Redemption. There is hope! Paul laid it out perfectly in Ephesians:

> *In Him we have redemption through His blood, the forgiveness of sins, in accordance with the riches of God's grace that He lavished on us with all wisdom and understanding. And He made known to us the mystery of His will according to His good pleasure, which He purposed in Christ, to be put into effect when the times will have reached their fulfillment—to bring all things in Heaven and on earth together under one Head, even Christ* (Ephesians 1:7-10 NIV).

There you have it. We are not slaves to the Lower Laws anymore. The Lower Laws are still in effect, but we are not *slaves* to them. There is newness, empowerment, freshness. We are sons and daughters of the living God almighty! We belong to Christ and we are His servants. There's a power from the future that is available to us right now, to enable us to live as new creatures in Christ—if we so choose.

Whether or not we choose, God's standards and His Moral Law still remain. We don't have to sacrifice on the temple altar anymore, but God is still against murder. He's still against oppressing others. Still against bigotry. And He still claims that the values of sexuality belong to Him.

I know a lot of Christian men and women who disagree deeply on this issue. They say that God's sexual prohibitions are only "cultural." In other words, they think those guidelines were only for the Israelite culture and don't apply to us anymore. However, if you claim that, then you have to reject other aspects of the Law, such as God being against oppression, God being against murder, and God being against idol-worship.

That's how we know God's guidelines for sexuality are not purely cultural. His instructions on sexuality are on the same playing field as His laws against murder. These laws are not cultural, and so they still apply today. Once again, God's creative and redemptive purpose involves how we enjoy this great gift of sex. We are to enjoy it *His* way.

SEXUALITY FOR SINGLES

A high school kid went into a 7-Eleven store on his way to a date. He grabbed a one-pound, a two-pound, and a three-pound box of chocolates and took them up to the counter.

"What are you going to do with all that candy, son?" the manager asked him.

"Well, I'm going on a date tonight," he explained. "I've never met her before—it's a blind date. After I have dinner at her house and meet her parents, we're going to a movie. And if she lets me hold her hand through the movie, she gets a one-pound box of chocolates. If she lets me put my arm around her, she gets the two-pounder. And if she lets me kiss her through the whole movie, she gets three whole pounds of chocolate."

"I see," said the manager.

The kid left the store and went to the girl's house, met her and her family, and when her father arrived home from work, they all sat down together for dinner. After the mother finished serving, the young man asked, "Do you mind if I pray?" They all looked at him, and he stood up and started to pray. He repeated the Apostle's Creed verbatim. He mentioned and thanked every missionary he could think of. Then he concluded by singing the Hallelujah Chorus *a cappella*. He then sat down while they all stared at him.

After a fairly quiet dinner, he walked his date to the car and opened the car door for her. As she got in, she said, "I didn't know you were such a man of prayer."

"And I didn't know your father manages the 7-Eleven down the street, either!" he replied.

Perhaps one of the biggest issues when it comes to God's standards on sex and sexuality is that of sex for singles. For single couples who are dating, "How far can we go?" is often the big question. What do we do with sex if we're not married? Are we still sexual? Is it OK to have sex outside of marriage?

I notice that junior high and high school kids get right to the point—they ask all the questions everybody wants to ask: "What can we touch?" "What can we do?" "What *can't* we do?"

Let's see what the average person has to say about the purpose of sex before or outside of marriage:

"There is nothing wrong with that; I agree with that all the way."

"It's OK if you love the person."

"I think it's fine. It's up to the individuals what they want to do; their beliefs, whatever."

"I think it's fun. It's a good time. I enjoy it."

"I think it's normal and it's healthy. I think that 99 percent of the world does it."

"I'm really not for it, but you know, that's today's society; I understand."

The bottom line seems to be, "If I enjoy it, and it's pleasurable, and other people do it, it's fine." But what does *God* say about sex? He's the One who created it after all! And He says that it is "covenant-making." Therefore, sex before you are married is breaking a covenant with somebody you have not yet met. Sex with someone other than your spouse after you are married is covenant-breaking with your spouse, and sex with someone while you are single is covenant-breaking with your *future* spouse.

So how far *can* we go outside of marriage? I'd like to propose that looking at the issue from this angle is looking at it upside-down. The question is not, "How far can I go?" The right question is, "What does a holy God want from me?"

Remember in Genesis 39 when Potiphar's wife was trying to seduce Joseph? Potiphar was the one who had gotten Joseph out of prison, and here was Potiphar's wife, hitting on Joseph all day long. One day she came and grabbed his robe—and he just ran, right out of his robe!

> *Now Joseph was handsome and good-looking. And after a time his master's wife cast her eyes on Joseph and said, "Lie with me." But he refused and said to his master's wife, "Look, with me here, my master has no concern about anything in the house, and he has put everything that he has in my hand. He is not greater in this house than I am, nor has he kept back anything from me except yourself, because you are his wife. How then could I do this great wickedness, and sin against God?" And although she spoke to Joseph day after day, he would not consent to lie beside her or to be with her* (Genesis 39:6a-10).

Notice what Joseph said to her when she tried to tempt him to go to bed with her? He said, "I will not do it. Period. I will not sin against God." He didn't ask, "How far can I go with Potiphar's wife? What am I allowed to do before it's officially considered sin?" No! He got out of there as quickly as possible, because he wasn't even going to *think* about doing something that would displease God. Sex outside of marriage is covenant-breaking, and Joseph knew this. He got out of there before the temptation had a chance to get any more tempting.

So, how far can *you* go? You can go as far as you think you can so that you can still pray to Christ and say, "Lord, bless what I'm about to do." You go as far as you'd feel comfortable with your future husband or wife going if it was someone else they were with at that moment. Some Christian leaders and counselors advise that there should be no touching below the neck until marriage. Since sex is covenant-making, the level of physical intimacy must match the level of relational commitment; thus, sex is reserved strictly for the marriage covenant relationship. Ultimately, bring the Lord God into all that you do. And whatever you feel comfortable doing in the presence of the Lord, who watches all things all the time, then go for it with gusto!

The eyes of the Lord range throughout the entire earth, to strengthen those whose heart is true to Him (2 Chronicles 16:9).

The Lord looks down from heaven; He sees all humankind (Psalm 33:13).

It would be hard to build a case for sexual activity outside of marriage, since sex is not merely for procreation or recreation, but for unification—two people becoming one.

SINGLENESS AND DATING

A dear member of my church staff is single. She's also attractive, intelligent, and funny. Recently I asked her (and dozens of others who I know are single) what they would preach to others about what it's like being a Christian single. What she told me disturbed me, but in all honesty it didn't really surprise me, because I had witnessed it time and again in the church. She said that far too often in church when someone asks if she's married and she politely answers, "I'm single," the response is always, "Why?"—as if something is wrong with her!

This attitude is not at all biblical. As Paul reminds us in Galatians, we are *all* the Body of Christ, whether we're married or single:

*There is no longer Jew or Greek, there is no longer slave or free, there is no longer male and female; **for all of you are one in Christ Jesus*** (Galatians 3:28).

Aside from that, we learn elsewhere in the Bible that there are distinct advantages to remaining single. The apostle Paul wrote that "those who marry will face many troubles in this life, and I want to spare you this" (1 Cor. 7:28b NIV). There are challenges as well, but all too often we forget to acknowledge the upside of singleness.

MESSAGE FOR EVERYONE

Before I go any further, I want to say something to you married readers: Keep reading! Don't skip over this chapter and think, "This doesn't apply to me. I'm not single."

The fact is, we all start out single, and unless you're the first to die or you die at the same time as your spouse, then you end up single, too. If the average lifespan in America is approaching 80 years of life, for most people the first 25 and the last 15 are single. In other words, half of our lifetime is spent in singleness. Even for the married!

It's also important for us married folks to understand single life so that we can be supportive of our single brothers and sisters in Christ.

ATTITUDE ADJUSTMENT

On the other side of the table are those single men and women who are bitter and angry about marriage in general and want everyone around them to know it.

A while back we did a service where married couples in our church could renew their vows. The whole thing obviously struck a nerve for one young lady because she went into quite an emotional fit about it. "I've tried dating," she stated angrily, "and no one will date me! I can't stand men and all their games. And the church and all their talk about marriage and kids—it makes me sick! Why won't men ask me out?" Hmmm…could it be your *personality*?

In all seriousness, we need to have a balanced biblical perspective about singleness, marriage, dating, and all the side issues that tack themselves to these topics. Are we all called to marriage? Should we all seek singleness? Is it more biblical to be married or more holy to stay single? Let's go to the Bible and find out.

A BIBLICAL VIEW OF SINGLENESS

Now for the matters you wrote about: It is good for a man not to marry. But since there is so much immorality, each man should have his own wife, and each woman her own husband (1 Corinthians 7:1-2 NIV).

This passage is used frequently when discussing issues of marriage and singleness. What is the apostle Paul saying here? There are many interpretations. Some think Paul was speaking *expressly* against marriage when he wrote, "It is good for a man not to marry." But that interpretation doesn't make sense in light of the fact that God instituted and ordained marriage. Why would Paul recommend against something that God created and ordained as "good" (see Proverbs 18:22)?

Others, however, believe this passage should be looked at as Paul expressing his *opinion* of marriage. Paul says that in this instance, he has no clear and exact word from the Lord (which he claims he definitely has on other things in the passage).

My sense of the best way to approach this verse—and any verse of Scripture, for that matter—is to consider the context. Paul was writing to the church in Corinth. Corinth was a very dark and dirty city. Sexual immorality was rampant. In fact, if you go back and look at the verses immediately preceding this passage, you'll see that Paul was telling the Corinthians to avoid sexuality immorality and remain pure.

At the start of chapter 7, Paul tells the Corinthian church that there is nothing inherently good or bad in marriage. "Now for the matters you wrote about: It is good for a man not to marry" (1 Cor. 7:1 NIV). In other words, deciding not to marry is fine, it is God-approved, it is "good." It's almost as if Paul is responding to those people in the church today who say to singles, "You're not married? Why?" Because, according to God's Word, it is good not to marry. If you're thinking about staying single, no problem—it's all good. And despite what some Christians might have you think, singleness can be just as God-honoring and God-glorifying as marriage.

CHALLENGES AND ADVANTAGES OF BEING SINGLE

In First Corinthians 7:2 (NIV) Paul goes on to say, "Since there is so much immorality, each man should have his own wife, and each woman her own husband."

What is Paul saying here? Is he going back on everything he just taught? Not at all. Again, consider the context. Paul is writing to Corinth, a city where there is much immorality. Paul is essentially saying, "If you want to stay single, that's great. But if you can't avoid the sexual temptations around you, by all means, get married. Then you can have all the sex you want to, but you'll be doing it God's way—the right way, within marriage."

Later in the same chapter, Paul talks more about the single life:

> *Now concerning virgins* [single women], *I have no command of the Lord, but I give my opinion as one who by the Lord's mercy*

is trustworthy. I think that, in view of the impending crisis, it is well for you to remain as you are [single]. *Are you bound to a wife? Do not seek to be free. Are you free from a wife? Do not seek a wife. But if you marry, you do not sin, and if a virgin* [a single woman] *marries, she does not sin. Yet those who marry will experience distress in this life, and I would spare you that. ...I want you to be free from anxieties. The unmarried man is anxious about the affairs of the Lord, how to please the Lord; but the married man is anxious about the affairs of the world, how to please his wife, and his interests are divided. And the unmarried woman and the virgin are anxious about the affairs of the Lord, so that they may be holy in body and spirit; but the married woman is anxious about the affairs of the world, how to please her husband. I say this for your own benefit, not to put any restraint upon you, but to promote good order and unhindered devotion to the Lord. If anyone thinks that he is not behaving properly toward his fiancée, if his passions are strong...let him marry as he wishes; it is no sin. Let them marry. But if someone stands firm in his resolve, being under no necessity but having his own desire under control, and has determined in his own mind to keep her as his fiancée, he will do well. So then, he who marries his fiancée does well; and he who refrains from marriage will do better* (1 Corinthians 7:25-28,32-38).

Paul was saying that while there are advantages to being married, the advantages of singleness are great, such as being more free to focus on the Lord's work. The argument is clear. A person without the encumbrance of a family has more freedom to focus single-mindedly and wholeheartedly on service to the Lord. Does this mean a married person can't serve the Lord? Not at all. It just means that, logically speaking, a single person has more time, possibly more resources, and probably more energy to devote to the Lord's work.

This isn't to say that the single life is without challenges. For one thing, as Paul states in First Corinthians 7:2, there can be great sexual temptations. But for those who are called to singleness, the Lord's grace is sufficient.

SINGLENESS AS A CALL

A person is complete if he or she is in Christ, whether that person is married or single. A person is not less whole, less complete, or less fulfilled if he or she is not married. If God has called you to singleness, then don't wonder and want. Just know that there will be a freedom—even a joy—in your singleness that others won't even be able to relate to.

Our fulfillment and completeness come in Christ, not in another person. The person called to being single has a distinct advantage over those who are married. There is a temptation common to mankind that is even more tempting when you're married—that of placing your trust in people instead of God.

> *Stop trusting in man, who has but a breath in his nostrils. Of what account is he?* (Isaiah 2:22 NIV)

Being single can be a vehicle for life transformation into Christ's image. It is an incredible opportunity to be completely surrendered to the Lord and to no one else, to be focused on Him alone. The call to singleness is not necessarily the call to become a monk or a nun. It's simply being open to the call of the Holy Spirit on your life.

Marriage is the norm for sacrificial love, but it's not exclusively representative of it. As a single Christian, you are called to a life of love just as much as married Christians are. I don't care if we are married or single, fulfilling this call is only possible when we're draped in the clothing of compassion, kindness, and forgiveness—in other words, when we're draped in Christ Himself.

> *For in Christ Jesus you are all children of God through faith. As many of you as were baptized into Christ have **clothed yourselves with Christ**. There is no longer Jew or Greek, there is no longer slave or free, there is no longer male and female; for all of you are one in Christ Jesus* (Galatians 3:26-28).

If you are called to singleness, embrace that call. Don't be defensive about it or use rudeness to defend your call. Just know that you are living out God's call on your life, and do it wholeheartedly, as unto the Lord.

PREMARITAL SINGLENESS

...Are you unmarried? Do not look for a wife (1 Corinthians 7:27 NIV).

For those who want to marry, it's easy to become discontent during the single season. But please, don't go there! Work toward contentment, toward realizing that *this* is where God has called you to be right now. If marriage is in your future He will lead you there, but for now, this time of singleness is as much a part of His plan and will for your life as your future marriage is.

Maybe you're single but you haven't specifically experienced a call of singleness on your life. Maybe you're single and want to be married, but you're afraid it won't happen. My advice to you is the same: *clothe yourself in Christ*. Use this time to learn more about yourself, more about others, more about Christ.

The time before marriage is a time for getting to know the opposite sex. It's a time of learning about them, about what makes them tick, about how God has wired them. It's a season of learning how to relate to them, of learning their dreams and desires, of learning their past and life history. It's a time to understand their joys and sorrows, and what their life is like. It may be about seeking a spouse, but it is also about simply dating and learning and enjoying getting to know them.

Whatever your personal history is, it is important to let the Lord in to touch those areas within you that need healing. Maybe you were wounded or betrayed or even attacked, and so you keep yourself in a safety bunker behind an emotional wall where no one can hurt you again. Let God lead you on your first steps into a world of new possibilities with wonderful new people.

Maybe the love of your life was taken from you and you just want companionship. Then simply be a companion to others. Or maybe you're going to ask someone out, but you're afraid that they might turn you down. My advice is to just go for it. If they say no, then simply ask someone else out. Keep moving forward and continue being a blessing to everyone around you. Don't postpone living until you find someone, but simply love on the level available in your life.

No matter where you are in the single life, my prayer for you is the same—that you don't get hung up in a predetermined mindset of what your life should look like. Treasure the happiness, life, and joy that you have in Christ, and trust that He will bring new seasons in His perfect timing.

POST-MARITAL SINGLENESS

Maybe you were married for a long time and have forgotten what it's like to be single. The wounds from divorce or losing a spouse to death can be deep as you deal with a "piece of you" that is now gone. Life is a series of attachments and of letting go—letting go of eras as well as people. It's not easy, but with the Lord it can be done. No matter what your loss, He knows and understands it. And He is with you, walking every step of the way.

Singleness prepares us for new relationships—new relationships both here on earth and in eternity. It is getting us ready to love others in this world during the short journey we have here. It is preparing us to make a landing zone for the Holy Spirit so that He can come and touch our emptiness, our hurt, our fear. He alone can do it.

As a pastor, I remarry people—but not everyone. If a person is a divorcee, I look to see if the virus that killed the first marriage is still there. If so, I counsel that person to work through it so that they are prepared and equipped for a new, healthy marriage.

No matter what you've been through, you are never too old, never too broken, never too "used" to marry. God can do wonderful new things!

PURPOSE OF DATING

So how do we enter into this wonderful, dangerous, and challenging thing called "dating"? The answer is in seeing that all relationships (even the ones that are transitional or temporary) are not different in purpose, even if they differ in duration.

The purpose of relationships is to glorify God and to mold us into the image of Christ. All of our horizontal (earthly) relationships are to be joyful, grace-filled responses from our vertical relationship with God.

It has been a long time since I dated. John Travolta had just starred in *Saturday Night Fever* and hadn't even heard of Scientology yet! But the biblical principles for dating are timeless, because the Bible is time-less. Those principles were the same in the '70s, they are the same today, and they'll be the same 30 years from now.

First, we have to understand that dating is a relational encounter that teaches us about three things:

1. Others.
2. Ourselves.
3. God and His marvelous grace!

Dating teaches us about others—what makes them tick, how God made them, what they treasure. It also teaches us about the un-realistic expectations of some—and the low expectations of others.

Dating teaches us about ourselves—our inner passions, our dreams, our desires. It helps us to understand our own unique "chemistry" and how to discern God's unique call on our life.

Dating teaches us about God and His marvelous grace. As we are entwined in relationships—any relationships—we begin to un-derstand more about God and His grace. When we have to extend grace to others, we more deeply understand the great gift God gave in extending grace to us. And when we receive grace from others on the horizontal plane, it makes us appreciate God's grace on the ver-tical level that much more.

The bottom line is that God is looking for not just Spirit-filled individuals but Spirit-filled *relationships*. I challenge you to get Christ into the middle of your relationship as quickly and as deeply as possible. There is no greater opportunity to experience God's power than in being close to others in committed relationships, whether those relationships are marriage relationships, friendships, or dating relationships.

One problem I've encountered in the church is that Christians often make too much of dating. They treat it like some big life-determining task, as if what they decide to do with their Friday night is going to irreversibly set the course for the rest of their life. *Don't date to mate!* Date to learn, date to grow, and date to enjoy some time with your fellow Christians.

Finally, if you don't end up marrying someone you're dating, make sure you leave them better off than when you found them. Remember, this is another human being—someone like you, with passions, dreams, hurts, and scars. Be gentle. And learn to be intimate without being physical. Work on affirming, caring for, challenging, and fellowshipping—and you can do all of that without unzipping. If marriage is all about preparing us to hand our spouses over to the Lord after this journey through life is over, to see if they grew more in His Image while they were in our presence, then dating has the same grand purpose as well.

One final thought while we're on the subject of dating—if you're dating an unbeliever, then you'd better think it through very carefully, because we are warned:

> *Do not be mismatched with unbelievers. For what partnership is there between righteousness and lawlessness?* (2 Corinthians 6:14)

God's primary purpose for dating is *fellowship*, not for sizing up a potential mate. As a child of Light, you cannot fully and truly fellowship with darkness. Seek out other Christians for dating, as any close, ongoing relationship is more comfortable overall when shared by people of like mind.

In Conclusion

Singleness is neither a curse nor a blessing in itself, but how we choose to live out our singleness can be one or the other. There are unique challenges and advantages in being single, just as there are unique challenges in dating and in being married. The ultimate aim, whether we are single or married, is to glorify God and love others. Period.

> *As God's chosen ones, holy and beloved, clothe yourselves with compassion, kindness, humility, meekness, and patience. Bear with one another and, if anyone has a complaint against another, forgive each other; just as the Lord has forgiven you, so you also must forgive. Above all, clothe yourselves with love, which binds everything together in perfect harmony. And let the peace of Christ rule in your hearts, to which indeed you were called in the one body. And be thankful. Let the word of Christ dwell in you richly; teach and admonish one another in all wisdom; and with gratitude in your hearts sing psalms, hymns, and spiritual songs*

to God. And whatever you do, in word or deed, do everything in the name of the Lord Jesus, giving thanks to God the Father through Him (Colossians 3:12-17).

In this passage, the Spirit of God through Paul lays out the framework for every relationship in the Lord. It's a question of clothing ourselves with Christ and His power, His compassion, His love. Whether you are single and seeking, single and staying that way, or married, the bottom line is the same: "Clothe yourselves" in Christ and "bear with one another." There is no higher calling than this.

There were prophets who married and prophets who remained single. Peter was married but Paul stayed single (see Matthew 8:14, 1 Corinthians 9:5, and 1 Corinthians 7:7). C.S. Lewis was single for most of his life until he married in his late 50s. The real call in life is not to marriage or singleness; it is simply to walk with the Lord.

ENDNOTE

1. Terry Vanderheyden, "Study Finds Normal Sexual Relations Have Health Benefit but Not Gay or Other Sex," *LifeSiteNews.com*: http://www.lifesite.net/ldn/2006/jan/06012607. html.

SECTION C

*Life in the Social World—Salt
and Light in a Free Society*

Introduction

The last three Commandments complete the life of holy love that we are called to live. So far we have seen that we are forbidden from harming our neighbor's physical life ("no murder"), and we are forbidden from harming relational lives ("no adultery"). Now we will examine the biblical prohibitions against harming our neighbor's economic life ("no stealing"), our neighbor's reputation ("no false testimony"), and even our neighbor's social position ("no coveting").

We will also examine women in ministry—can they teach in church? Can they preach? What does the Word of God have to say about this? And we'll look at using our mouths for the good of others (like the third Commandment of blessing the Lord's name) and the second Commandment call to have no other gods than the Lord ("no idols").

George Washington's question of whether the Great Experiment called America would work without a king is still up for debate. America is much younger than the mighty Roman Empire was when it finally toppled.

The values of the Bible are at the foundation of our democratic republic—and yet those biblical values came from a people who never even heard of the concept of democracy. Since neither the Old nor New Testament mentions the concept of electing leadership

171

over the community, how do we know how we are to structure a democracy and function within it?

This raises a whole host of side questions, such as how can Christian Republicans and Democrats be so far apart on key issues? Why can't we seem to vote all the values of the Bible? When are we involved with governing, when are we exercising our biblical duty—and when are we looking to "princes of flesh" to save us rather than to the Lord? Should we be more concerned about the Federal government intruding into our wallets via taxes—or not intruding when it comes to issues of establishing law and order?

If we are free in Christ to do all things as Romans 8:1 seems to suggest, when—if ever—must we be concerned about what others think? When does acting out our liberties simply show freedom from the "Pharisee mindset"—and when does is it cause stumbling for others?

How do we resolve the issue of alcohol being called a gift from God in the Scriptures (see Proverbs 31:6-7 and Psalm 104:15), and yet it is by far the greatest, most devastating drug of all time. Is the Lord more concerned about the dangers of substance abuse or the judgementalism of our fellow Christians? How did the apostle Paul handle the legalists and ascetics and the self-destructive over-indulgers of his day?

Beside physical stewardship, there is also mental stewardship. What does it mean to have a "biblical worldview" concerning entertainment? What is the difference between art and entertainment, and what are the boundaries for the Christian? What does it mean to be "media literate" *and* a follower of Jesus?

Does God care if we watch R-rated movies? What about video games and plays? How can we as the Church reclaim the arts for Christ and redirect the current river of poison gushing at us every day?

These are some of the issues we will examine in this section—and how we, as Christians, can be salt and light in the realm of these cultural issues.

CHAPTER 14

Issue Seven—Women in Ministry

The Role of Women in the Church

One of the great debates that that has been going on in Christ's Church is, "Can women be in leadership?" Other than divorce and remarriage, in certain theological circles this is a commonly asked question I receive as a senior pastor.

The issue of women in ministry is not an "essential"—salvation and sanctification don't hinge on it. But like many other issues, it is essential to understand this issue for edification and for spiritual maturity.

Let me begin by saying that I believe there are more Scriptures that support certain women being in leadership than there are those that seem to speak against it. But I do want to take time to examine those passages most frequently used to forbid women being pastors, primarily verses from First Timothy and Titus.

It should be noted that Paul had no problem with women in leadership in Greece and Rome. He even addressed a female deaconess, Phoebe, in the Book of Romans (see Romans 16:1-2). Paul is able to theologically explain these issues of leadership without being rigidly boxed in, much the same way he could discuss and explain issues surrounding controversial topics of his day like circumcision, for example.

Let's examine the words of Paul concerning women in leadership in the church to get a "biblical word" on this issue. Then let's make sense of the issue with a "theological word." Finally we'll bring them together in a "pastoral word" that helps us determine how to live a life of Christ's love.

BIBLICAL WORD: PAUL'S ADMONITION TO TIMOTHY

A primary rule of understanding Scripture is to know what God *has said* before we look at what He *is saying* to this culture and society. God revealed Himself through events of holy history, culminating with the birth, ministry, death, and resurrection of His Son, the Lord Jesus. These incredible events were reduced to writing by historical grammatical means. So we must first read a passage according to the text that pertains to the original event, story, parable or teaching, in order to then begin putting it into context for today, because a text without context is only pretext.

Second, we must allow the light of God, though the Holy Spirit, to quicken, to speak, and to apply His words to our everyday lives.

With this in mind, let's look at Paul's words regarding women in ministry.

> *Let a woman learn in silence with full submission. I permit no woman to teach or to have authority over a man; she is to keep silent. For Adam was formed first, then Eve; and Adam was not deceived, but the woman was deceived and became a transgressor. Yet she will be saved through childbearing, provided they continue in faith and love and holiness, with modesty* (1 Timothy 2:11-15).

Paul was writing to his beloved Timothy, probably in Ephesus (see 1 Tim. 1:3). Remember that his purpose in this exposition was to encourage the worship of God *in peace* and *in harmony*, specifically in Timothy's church. But although he's concerned with a specific instance (Timothy's church), he appeals to cross-cultural arguments, one of which is that women are to remain silent and not teach. Why? Because of who was created first (Adam) and who sinned first (Eve).

To truly understand this passage of Scripture, we need to understand the world's view of women in the Greek, Roman, and Jewish cultures 2,000 years ago. Each of these societies viewed women, in varying degrees, on a lesser level than men. There were also stark differences in how women were treated in relation to the Law. For instance, the Jews interpreted Moses' laws about divorce (see Deuteronomy 24:1-4) to mean that a man could give a bill of divorcement to his wife if there was something about her he simply didn't like. So if one day a man decided he didn't like his wife's cooking or the way she dressed, he could divorce her.

Unfortunately, our culture also operates under this premise. But when Jesus came He said:

> *It was also said, "Whoever divorces his wife, let him give her a certificate of divorce." But I say to you that anyone who divorces his wife, except on the ground of unchastity, causes her to commit adultery; and whoever marries a divorced woman commits adultery* (Matthew 5:31-32).

So why did Moses allow a man to put away his wife? As Jesus explained to the Pharisees:

> *Moses, because of the hardness of your hearts, permitted you to divorce your wives, but from the beginning it was not so* (Matthew 19:8 NKJV).

Hardness of heart was the recipe for divorce—and also for pigeonholing women into a certain role. So how do we reconcile a woman's role in the church with the passage in First Timothy 2? Paul had the ability to discern what was truly God's intention. When he was addressing the leadership of women in the church, he was able to sense the fluidity of the culture and the leading of the Holy Spirit.

To further understand God's order of things, let's go back and look at the creation of humankind.

THEOLOGICAL WORD: GOD'S ORDERINGS—ORDER OF CREATION

In First Timothy 2:13-14, we are given the order of creation as the reason for authority. Notice that Paul said, "For Adam was formed first, then Eve; and Adam was not deceived." Because man was created first, he was given authority; and woman, created after man, was to be in subjection. This doesn't at all imply that the woman was inferior to the man.

Theologically there are three "orders" in God's way of administrating life (that is, the way God does things or desires that they be done). These orders are the general relational and societal structures and means that God uses to achieve His purposes. First, there was the original order of creation. Second, there was the order after sin entered the creation and distorted the original harmony. And third, there is the redemptive order of what God is moving us toward now that Christ has redeemed the creation.

In Moses' account of creation in Genesis, we discover that men and women were created *equally*, in the image of God:

> *Then God said, "Let Us make humankind in Our image, according to Our likeness; and let **them** have dominion over the fish of the sea, and over the birds of the air, and over the cattle, and over all the wild animals of the earth, and over every creeping thing that creeps upon the earth." So God created humankind in His image, in the image of God He created them; male and female He created them* (Genesis 1:26-27).

From this passage comes the theology of the Order of Creation, where male and female had mutual shared dominion over creation. This demonstrates the beauty of man and woman in paradise. One is not over the other. Paul will use the passage in First Timothy 2 to describe the priority of male leadership. What makes his admonition to Timothy so difficult is that Paul will use women in leadership outside the Jewish synagogues he is evangelizing. Once again we ask, "Is Paul being wishy washy?" Not at all. He is using a classic rabbinic application for "the highest good" in any situation.

In Genesis 2, there is a more detailed examination of the creation of humankind. It unveils the glory of relationship between man and woman, with Adam being created first and Eve created to be his helper. Although they were equal, each had a specific role to fill— and they flowed together in perfect harmony.

ORDER OF THE FALL

The second theology as it relates to the role of women in the church is the "Order of the Fall," introduced when Paul said, "And it was not Adam who was deceived, but the woman being deceived, fell into transgression" (1 Tim. 2:14 NASB). Paul was referring to the transgression of humankind as recorded in the Book of Genesis:

> *Now the serpent was more crafty than any other wild animal that the Lord God had made. He said to the woman, "Did God say, 'You shall not eat from any tree in the garden'?" The woman said to the serpent, "We may eat of the fruit of the trees in the garden; but God said, 'You shall not eat of the fruit of the tree that is in the middle of the garden, nor shall you touch it, or you shall die.'" But the serpent said to the woman, "You will not die; for God knows that when you eat of it your eyes will be opened, and you will be like God, knowing good and evil." So when the woman saw that the tree was good for food, and that it was a delight to the eyes, and that the tree was to be desired to make one wise, she took of its fruit and ate; and she also gave some to her husband, who was with her, and he ate. Then the eyes of both were opened, and they knew that they were naked; and they sewed fig leaves together and made loincloths for themselves* (Genesis 3:1-7).

Here, a new element was added to the mix. Eve had succumbed to the lies and temptation of the serpent in the Garden of Eden. She made a decision to partake of the forbidden fruit from the Tree of Knowledge of Good and Evil without seeking Adam's insight or leadership. And then she led her husband into sin. Because Adam and Eve sinned, the roles established by God were jeopardized. However, the fact that a woman is now under the "subjection" of a man as punishment for the fall (see Genesis 3:16) shows that originally there was coleadership.

The Order of the Fall brought with it a fourfold curse:

1. Pain in childbirth.
2. Living from the "sweat of man's brow."
3. Woman's submission to man.
4. Death and return to the dust.

It would be improper to elevate or emphasize one curse (such as female submission to man) while trying to minimize the other three. You cannot push Paul beyond traditional accepted rabbinical teaching methods with this difficult passage. As a coequal "team," Adam and Eve both succumbed to the enticement of temptation, and they therefore *both* suffered consequences for their mutual decision to disobey God. Even though the results were that sin entered the world through their sin, it is not reasonable to embrace the result of female subjection to man while resisting change to the other three results of sin. For example, no Christian encourages "pain in childbirth" or "living from the sweat of man's brow" or certainly not "death;" so why embrace "woman's submission to man" alone? It is a tough issue, indeed.

ORDER OF REDEMPTION

Finally, to fully understand Paul's writings concerning the leadership of women, we must discern the Order of Redemption, which means that all are one in Christ—but not necessarily equally gifted. How does God best use people for ministry on this side of the Cross and risen Christ?

Because of the Fall, men and women are both under the curse of sin, "since all have sinned and fall short of the glory of God" (Rom. 3:23). But they also can partake in the same gift of redemption, because "they are now justified by His grace as a gift, through the redemption that is in Christ Jesus" (Rom. 3:24). Equality, however, does not imply that God has given to everyone the exact same role in the life and work of the Church.

You see, the grace of God comes into our brokenness, cutting through our "power games" and self-absorption, and ultimately empowering us to change. He gives gifts and internal "wirings" for the good of others—to bless and not to take, to celebrate and not to use. The bottom line is that there *are* women who are called, gifted, and mightily used by God in positions of leadership in the ministry—but it must be of the Lord.

Paul said, "There is no longer Jew or Greek, there is no longer slave or free, there is no longer male and female; for all of you are one in Christ Jesus" (Gal. 3:28). The new order of redemption is only available in "splinters" from the future. For example, we will never be more forgiven than we are right now—but the new world and new heaven are still in the future.

Generally, because we live in the Order of the Fall, men tend to become leaders more easily than women. (Certainly, however, there are individual cases where just the opposite is true!) Whether this is sociologically learned or biologically "wired," it is a statement of observation.

This is also why I believe that, in the institution of marriage, the male is the head of the two equals. This means the call on the head of the equals is to strive to make decisions together, and when that's not possible, to only make them with an eye toward the woman's welfare (in the same spirit that Christ showed when laying His life down for the Church). This is not some cloaking for male chauvinism or oppression, not by any means. It is born from a loving, working relationship. Someone has to make a final decision when both cannot, and the burden falls on the husband to make it solely for the good of the wife. If you operate properly within God's biblical marriage structure, then there will be true harmony within the husband-wife relationship. When this order breaks down, however, the marriage can become a manipulative, self-positioning struggle for both parties.

There are certain women, however, who were wonderfully gifted and definitely called to leadership, such as Deborah, Esther, Lydia, and Mary, to name just a few. By exercising their God-given gifts, these amazing women brought great blessing to those whom they were called to lead. There are more Scriptures that speak of women in leadership than speak against it. The sentinels of Scripture, Reason, Wise Counsel, and the Inner Calling of the Spirit, all speak to supporting women (as well as men) who are called to ministry.

PASTORAL WORD: LIVING IN BIBLICAL RELATIONSHIPS VS. ROLES

The conclusion of the matter is that we need to understand the difference between biblical *relationships* and biblical *roles*. In other words, we must determine each person's unique make-up and various giftings in order to identify their appropriate place of service in the church—whether male or female.

I have discovered that (not surprisingly, since God made it this way) moms are best at being moms and dads are best at being dads. But let's look at it another way. Does God care who fishes in the village as long as someone catches the fish for dinner? Probably not. We each have a specific purpose, design, and plan from God within the home, workplace, and church—but the ultimate goal is to get His work done, no matter who's doing it.

Paul put it most eloquently:

> *For as in one body we have many members, and not all the members have the same function, so we, who are many, are one body in Christ, and individually we are members one of another. We have gifts that differ according to the grace given to us: prophecy, in proportion to faith; ministry, in ministering; the teacher, in teaching; the exhorter, in exhortation; the giver, in generosity; the leader, in diligence; the compassionate, in cheerfulness. Let love be genuine; hate what is evil, hold fast to what is good; love one another with mutual affection; outdo one another in showing honor* (Romans 12:4-10).

Whatever your role—whether you're a woman or a man—be convicted by the whole of Scripture and not just a few "favorite passages" that you can tear out and wear like bumper stickers. There's no place for closet humanists who disregard the Word, nor is there any room for closet bigots who use cardboard theologies to oppress others. It's God's universe, and He knows best how to run it to His glory and our happiness. So trust Him.

The truth is, we need to live God's core basics and avoid what not to do. We shouldn't "major on the minors," but rather—and more than anything—live the Word and display Christ's life in and through us.

Ladies, whether you are faithful to serving at home or in school or in the marketplace, your role in life is important—and Christ is crazy about you and wants to use you in many amazing ways.

CHAPTER 15

Issue Eight—Christians and Money

The Bible and Money Matters

The Bible has a lot to say about money matters—because *money matters!* Wealth and the creation of wealth is one of the greatest drives all of us have in life. The reason Scripture—and in particular, Jesus—has so much to say about money is because our hearts are wrapped around the stuff. And God wants those hearts—He wants them to be free and He wants them to be His.

Preachers are as guilty of obsessing about money as anyone else because…well, they're people, too! A preacher, a priest, and a rabbi were talking about money and how they determine the amount of the offering that should go to God and how much should go to them.

The priest said, "Well, in my church we bring all the money forward. I draw a big chalk circle on the floor. We throw all the money up in the air. Everything that lands on the outside of the circle goes to God; everything on the inside goes to me."

The Rabbi responded, "Yeah, we also bring all the money forward like that, and we too draw a big circle and throw it all in the air, same as you. The only difference is that everything on the *inside* goes to God, and anything on the *outside* goes to me."

The preacher chimed in, "Gentlemen, I am shocked—*shocked*—at how you decide. In my church, we bring all the money forward, draw a circle, and throw the money into the air. Anything God wants, He can take while it's in the air. Everything else belongs to me."

It is easy to judge others on their own financial convictions or lack thereof. The Scriptures have much to say about all three dimensions of wealth—how we make it, how we spend it, and how we share it.

MONEY: HOW WE MAKE IT

Some people think God only cares about what we give to Him and to others. But God cares about the other 90 percent just as much—and how we make it.

Creating wealth and the making of money can be very good. From the very beginning, God declared the world *"good"* (see Genesis 1:4,10,12,18,21,25,31). The physical creation is the reflection of the joy of its Creator, and that includes all things that are merely pleasing to the eye.

One day in World War II, Prime Minister Winston Churchill was being briefed about the war in North Africa by one of his generals. Churchill, who was notorious for loving good food, fine cigars, and a stiff drink, offered a general some caviar.

The general responded sternly, "There is no way in God's earth I will eat caviar while our boys are dying of thirst and hunger on the battlefield."

"If you can show me how my not eating this caviar would save one soldier one moment of pain," Churchill calmly replied, "I will never touch it again in my life. But if not…would you mind passing me one of those crackers, General."

God is a God who gives good things, and He wants them to be enjoyed. Rabbis say that we will give an account for every blessing we refused to enjoy. "Going without" does not necessarily mean that others will "go with." There will be times when our hogging the meal means others go hungry, but there are other times when our refusing to let God bless us with material blessings is not because of our love for God or others, but because of some deeper stoic tendency that says abstaining is somehow holy. Paul blasted his churches on more than one occasion for such a Greek worldview. We cannot allow ourselves to think that we are "more holy" because we don't make more money. Money has value, but in a different way.

INSTRUMENTAL VALUE OF MONEY AND INTRINSIC VALUE OF PEOPLE

Money has great value and power, but only in how it is used. Money has only "instrumental power." It has no value in itself unless it used—and used rightly. Spending money can be life-giving or life-strangling.

People, on the other hand, have value intrinsically. Whether they know it or not, people are made in the very image of God, and they have value as they are for who they are—not for anything they do. This is why God is so concerned that we have money in proper perspective. When Jesus quoted Deuteronomy 8:3 to satan and reminded him that man does not live by bread alone but by every word that proceeds from the mouth of God, He was telling us to keep our lifestyles in perspective.

World history is one story after another of those who gained the world but lost their soul (see Matthew 16:26, Mark 8:36). The greatest conflicts and wars of history were ignited by lust for gold and the power of wealth. Many lives and families have been sacrificed on the altar of financial gain. But some things are far more costly than money, such as the relationships sacrificed to get it.

BIBLICAL VIEW OF WORK

Creating wealth, however, is very different from living *for* wealth. There is a vast difference between how a person makes a living and what that person lives for. As a great saint once said, "Until all we have left is God, we will never know God is all we need." And as the old saying goes, the richest person in the world is the one who has a hundred dollars more than they want, and the poorest one is the one who has a hundred less—even if they have millions! It all boils down to where you heart is and what you value most.

When handled properly, work has a goodness and dignity to it. When Adam was helping God name the animals, there was no sin in the world. Adam—and later both Adam and Eve—took care of the Garden, and it was a delight. There was dignity in the work they did.

The same holds true today. To offer to God our talents and service is to praise Him in the marketplace, at school, at home, and everywhere else on earth—as long as we do it unto the Lord, as we are admonished in Scripture (see Colossians 3:23).

Are there more godly careers and jobs than others? Not as long as they are unto the Lord and a blessing to others.

I saw a thing of beauty the other day. I was watching a waitress in a small greasy spoon restaurant that I love. As I saw her take care of the whole place, I noticed how she was a virtual one-woman ballet dancer in the food industry. She smiled, took orders, brought coffee, slung toast, and greeted people with a joy that I wish I had all the time. She also had a little beat-up pin that read, "God loves you so much He has your picture on His refrigerator!" Who knows how many people she has changed by her quality of work and sweetness of spirit in that burger joint. It wasn't so much *what* she was doing as much as it was *why*, and for *Whom*, and *how* she was doing it.

Are you offering an honest service or product? Are you in your job because of a sense of being stuck—or a sense of what Christ can do with it? Do people know they can trust you to look out for their interests—or are you just using them for your own agenda? God cares *how* you make your money!

HOW WE SPEND IT

The Lord makes it clear in Scripture that He also cares how we *spend* our money. He wants us to enjoy it, but He also wants us to not be addicted to it. Money can be a powerful "narcotic." Narcotics can do wonderful things to help heal the body, but they are also the source of countless lives being destroyed.

There is an old proverb of the streets: "Never get between an addict and their drug." Why? Because they'll kill you for it. The horrible law of diminishing returns says that the more and more you use of a drug, the less and less of a high you get from it—and the more you need to get that same high.

The more you drink, the less you feel it and the more you need and want it. No one drinks themselves dry or spends themselves free. Likewise, no one stashes away to financial freedom.

We live in a culture addicted to many things—the chief of which is money. It's like the old comedy sketch of the gunman holding up the notorious cheap executive. The robber says, "Your money or your life!" The executive says nothing. The thief says again, "I said, your money or your life!" To which the cheapskate snaps back, "I'm thinking, I'm thinking!" Too many Christians trade away spiritual security for financial hoarding.

DEBT

The general rule of finances is to get out of debt, keep out of debt, and stay out of debt. Debt takes away your options and the freedom that God wants to give you. There are times when debt can be a wealth creator—such as a home mortgage in a rising housing market—but debt must be carefully considered before it's incurred. It shouldn't be taken lightly.

Too often, debt is just you paying someone else's living expenses. What's ironic is that the source of this problem is the same as the spendthrift. The person who thinks they cannot enjoy life without spending money has the same affliction as the person who sits on mounds of cash and won't spend a dollar. That is addiction at its worst and idolatry at its zenith.

How much should we have? Whatever freedom feels like to you. As John Wesley said, "Make as much as you can, save as much as you can, give as much as you can."

HOW WE SHARE IT

I often have people who tell me that tithing the first 10 percent to the Lord is legalistic. I tell them, "Fine. Then start with 15 percent." It's true that we don't want to be legalists and get hung up on nickel and diming God for our tithe back to Him.

In the Old Testament, the harvester was to leave some of the good fruit unpicked for the stranger, and some of the field uncut for the poor (see Leviticus 23:22). I don't think God wants us out there with a calculator and chalk line measuring off to the apple how much to leave behind. He wants a generous people who care for others. He wants a people who trust the Giver of all wealth to continue giving in spite of how much we give to needy causes.

If you look at the New Testament, the people there shame the Old Testament in giving amounts. In the New Testament, they either liquidate all their assets and put them in a common trust (as in Acts) or repay any debt fourfold and give 50 percent of their wealth to the poor (Zacchaeus)! They don't just give a tithe—they blow the top off! And they do it with great joy and gratitude.

If you offer any toddler an ice cream cone or a check for $1 million, they'll take the ice cream cone. They don't know the check can buy the whole ice cream store. In the same way, when we share and give to others, God offers us the passing riches of this earth (which He gives us to enjoy) or the signed check of belonging to His family—along with the riches of the King Himself.

CHAPTER 16

Issue Nine—Tithing

Giving: An Act of God's Mercy

Early in his adult life, American industrialist John Davidson Rockefeller played a pivotal role in the establishment of the oil industry. He became a millionaire by the age of 23 and was the world's first billionaire by the age of 50. His company, Standard Oil, became the most profitable company in the world. And then, at the age of 53, the world's richest man became violently ill and was confined to what appeared to be his deathbed.

In utter agony, Rockefeller—a man who could have anything he wanted—could barely eat a bite of food. Although he had the best physicians in the world at his disposal, the best they could hope for was one final year of life. Rockefeller's life grew meaningless.

As death drew closer, Rockefeller awoke one morning from a vague but troubling dream. Though the details of the dream had faded, its meaning had not. From his dream Rockefeller learned that success, wealth, and fame were fleeting and temporal. Through that dream, the man who once controlled the largest oil company in the world came to understand that he could not control his own destiny. This revelation became the turning point in his life. He began to funnel his assets into hospitals, research, and education.

He also went on to live for another 45 years after this decision.

Through his philanthropic work and development of medical research in North America, Rockefeller was instrumental in eradicating hookworm and yellow fever. As a devout Christian, he also supported many church-based organizations. The list of discoveries resulting from his financial donations is incredible.

The old saying, "The road to hell is paved with good intentions," means that all the ideals and mixed motives mean nothing without actions. It is results that count, as evidenced by the life of the great industrialist John D. Rockefeller.

HISTORY OF TITHING

In order to understand the history of tithing, let's take a look at the first recorded instance of an offering given to God:

> *In the course of time Cain brought to the Lord an offering of the fruit of the ground, and Abel for his part brought of the firstlings of his flock, their fat portions. And the Lord had regard for Abel and his offering, but for Cain and his offering he had no regard. So Cain was very angry, and his countenance fell* (Genesis 4:3-5).

Notice that Abel brought the first and choicest of his flock, but Cain did not bring the first fruits of his crops. Not only did Cain bring the "leftovers" from the land (which God had cursed), but he took his sweet time in bringing it.

What we must remember is that it's not so much the offering we prepare that matters—it's the condition of our heart when we give it. Paul told the Corinthians, "Each of you must give as you have made up your mind, not reluctantly or under compulsion, for God loves a cheerful giver" (2 Cor. 9:7).

The principle of giving was also in operation as Abraham was asked to offer Isaac:

> *He [God] said, "Take your son, your only son Isaac, whom you love, and go to the land of Moriah, and offer him there as a burnt-offering on one of the mountains that I shall show you"* (Genesis 22:2).

Abraham tithed to Melchizedek even before the law was given by the Lord to Moses:

> *And King Melchizedek of Salem brought out bread and wine; he was priest of God Most High. He blessed him and said, "Blessed be Abram by God Most High, maker of Heaven and earth; and blessed be God Most High, who has delivered your enemies into your hand!" And Abram gave him one-tenth of everything* (Genesis 14:18-20).

In other words, tithing was established 400 years *before* the Law was handed down. Then, when the Law was given to Moses on Mount Sinai, the tithe (which means "the tenth part") became a part of it:

> *All tithes from the land, whether the seed from the ground or the fruit from the tree, are the Lord's; they are holy to the Lord* (Leviticus 27:30).

Later on, in the Book of Malachi, the last book of the Old Testament, God declared:

> *Bring the full tithe into the storehouse, so that there may be food in My house, and thus put Me to the test, says the Lord of hosts; see if I will not open the windows of Heaven for you and pour down for you an overflowing blessing. I will rebuke the locust for you, so that it will not destroy the produce of your soil; and your vine in the field shall not be barren, says the Lord of hosts. Then all nations will count you happy, for you will be a land of delight, says the Lord of hosts* (Malachi 3:10-12).

TITHING IN THE NEW TESTAMENT

Even though the Old Testament ceremonial law is gone because of Christ's Cross, you will discover that Christ didn't come to do away with the Law but to complete it. Jesus stated,

> *Do not think that I have come to abolish the law or the prophets; I have come not to abolish but to fulfill* (Matthew 5:17).

Some try to diminish the Law by citing the concept of grace, but Jesus' coming to earth didn't make the law null and void. If you killed someone, it was still considered murder. Adultery was still forbidden. And the issue of the tithe was still in force.

But under Christ, the driving force for keeping the Law is not fear, but love born out of a relationship with God's only Son.

As the Lord said,

> This is the covenant that I will make with the house of Israel after those days, says the Lord: I will put My laws in their minds, and write them on their hearts, and I will be their God, and they shall be My people (Hebrews 8:10).

Other examples in the Book of Acts show how the church not only gave part of their possessions, but liquidated all of their assets and gave the proceeds to care for the poor. We also have Paul's admonition for sacrificial helping of the poorer churches. Eternal principles are woven throughout the fabric of God's Word, and tithing is clearly one of them.

Everything belongs to God, but He richly gives us all things to enjoy, which equates to stewardship responsibility over everything. It's not difficult to give a measly 10 percent to the Lord, because it's all from Him in the first place. As the apostle Paul said, "As for those who in the present age are rich, command them not to be haughty, or to set their hopes on the uncertainty of riches, but rather on God who richly provides us with everything for our enjoyment" (1 Timothy 6:17).

We are commanded to be good and trustworthy stewards (see 1 Corinthians 4:2). When we give God the tithe, we are demonstrating our faithfulness in stewardship, showing God that we recognize that we are stewards, and not owners, of everything we possess.

Jesus said:

> Do not store up for yourselves treasures on earth, where moth and rust consume and where thieves break in and steal; but store up for yourselves treasures in heaven, where neither moth nor rust consumes and where thieves do not break in and steal. For where your treasure is, there your heart will be also (Matthew 6:19-21).

The pattern of giving for Christians is to offer to the Lord our tithes and offerings, which are given to the Church, and to give to the needy out of our love for Christ.

The power of God to provide for us above and beyond our mere needs is found when we step out in faith, trust His Word on this issue, and give. The objective is to be free. Whatever amount we make, then we should learn the power of having money as our servant and not our master. Just like fire, money is a wonderful servant but a horrible master. Keep a fire in the fireplace and it will warm a home. Let it get out of place and it will burn the whole house down. The same it true of money.[1]

WHAT JESUS SAID ABOUT TITHING

In one of the dozens of parables we have of our Lord, Jesus declares to us a sobering message in a three-scene story:

Scene 1: When We Need Mercy From the Master

Scene 2: When Others Need Mercy From Us

Scene 3: How the Master Responds to the Unmerciful

Let's examine each scene.

SCENE 1: WHEN WE NEED MERCY FROM THE MASTER

One of the great truths of life in this parable is that we should treat others as God has treated us, because know that how we treat others is how God will finally treat us.

Then Peter came to Him and said, "Lord, how often shall my brother sin against me, and I forgive him? Up to seven times?" Jesus said to him, "I do not say to you, up to seven times, but up to seventy times seven. Therefore the kingdom of heaven is like a certain king who wanted to settle accounts with his servants. And when he had begun to settle accounts, one was brought to him who owed him ten thousand talents. But as he was not able to pay, his master commanded that he be sold, with his wife and children and all that he had, and that payment be made. The servant therefore fell down before him, saying, 'Master, have patience with me, and I will pay you all.' Then the master of that servant was moved with compassion, released him, and forgave him the debt" (Matthew 18:21-27 NKJV).

The first thing that stands out in this passage is the stunning amount of debt owed by the servant. Look at the outrageousness of the master's response before the servant begged for forgiveness. Without the compassion of the master, the servant would have been made to pay all that he owed—in addition to losing his entire family! Yet, in an act of inexplicable mercy, the master forgave all of the servant's debt. Through this parable, we learn that we will face a full accounting for the actions we take or neglect to take during our lives.

Mercy in Greek is the word *hesed*, which means "unmerited favor." Mercy is more than just ignoring someone's situation—it is paying for another out of "unmerited love" for them. We often feel that life is unjust to us, and it can certainly be. But how we respond in times of injustice, tragedy, and disappointment is what makes all the difference. God's mercy is on display to us in all of life, although we may not always recognize it.

Deuteronomy 8:18 says, "Remember the Lord your God, for it is He who gives you power to get wealth, so that He may confirm His covenant that He swore to your ancestors, as He is doing today." God has given us the ability to create wealth, and He has given us the talent, the dreams, the happenstance, and His help all along the way. He wants you to enjoy what you have been given and not keep it at arm's distance.

SCENE 2: WHEN OTHERS NEED MERCY FROM US

Notice that the servant who was forgiven much then went to collect a small debt from a fellow servant. The servant had just been forgiven his entire, massive debt—yet he immediately goes out and collects a miniscule little sum from one of his own debtors:

> But that servant went out and found one of his fellow servants who owed him a hundred denarii; and he laid hands on him and took him by the throat, saying, "Pay me what you owe!" So his fellow servant fell down at his feet and begged him, saying, "Have patience with me, and I will pay you all." And he would not, but went and threw him into prison till he should pay the debt. So when his fellow servants saw what had been done, they were very grieved, and came and told their master all that had been done (Matthew 18:28-31 NKJV).

The mercy that others need is not based on justice. It's about the "river of God's grace" flowing through us. The challenge is to get people to open up the gates of God's blessings.

Some who are poor sometimes got there of their own accord. At other times, unforeseen circumstances or a great sickness caused them to fall into poverty. But it doesn't matter how people find themselves lacking—we must show mercy to them all the same.

SCENE 3: THE MASTER'S RESPONSE
TO THE UNMERCIFUL

Then his master, after he had called him, said to him, "You wicked servant! I forgave you all that debt because you begged me. Should you not also have had compassion on your fellow servant, just as I had pity on you?" And his master was angry, and delivered him to the torturers until he should pay all that was due to him. So My heavenly Father also will do to you if each of you, from his heart, does not forgive his brother his trespasses (Matthew 18:32-35 NKJV).

How does God feel when His children hurt His other kids—when they themselves have been loved? We have the answer in this passage of Scripture—it is a righteous indignation. God is clear what happens when we fail to forgive those who have harmed us:

If you forgive others their trespasses, your heavenly Father will also forgive you; but if you do not forgive others, neither will your Father forgive your trespasses (Matthew 6:14-15).

The self-induced judgment of refusing to let God live His life through us is a sentence of punishment all its own. It's like the smell of "grace gone sour."

We are to use our lives to show mercy to others, both to those in our churches and to those within our families, communities, workplaces, and schools. Galatians 5:14 says, "For the whole law is summed up in a single commandment, 'You shall love your neighbor as yourself.'" God wants His love to shine through our actions and compassion toward others.

So how much is enough when it comes to giving? Your heart knows. But you need to give enough to let the river of Living Water out. There are so many people who need to experience the life-giving message of Jesus, and we have the power to share it with them through our giving and acts of mercy.

ENDNOTE

1. For an excellent study in money from God's perspective, see Dr. Kenneth Ulmer's *Making Your Money Count: Why We Have it—How to Manage it* (Regal Publishing Group, 2007).

CHAPTER 17

Issue Ten—Christians and Politics

Politics

Ever since Jesus told His critics to render unto Caesar the things that are Caesar's and to give to God what is God's, His followers have been trying to figure out how to live with "government."

The concept of choosing your government, like we do in democracy, was unheard of in Jesus' day. Most people simply prayed for a godly royal family, and learned to live with whatever was decreed.

Unquestioning obedience is more complex for Americans because we belong to a secular democracy—something the vast majority of people we meet in Heaven will probably never have lived under. In fact, if the Lord comes soon, when we get to Heaven, most women and men there will never have done three things:

1. Read a book (though there were many literate people throughout the ages, most have not had that privilege).

2. Swim (some, but even the sailors of old did not know the skill before the 1800s).

3. Vote (most of our brothers and sisters throughout the ages lived under kings, queens, and emperors). American citizens have had a hands-on privilege when it comes to the process of making laws and drafting rules to live by.

So how should we as Christians involve ourselves in politics?

POLITICS: A BIBLICAL VIEW

God has much to say about government and politics, in both the Old and New Testament. The rationale behind any government can be reduced to two purposes:

1. Avoiding anarchy.
2. Distributing wealth.

There are hundreds of verses in the Bible dedicated to addressing the leaders and governance of God's people and the world. We'll look at some of them in this chapter.

AVOIDING ANARCHY

God is a God of order. He loves to bring harmony and clear process into living organisms and groups. With humans, whether it's a family, a group of friends, a business, a ministry, or an entire nation, it's important to make decisions in an orderly manner. From Stone Age cultures in the outback of Australia to admirals and generals in the Pentagon, groups tend to agree upon procedures for deciding what to do and how to keep chaos from reigning.

However, we must strive for a balance between *efficiency* and *effectiveness*. By far, the most efficient form of government is the dictatorship, where one person's will is the law. Dictatorships are very efficient in the decision-making process—no messy discussions, no executive committees, no policy boards, no exploratory commissions, no long and drawn-out procedures. Efficient? Yes. Effective? No.

The Greeks said that when the gods wanted to destroy someone, they gave them power. Why was that? Because of the great axiom that *power corrupts, and absolute power corrupts absolutely.* We fallen creatures very easily become tyrants and oppressors. Power in the hands of almost any of us is like car keys in the hands of a precocious 6-year-old—we have a habit of wrecking cars, people, and ourselves!

OLD TESTAMENT KINGSHIP

In the Old Testament, God told the prophet Samuel that the people had rejected God as their Leader when they cried out for a king.

In response to their cries, God gave them a king, Saul—who soon became a tragic story of the *might have been.*

Having a king wasn't wrong in itself. In fact, it was a much more efficient process than having 12 loosely bound tribes trying to follow God. But a king was ineffective in keeping the people mindful of the fact that they belonged to God—not to a human king. God had warned them of this danger, and Saul proceeded to fulfill God's warning. He took the peoples' money and pressed them into labor to build monuments to his own massive ego!

There were great kings in Israel's history—like David, Asa, Josiah, and Hezekiah—and there were horrid kings—like Ahab, Jeroboam, and Ahaz. It's interesting that God never did step back in and put into place a pure theocracy once a king was ruling. At any time He could have said, "This king thing is not working—it's over!" But He never did. Instead, He called the kings to be agents of justice and fairness and concern for the people, hoping that they would wholeheartedly agree and behave accordingly.

In the intertestamental period, Israel's Sanhedrin (their "Supreme Court") was developed even further. There was a king, but there was also a deliberate checks and balance system with the priests, prophets, and other elders of the nation. Power became more vested in "ordered groups" rather than in one sole individual. There was oversight, in an effort to avoid people imposing their own will on others. God was still in control, but now through His leaders.

NEW TESTAMENT GOVERNANCE

In the New Testament, the church in the Book of Acts had a fairly fluid form of government, but it closely followed the synagogue pattern of decision-making. There were now disciples, elders, deacons—and even the apostles, who had walked with Christ.

Acts 15 gives us delicious insight into how the government in the early church made decisions. There are the witnesses of the apostles Paul and Barnabus; there are leaders such as James; and then there is the consensus of the entire believing community. Any denomination can find biblical support for its form of government from the Acts 15. It seems that God can (and does) use many different types of government in creating an orderly world in which to live.

The apostles Paul and Peter told the people to submit to the authority of the pagan emperor of Rome, even though he was hardly pro-Jesus. They did that because they acknowledged such submission as God's way of keeping order in the world. The New Testament makes clear that there will come a time when the victory of Christ will be found in resisting the government to the point of martyrdom, but unless the government was demanding idolatrous worship or violation of God's laws, then good citizenship was taught under Roman government.

To love God and to love our neighbor means that we care for others, regardless of whether they deserve it or not. It also means that we are to be people who abide by social laws—and there are consequences for lawbreakers.

DISTRIBUTING LIFE PROVISIONS

The second purpose of government goes beyond keeping an orderly world in which people, families, and businesses can prosper. There must be administration and distribution of goods and services, as well as protection of citizens.

Think about it in the realm of the home. Parents must not only provide a safe and orderly home—they also need to feed their family members and supply for their needs. It's the same in the business world. Corporate leaders need to have more than rules and procedures for their employees' safety and their customers' interests; they must also create wealth and value, and they must distribute the proceeds justly to all involved. Logically, these principles apply to the political realm as well. Presidents, parliaments, kings, and queens must have more than just order and harmony—they also need systems that create and share the wealth and goods produced.

Who decides the specifics of wealth distribution? How much government is the best way to honor God and love His people? How involved should a Christian become, since we belong to God's Kingdom and not to the kingdom of this world? Should we ever resist the government—or in every instance, obey it? Would God prefer professional politicians—or would it be better to have objective but inexperienced leaders make the big decisions?

We've all heard the saying, "The way to tell if a politician is lying is if their lips are moving." The reason there is such cynicism and distrust of politicians is because we have created a system in America where the most money, image-spinning, and unkept promises are what really gets a person into office.

We live in a culture that has become dumbed down and seemingly unable to address the important issues of the day in an intelligent, informative, and non-defensive manner. We even have political experts and media pundits who try to win the debate by shouting each other down under the guise of "conviction," when it is actually little more than mind-numbing staged entertainment to foster the dumbing down of society. It's like the politician who said with great passion, "Those are my convictions. If you don't like them, I have other ones, too."

Christian men and women throughout the centuries have tried to live in a world rife with real dangers and real challenges while recognizing that we are dual citizens who live here on earth but whose real home is in Heaven (and the new earth, as foretold in the Book of Revelation).

In the A.D. 400s Augustine lived under the gradual decline of the pagan Roman Empire. In *City of God* (a work Augustine wrote over a period of 13 years) he stated that we belong to two cities—the city of God coming down from Heaven, and the city of man we live in now.

Augustine was wary of trusting the Church being close to the government—you would be too if, for the last 300 years, they'd been killing people just for being Christians! Even though Christianity became accepted in A.D. 325 under Constantine, and even though it became the *only* religion in Rome under Emperor Theodosius I in A.D. 385, Augustine was still wary of government and agreed with the adage, "He who dines with the devil should use a long spoon."

Thomas Aquinas, writing in the 1200s, lived when the Church and the state were one and the same. The Holy Roman Empire was the government of Europe, and the laws of the land were supposedly taken directly from the Bible. Aquinas challenged Christians to be devout in both their spiritual as well as their civic lives. He saw no conflict between the purposes of the Church and those of the state. He said it was more an issue of power—the one with the power now was the state, but the real power lay in the hands of Christ and His followers.

Three centuries later, Martin Luther would write in his home of Germany about the Church being submissive to the government. This was probably a natural response to his environment, as he lived during the bloody Peasants' War of 16th-century Europe and saw rising fear and chaos overtaking society.

Even though these three giants of spiritual and intellectual life lived far apart geographically and during different centuries, all agreed on the two purposes of Christians in government: to keep loving order, and to give loving care to all people.

TENTACLES OF GOVERNMENT AND THE GREAT EXPERIMENT

Some 230 years ago, a handful of brilliant men sat down and drafted the boldest plan of government the world had seen to date. George Washington called it, "The Great Experiment: Can a people govern themselves without a king?" They were going to create a new nation without a ruler to keep order.

The American Revolution was being born. Jefferson, Franklin, Washington, Adams, and the rest were students of history. They knew democracies had existed before—such as some of the Greek city-states—but none had lasted. Even the Republic of Rome became the Imperial Roman Empire in a flash.

Why? Because if not properly structured, a democracy can become an anarchy—and a dictatorship is necessary to bring it back to order. The founders feared two things—the king and the dictator. But there was one thing they feared even more—the mob. The tendency for societies to fall apart was the greatest threat in their minds.

The founders surmised that, in order to have true freedom, three things were needed. The three sides of this "freedom triangle" were:

1. Values of justice and concern for all others from every citizen (what the founding fathers called "manners").

2. Religion (or "spirituality"), which helps to develop values of justice and concern.

3. Freedom from the government's involvement in religious matters.

America's founders would be blown away at the success of their experiment! However, they instinctively knew, way back then, that success required the values and strength of a deeply religious people.

THE BIBLE AND AMERICAN GOVERNMENT

Thomas Jefferson was an interesting Deist and hard to pin down spiritually, but he was not a confessing Christian. His Bible is on display in Monticello, and you can see where he physically cut out verses he thought were redundant or unimportant!

Supposedly, John Adams commented one day, seeing Jefferson lugging a Bible with him, "Thomas, why are you carrying about that Bible? You don't believe in it like we do!"

To which Jefferson allegedly smiled and replied in earnest, "Ah, but the republic needs it!"

Whether that tale is true or not, Jefferson and Adams would both be scared out of their buckle shoes to know that we have reached a point in America where people are turning upside-down their attempt to create an America based on biblical values—with the result being a sterile democracy increasingly devoid of all religion and spiritual influences.

So where should we stand politically as heirs of America who also belong to Christ's Kingdom? Should you vote Democrat, Republican, *and* Independent—in other words, voting the issue and not the party? Should we vote strict party lines, regardless of individual issues? Should we not vote at all?

PARTY LINES

If you were to look at the government as an octopus, you would see it differently depending on whether you are a Democrat or a Republican. Democrats generally see the tentacles of this political octopus as friendly, because the octopus of government is simply *us*. The arms are there to help you. They protect you, hold you, feed you, and give guidance as you feed it.

But if you're a Republican, you generally think this octopus is there to hold you back. It will strangle your freedom and take the food off of your plate, so the best thing to do is have as small an octopus as possible.

The Republican octopus abides by the Thomas Paine quote: "That government is best which governs least." The Democrat octopus sings, "We are stronger together than any of us alone." You can see that both have legitimate, and even noble, perspectives.

The point is not to label whether Democrats or Republicans are more Christian, but to determine how all of us can together create the biblical values and world perspective of Christ and His followers. There is no perfect political organization, nor will there ever be. If we are Republican, we had better keep up the effort in helping the poor and the outcast. If we are Democrat, we had better take seriously this thing called "boldness for the Gospel," and a life of purity within our society. The challenge for both is how to best use the tentacles of government to keep order, reward hard work, care for the downcast, and yet not get in the way of peoples' freedom.

How do you distribute and create wealth so that you reward good behavior and give all equal opportunities, while not letting a "privileged" few take advantage of others? The Bible would simply say something like, "If you think you should have a small government, then make sure others are being helped and cared for in other ways. And if you think the government should be large, then make sure peoples' self-initiative is protected."

MATTHEW 25 AGENDA AND LEAKY BUCKETS

When the Son of Man comes in His glory, and all the angels with Him, He will sit on His throne in heavenly glory. All the nations will be gathered before Him, and He will separate the people one from another as a shepherd separates the sheep from the goats. He will put the sheep on His right and the goats on His left. Then the King will say to those on His right, "Come, you who are blessed by My Father; take your inheritance, the kingdom prepared for you since the creation of the world. For I was hungry and you gave Me something to eat, I was thirsty and you gave Me something to drink, I was a stranger and you invited Me in, I needed clothes and you clothed Me, I was sick and you looked after Me, I was in prison and you came to visit Me." Then the righteous will answer Him, "Lord, when did we see You hungry and feed You, or thirsty and give You something to drink? When did we see You a stranger and invite You in, or needing clothes and clothe You? When did we see You sick or in prison and go to visit You?" The King will reply, "I tell you the truth, whatever you

> *did for one of the least of these brothers of Mine, you did for Me."*
> *Then He will say to those on His left, "Depart from Me, you who*
> *are cursed, into the eternal fire prepared for the devil and his an-*
> *gels. For I was hungry and you gave Me nothing to eat, I was*
> *thirsty and you gave Me nothing to drink, I was a stranger and*
> *you did not invite Me in, I needed clothes and you did not clothe*
> *Me, I was sick and in prison and you did not look after Me."*
> *They also will answer, "Lord, when did we see You hungry or*
> *thirsty or a stranger or needing clothes or sick or in prison, and*
> *did not help You?" He will reply, "I tell you the truth, whatever*
> *you did not do for one of the least of these, you did not do for Me."*
> *Then they will go away to eternal punishment, but the righteous*
> *to eternal life* (Matthew 25:31-46 NIV).

On that day when we each stand before the Lord, the shock to us will be how Jesus evaluates our love for Him. In His great parable of compassion in Matthew 25, Jesus plainly states that how we treat the least of the least is how we treat Him. He said that when He was "in need," they either helped or ignored Him. Surprised, the disciples asked when that had happened. He declared that it was when they did it to those in their communities, the people they encountered. Those without clothes, food, or drink…those in prison…the lonely.

As followers of Christ, we must be diligent in caring for the widows and orphans, the lepers of our day (those with AIDS), and the outcasts. Since we have government, we must make sure that it cares for them. We are to give a "cup of water" in Christ's name and be prepared to receive His gratitude.

The challenge is the old *leaky bucket syndrome*—you take in billions of dollars of taxes from the citizenry, and by the time you get it into the hands of the needy, it has leaked so much into the system itself that little actually gets to the people who need it most. Or worse, the government's priorities are so out of balance that more money goes to causes that don't improve society or help the needy than to those that do.

We cannot let the government be the sole givers of help. God have mercy on any sane follower of Christ who says, "It's the government's job to take care of everyone." It is *our* privilege and command as the church—and certainly as individuals as well as corporate America—to help. But it requires intelligent, fresh, and diligent responses, and it demands that we hold government accountable for when the leaks in the bucket of bureaucracy prevent help from reaching the poor, the children, and the infirm.

THE KINGDOM AGENDA

I have heard people say so often, especially at election time, "How can you be a Christian brother or sister and beat my brains out in the voting booth?" However, after having been one of the only white Republican members of an African-American Democratic alliance, I can say with confidence that both majority and suburban Christians and minority and urban Christians all want pretty much the same things. The difference is in the emphasis on what is the most urgent need to tend to right now.

We in suburbia would say that the great, immediate cultural needs that God wants us to attend to are the big moral issues of pornography, abortion, substance abuse, and sexuality. The urban church, however, would say it is jobs, careers, caring for the elderly, and feeding the children. If you brought the two together, that would be called *The Kingdom Agenda*. Both halves reflect Kingdom values, and we can't abandon one for the sake of the other.

One of the early emperors of the Byzantine Empire ruled over his empire as a Christian, but he had never had the privilege of actually reading a copy of the Gospels since they were so rare. When he finally was presented with a copy of the Gospels as a gift and tribute, he took them to his palace and read them for a week. He then came back, summoned his council, and declared, "Either these are not the Gospels, or we are not Christians!" After finally being exposed to the pure words of Christ, he was struck at how far off his life and empire were from God's words and ways.

We are to be an open book for Christ. When people "read" us Christians and observe how we get involved in governing this great experiment of American politics, may they not say of our lives, "Either the Gospels aren't true, or they're not really Christians!" May we be found caring for others because of Christ's care for us first.

CHAPTER 18

Issue Eleven—Everyday Pleasures Entertainment and the Arts, Smoking and Drinking

We hold these truths to be self-evident, that all men are created equal, that they are endowed by their Creator with certain unalienable Rights, that among these are Life, Liberty and the pursuit of Happiness.

—The Declaration of Independence of the United States of America

As followers of Jesus Christ and as people bound by the Word of God, how do we live the pursuit of happiness mentioned in our Declaration of Independence? Contrary to the stereotypes and misconceptions of the world, God is not a cosmic killjoy seeking to stop us from enjoying His creation. So how can we take this important need and bring it under the light of God's Word? We need a "theology of fun."

WHAT IS "FUN"?

I said to myself, "Come now, I will make a test of pleasure; enjoy yourself." But again, this also was vanity. I said of laughter, "It is mad," and of pleasure, "What use is it?" I searched with my mind how to cheer my body with wine—my mind still guiding me with wisdom—and how to lay hold on folly, until I might see what was good for mortals to do under Heaven during the few days of their life (Ecclesiastes 2:1-3).

Many Bible scholars believe that King Solomon was the author of Ecclesiastes. We know that at the time he was alive, he was the wisest, wealthiest, and most powerful man on earth. He could do whatever he wanted—and yet he described pleasure and the things of this world as "meaningless."

God is the Creator of pleasure, but exactly what is *pleasure*? One of the Greek words for *pleasure* is *hedone*, which deals with the physical, or the good feelings of the body and the senses. It might be a cup of hot cocoa, the smell of fresh pine boughs, the feel of a hug, the sound of a symphony, the sight of fresh snow on the forest floor, or a warm shower. These are just a few of the many examples of the pleasures to be found in God's cosmos. For humans, the acts and feelings of pleasure can be endless.

HAPPINESS

The word *happiness* comes from Greek word *makarios*, meaning "blessed." Happiness can come from achieving a goal or performing a great feat. The philosophical term is "overcoming finitude." When you make something with your hands, or accomplish something, or take a test and pass it, or make the winning goal in a big game, you experience a sense of happiness.

The only trouble with happiness is that it's based on *happenings*—and many people are always running to the next new thing, seeking to keep that "high" of accomplishment and avoid the "lows" of life. It's good to accomplish things and to take pleasure in doing so, but to get caught in a never-ending cycle of seeking "happy happenings" is dangerous—and will ultimately be unfulfilling.

Paul said to the Corinthians, "All things are lawful for me, but not all things are profitable. All things are lawful for me, but I will not be mastered by anything" (see 1 Corinthians 6:12; 10:23 NASB). The bottom line is that you have freedom in Christ to do what your conscious permits you to. But the reason you say "no" to certain desires is because you don't want to be addicted to anything. We have to be wise in how we live out our freedom to pursue happiness.

Those who eat must not despise those who abstain, and those who abstain must not pass judgment on those who eat; for God has welcomed them. Who are you to pass judgment on servants of another? It is before their own lord that they stand or fall. And they will be upheld, for the Lord is able to make them stand. Some judge one day to be better than another, while others judge all days to be alike. Let all be fully convinced in their own minds. Those who observe the day, observe it in honor of the Lord. Also those who eat, eat in honor of the Lord, since they give thanks to God; while those who abstain, abstain in honor of the Lord and give thanks to God (Romans 14:3-6).

JOY

The question remains as to how you can have fun and enjoy everyday pleasures while loving God and those around you and not giving a negative image of Christianity.

Have you ever been driving along and you see a sunset, or you hear a particular song, and all of a sudden something bubbles up inside of you and you think, "Yeah, *that's* it! That's great!" You are experiencing a flood of joy.

The Greek word for *joy* is *chara*, meaning "gift of God." C.S. Lewis was right when he said, "Joy is a hunger for God." That hunger is more wonderful than anything we consume here in life.

It is important for Christians to show the world what a good time is all about. It's not about an escape into self-medication. It's about enjoying the good things of God and His unspeakable joy. You can get as high as a kite and go get blasted drunk and feel wonderful—but then you come down and it's empty. And even when you're wearing nice clothes and your stomach is full, you can still feel empty.

Happiness comes from *achieving* or *attaining* something—but the sense of happiness at that accomplishment is temporary. It's not the all-engulfing, undying joy of God.

Someday we're going to drink from the fountain of joy Himself, when we stand in front of the Lord. I believe we'll need a perfect body just to be able to not have a meltdown from the joy that we're going to have when we stand in front of God!

PLEASURE

Pleasure is one of the basic foundational areas of life. King Solomon was a king—he could buy anything he wanted. He had the best wine, threw the best parties, did the best celebrating. And he still said, "You know what? I'm empty. It's not all it's cracked up to be."

Pleasure is originally from God—He created pleasure. In the story of the Garden of Eden, God made some trees to eat from, and others that were simply beautiful and pleasing to the eye. They were intended for pleasure. God likes pleasure—that's why He gave us our senses, so we too could share in the beauty and wonders of His creation. Pleasure is good! Pleasure is *God-given.*

> *Therefore we also pray always for you that our God would count you worthy of this calling, and fulfill all the good pleasure of His goodness and the work of faith with power* (2 Thessalonians 1:11 NKJV).

PLEASURE CORRUPTED

The problem in today's culture—and throughout the history of humankind—is that pleasure has been corrupted by sin. When Adam and Eve rebelled against God, we were rendered as slaves to the Lower Laws, and our values and priorities became all tangled up. Now, what was supposed to be a just "means" has become the "end." God gave us pleasure as icing on the cake—not as the main purpose in life. But many have made pursuit of the icing their chief end for being. That's where all the disease and addiction and problems came from.

The word *longing* comes from the Greek word *epithumia—epi,* meaning "inside," and *thumia,* meaning "lust." It refers to the lust we have inside, the *longing.* Lust isn't only sexual. It also means any form of wanting something so much that you're not willing to say no to it.

People have always had problems with pleasure. When Henry the Eighth came to the throne in 16th-century England, the people had high hopes. He was an athlete, he was good-looking, and he was brilliant. But Henry was also a pleasure addict with a severe sexual addiction. Not only did he have six wives, but he beheaded some of them so he could marry someone else whenever he wanted a new wife. He did this because the Pope wouldn't allow Henry to get a divorce, so Henry would kill them in order to get around that papal edict. That's why he eventually broke away from the Roman Catholic Church and supported the Church of England.

In addition to being a sex glutton, Henry was also a food glutton. He got so fat he couldn't walk up the stairs. They had to rig up an elevator to hoist him to the upper floors of the castle. And this was the "great hope" of England! Instead, he ended up becoming a miserable, bloated, sexoholic wretch. All because of his out-of-control *epithumia*.

However, the number one sex addict of all history may have been Cleopatra the Seventh, Queen of the Nile. Octavius wrote about her that not only did she bed down Mark Anthony, Julius Caesar, and her own brothers, but she also kept a harem of a hundred men, just to satisfy her sexual pleasure! She gave herself over totally to satisfying her sexual lust, and then committed suicide when she was only 39.[1]

> *If you have found honey, eat only enough for you, or else, having too much, you will vomit it* (Proverbs 25:16).

Isn't Proverbs 25:16 a great verse? What this means is that God gives us a lot of sweet things in life that are wonderful—but when we overindulge, the resulting pleasure diminishes with each occurrence, and eventually makes us sick.

ENTERTAINMENT AND THE ARTS

The relationship between faith and the arts has been a hot topic throughout history—but the issue has reached an especially fevered pitch in the 21st century. In this entertainment and media-mad society of television, movies, magazines, video games, and the ever-increasing demand for *fun*, how should Christians handle the onslaught of audio and visual input?

Should the media *reflect* or *direct* culture? In Southern California where I live, that's a nonsensical question, because the media literally is the culture in Los Angeles. What's more, it's becoming the culture of America.

The Church needs to reclaim the arts for Christ. In the Middle Ages, if you wanted to see the best in art, you went to the church. Whether you agreed with Christianity or not, the church had the best music, the best sculptures, the best paintings. If you wanted to find out what was happening, you went to the church. When was the last time you said, "If you want to see what's on the cutting edge of the arts, go to the local church"? We don't—and *that's* the problem.

TIME FOR A CHANGE

I think evil smiles at some of the poison that's being piped into the heads and hearts of people today through the media. But just as I believe that evil itself delights in much of what we call art and entertainment today, I just as firmly believe that God Himself delights even more in people using their God-given creativity to express themselves, because God gave the ability to create in celebration of His own creativeness. I believe that as we approach the return of the Lord, some of the greatest music, books, plays, cinema, and art are yet to be created. I believe Christ wants us to reclaim the arts that were hijacked from the Creator and use them to our blessing and His glory.

I want to propose to you three brief guidelines on this issue, taken from principles in God's Word:

1. God enjoys others enjoying His creation.
2. God is concerned with the power of images and thought.
3. God calls us to be stewards of the gift of art.

Proposition #1:
God Enjoys Others Enjoying His Creation

In Genesis, God tells the marvelous creation account, where He makes everything and it's all "good." In the second chapter, He makes Adam—although he's not fully man yet, not until woman, Eve, is taken from his side. Then we come to:

> *And the Lord God planted a garden in Eden, in the east; and there He put the man whom He had formed. Out of the ground the Lord God made to grow every tree that is **pleasant to the sight**...* (Genesis 2:8-9).

Notice that God made some things for the sheer purpose of *His pleasure.* They have no function except that God thinks they look cool. Can you imagine how many plants and flowers are blooming on the backside of mountains that no human eye will ever see? They're there just for God to enjoy.

There is plant and animal sea life in the oceans that humans will never even discover. And it's not all there just for the ecosystem. God makes them because He loves what He has made and He likes making it. God is so creative that He doesn't even make two snowflakes alike. He is constantly creating.

Pleasure should be celebrated in God's way. God often wants to give us things merely to enjoy. But sometimes when He tries to bless us we say, "No. I don't have time. I'm in a bad mood. I'm just too stressed." But God has a purpose for pleasure, and we should embrace it as a gift.

> *You show me the path of life. In Your presence there is fullness of joy; in Your right hand are pleasures forevermore* (Psalm 16:11).

The problem with our culture today is that it treats pleasure as the end-all, be-all. Pleasure is *not* an end in itself, it is for two important functions—to reflect God's glory and to refresh and restore His people.

Proposition #2:
God Is Concerned With the Power of Images and Thoughts

> *Love the Lord your God with all your heart, and with all your soul, and with all your mind* (Matthew 22:37).

Entertainment usually means "escaping reality," but *art* generally refers to "raising your awareness of reality." Of course entertainment can be artistic and art can be entertaining, but often with many forms of entertainment, people are tired of the same ol' same ol'—they want to go to Fantasy Land! They want to "zone out" for a while.

Art, on the other hand, is supposed to raise our awareness of reality. That's why sculptures, paintings, symphonies, dances, or anything throughout the ages demanded "work" on the part of the observer. Yes, art serves as a reprieve from the daily grind of life, but the manner in which it helps to "refresh" observers is tied up in the fact that observers must participate in the work of art. You can't just see it and understand it—it pulls you up to a greater awareness, because you have to dig deep and consider what is before you. It is refreshing, but not numbing.

Have you ever taken a long walk and enjoyed a cool, refreshing drink of water at the end? Or taken a bite of food after many long hours of not eating? Or taken your shoes off and put your toes into a mountain stream? Doesn't that refresh you? Sometimes we forget that our lives are not just about working all the time and keeping busy, busy, busy. We need refreshing—not constant bombardment.

We live in a culture where people are just shells of humanity, looking for something to thrill and excite them. We want something to remind us we're *alive*. That's what the addiction to sex is all about. That's why some people are obsessed with violence. Sometimes people just get numb and don't realize those ways are wrong, because they're so used to it—like frogs in slowly boiling water. We need to be alert to what we're exposing our minds to, and God is the One to give us the wake-up call.

Seek Enrichment—Not Just Entertainment

Nothing is *just* entertaining. Whether it's a movie, a book, a play, or anything else that tells a story, the big themes are ultimately issues that deal with the eternal, the religious, the spiritual. They all have God in the undercurrent. In his book *The Divine Romance*, author Gene Edwards says that all story plots are really just different takes on the one big plot of the universe: God is the Hero, evil enters, the Hero rescues the beloved, and evil loses in the end. The story of redemption and love is behind every great story, for the simple fact that it is the story behind the universe itself. It rings true to our souls because God Himself wrote this story of lost love recovered and redeemed.

The challenge for us as "foreigners" on planet Earth is to remember that Heaven is where we're going; that's our final destination, our home. Our journey requires that, while we're here, the process of sanctification, or spiritual growth, take place. Entertainment can actually be part of that process.

Some art is not only acceptable, it's actually beneficial, enriching. Some art is wonderful—a cup of cold water to a parched soul. But a lot of entertainment is like strychnine to the soul. Whether you sip it or chug it, it takes the life from you. We have to be able to discern between that which is good for us and that which is destructive.

We are called to search out and create that which is of high quality *and* high virtue. I believe we need to use entertainment in the right ways. We need to put out the call to vote with our wallets, to watch and to create only high-quality, high-virtue entertainment. We need to embrace good art with a good message that God would appreciate. Decide on what you're going to watch and what you're going to read, and make those decisions based on how God would support it if He were sitting right there with you…because He is!

Put a barrier between yourself and what you take into your mind. You're not immune to temptation any more than you're immune to the laws of gravity.

Power of the Image

Ultimately, our challenge is to understand the power of images. The assault on language, communication, and entertainment in our culture has lead to the "dumbing down" of America. It's not that people themselves are dumb—they're not. But there's an inability to connect, because we are out of touch with words, with thoughts, with ideas.

Symbols profoundly affect our idea systems and thought grids. As an example, think about flags, which are themselves symbols. For a proud American, the sight of the American flag conjures up certain ideas, thoughts, and ideals of pride, belonging, significance, and purpose. For that same American, seeing images of the flag of Nazi Germany would likely conjure thoughts and feelings of disgust, sadness, pain, and grief. The reason is because symbols are powerful. They hold a world of meaning behind them.

We need to be aware of the impact of images. Movie images have a vast, instant impact. In the movie *Schindler's List*, for example, there is a scene in which Oscar Schindler is coming up with the final list of the people whose freedom he can afford to purchase; those not on the list will go to the gas chamber. What a powerful and poignant image as Schindler agonizes over who to add to his list! Then there's a scene in *Chariots of Fire* where the runner falls…and then gets back up and finishes the race. These images, these scenes, deeply affect us.

God is concerned about the power of images, as they can be very powerful indeed. They can nullify logic or transcend it. The Cross is the ultimate symbol, and that's why many churches choose to prominently display one in their auditorium or sanctuary. What does it say? It says how horrific sin is in the eyes of God that it would cost Him that much to cover the evil we commit. It declares how immeasurably God loves us, in that He gave His only Son. And it speaks volumes of hope since the empty Cross reminds us that Christ is coming back. All that wrapped up in one wooden symbol.

Interplay of Image and Thought

While they can be strongholds of meaning, the problem is that images and symbols can also nullify rational thought. Today in the 21st century, we more often than not connect out of imagery and symbols—not out of logic and reasoning. We are an image-driven culture, and words no longer hold the power or the significance they once did. The problem with this is that spiritual growth must begin with our mind—because that's the first place we turn away from God and it's what controls our actions. Jesus said to love the Lord with our *entire* mind (see Mark 12:30)—but we can't do that if we've forgotten *how* to use our mind.

The power of a logical discussion is that dialoguing about issues requires us to take abstract ideas and present them in ways that can be clearly communicated to others. Talking about abstractions and wrestling through them is good exercise for the mental muscles. The power and danger of the visual image is we can't really "argue" with it. We see it and are moved to "agree" with the emotional response whether it is accurate or not. Images are powerful, but like emotional reasoning, they are prone to contradictory thinking. Imagery is a super effective motivator. It is a great engine that releases movement. What it doesn't do is sift the decision to do something through the grid of sound thinking. There is a reason that politics and advertising are image driven. Our minds naturally associate the product with some happy image or desire. We need words and language to understand, to function—and to clearly evaluate images. That is the way God has made us. We must increase our reading to the level of our watching. We must strive to critically think as much as we simply consume media.

In 1985 Neil Postman wrote a book called *Amusing Ourselves to Death*. He is not a believer, but he makes a lot of good points. He says that the problem with America is not so much *that* we watch entertainment or the arts, nor is it even so much of a problem *what* we watch. Rather, he says, the problem is that we watch to the *level* that we do, because it compromises our ability to reason, think, understand, and comprehend.

These principles hold true nowhere more poignantly than in the spiritual realm. The more you have God's Word in your mind, the more you can actually see His image. We need to bathe our minds in God's Word more than in the images of this lost and dying world, so that we can see and understand rightly.

Proposition #3:
God Calls Us to Be Stewards of the Gift of Art

Does God care what we see? Absolutely. But to what degree? Can watching a play ever do you harm? When is art actually good for you, and when is it destructive for you? For those of us who make our living directly or indirectly from the entertainment industry, what does the Lord ask us to do? Are we called to embrace our culture? Are we called to drop out and start our own little Christian subculture on to the side, where only Christian movies and books and shows and entertainment are produced and enjoyed?

I believe that we are not to flee from entertainment or arts. I believe we are instead to enter, infuse, and drastically impact the entertainment business—to use it for God's glory.

I once talked to a church member who worked at one of the television studios. She told me they were filming a scene that made fun of Christians, and the producers decided to cut the scene out because they love their receptionist, who is a Christian, and they didn't want to offend her. Now *that* is affecting Hollywood from the inside. Here's the remarkable thing—she was their *only* touch-point with Christians!

Should she, as a Christian, be working there? Yes! She caused millions of people not to see a scene that put down Christians! Without a fuss, without a fight, without begging or whining or threatening or pleading—but just by her mere presence—she caused a scene that would have put our Lord in a negative light to be cast out. She affected

Hollywood for God by merely being in a relationship with the studio where they respected her integrity and work.

I believe that one reason Hollywood puts out so much negativity about Christianity is because most of what many of them see of Christianity are televangelists. That's their only sphere of observation. We need to improve their image of Christianity by giving them alternative images of us.

There are countless Christians involved in the film industry—some successful, some struggling. Those Christians who are in the industry not for fame or fortune, but simply to express the greatness of God, need our support. We need to be praying for them, encouraging them, supporting them in every way we can.

That doesn't mean applauding artistic mediocrity simply because they love the Lord. It means being a light in the world and striving for artistic excellence that is glorifying to God. There are so few truly dedicated Christians working in the entertainment industry. It is a vast mission field in need of light. They have the potential to reach an incredible mission field.

In 2006 the population of America reached 300 million. The average American spends nearly 30 hours per week in front of the television[2], and more than 20 million people purchase tickets to see movies each week. Just imagine the impact Christian men and women in the film industry can have on these millions of people!

We Christians who are not part of the entertainment industry must stand by, support, pray for, and cover those Christians who are working in the industry. I can't tell you the number of people I've talked to who've said, "My Christian friends say they can't believe I work in the entertainment business. They just don't understand my career. And people in Hollywood don't understand my faith, my love for Christ. I'm like a person with no country!" We must support and pray for those people.

HONOR THE SHEPHERD

I heard a story once about an actor in the 1950s who was going to recite the Twenty-Third Psalm in church. In the pews was an older pastor who was visiting. The actor, who had a Shakespearean voice, recited the Twenty-Third Psalm flawlessly. Everybody applauded.

Then they asked the elderly pastor to quote the psalm. He stood and began to speak. When he was done, nobody applauded—they were all quiet. Many were weeping. Someone later asked, "What was the difference between the two?" The answer is that one man knew the psalm…and the other knew the Shepherd. We need more men and women in Hollywood who know the Shepherd.

At the same time, those Christian men and women involved in the entertainment industry need to stand guard. Don't get sucked into what you know is wrong all in the name of "expanding your mission field." It's tough to turn down work, I know, but turn it down if it doesn't uplift the Lord. You might get labeled as someone hard to work with, but believe me, the Lord will honor those who honor Him. God is your ultimate audience, not the entertainment industry or a fickle public.

For those who are working in the entertainment industry in an area that somehow touches on or benefits the pornography business, I'm going to speak very plainly to you—you are up to your eyeballs in sin! That is not the so-called "celebration of freedom" or "art of the body." The sad thing is how many lives have been fed the lie that the "adult industry" will lead to a career in the mainstream studios. I counsel these broken lives all the time. It is the economic rape and oppression of women, men, and children, and it is a drug to a sexually addicted culture. God is not mocked. Knock it off *today*! Shut it down and turn it off! God will open doors to better work for you.

You can't stop the river of violence and emptiness and dehumanization, but you can help redirect it by making a decision to support only art and entertainment that deserves supporting and that does not degrade or sexually exploit any person.

THE LOOK OF CHRISTIAN ART

When Paul wrote the Book of Romans, he was writing from the heart of the entertainment world, Imperial Rome. He said of the citizens of Rome, essentially, "They are without excuse, for God is evident because of His creation" (see Romans 1:20-21). God is evident. Creation reflects His glory, and He wants us to reflect His glory as well.

"Christian art" doesn't mean there always has to be a picture of Jesus, or a cross, or Moses. Christian art is a celebration of God. So every time you say, "I'm an artist and I need to do something," you don't have to create a Bible with a popup of the apostles. Sometimes art is just a celebration. Sometimes it's just meant to refresh us.

The same goes for film. A Christian film doesn't necessarily mean that someone has to say "Jesus." And just because a film *does* have the name "Jesus" in it doesn't mean it is God-honoring art, either.

Frances Schafer said it best: "The purpose of all art is to have good message and good art." Unfortunately, many Christians miss the second half of the equation. They've got the "good message" part down, but they totally ignore the "good art." Many Christian movies have a great message, but they are bad art if they're not well produced.

"Christian schlock" is a term that needs to be made inapplicable in the world of entertainment. For some reason, Christians tend to think that just because something has a good, moral, Christian message, then it's good entertainment, no matter what the artistic quality. Not necessarily so. Our God is a *creative* God, and we need to demonstrate this creativity too, in the art and entertainment we create.

A HIGHER CALL

Finally, brothers, whatever is true, whatever is noble, whatever is right, whatever is pure, whatever is lovely, whatever is admirable—if anything is excellent or praiseworthy—think about such things. Whatever you have learned or received or heard from me, or seen in me—put it into practice. And the God of peace will be with you (Philippians 4:8-9 NIV).

Notice what Paul is teaching in this passage. He's saying, essentially, that when you direct all the focus of your thoughts, your will engages. We can't simply *will* to stop being evil; we have to be redirected *away* from evil and *toward* good. We have a disease called sin; we can't just will it away on our own. But if we are willing to be willing, and ready to say with conviction, "Lord, guide me," and if we firmly regulate what we put into our minds through our senses, then it is remarkable the power that God then puts into us to be able to take the next step up.

When the serpent came against Adam and Eve in the Garden, he didn't come with a stick and beat them into sin. He came subtly, with an idea, through an image. The image went like this: "God is not trustworthy. God wants you to have a boring life, and if you obey God, you'll miss out on something good. So you need to take care of yourself. On your own. Without God."

That's how it started. It wasn't a logical discussion. It was simply an image that the devil planted in Eve's mind: "God is not trustworthy." We live in a world of lost people who actually believe that about God. Satan's false image has persisted. We need to show the world differently by bringing in *new* mental and visual images.

St. Francis of Assisi is often attributed with having said, "Preach the gospel always, and if necessary, use words." Words are vital, and you certainly can't have the full gospel message without words. But images are powerful—and we need to realize their importance in reaching our culture today. This image-saturated society won't understand words alone. It needs us to communicate on its level—with images *and* words. Images that make life itself a demonstration of the love of God, so that people will say, "Oh…*that's* what Christianity is all about."

ARTISTIC STEWARDS

God calls us to be stewards of what we consume and what we create. If you like to watch a lot of television or movies, that's fine. Just make sure that you read as much as you watch, and make sure that what you read and watch is of a good caliber to be putting into your mind and heart, which is the temple of God (see 1 Corinthians 6:19). Also, try to keep your reading time to an amount at least equal to what you spend sitting in front of the screen, whether it's the big screen or a television screen. Raise your reading level!

Just as importantly, raise the amount of time you spend with people to the level of time you spend watching entertainment or reading. God calls us to not just to love His Word but to also love the people around us. I can't tell you how many people say, "I love the Word of God. I just

WHAT'S YOUR SPIRITUAL QUOTIENT?

can't stand Christians." I'll tell you why that is—because the Bible never has coffee breath!

In Exodus, the people were instructed by God to build the tabernacle, a place where He would meet them. He was in their presence, but this was to be a place set aside (which implies that there are some places where God will *not* meet us):

> *Moses then called Bezalel and Oholiab and every skillful one to whom the Lord had given skill, everyone whose heart was stirred to come to do the work; and they received from Moses all the freewill offerings that the Israelites had brought for doing the work on the sanctuary. They still kept bringing him freewill offerings every morning, so that all the artisans who were doing every sort of task on the sanctuary came, each from the task being performed, and said to Moses, "The people are bringing much more than enough for doing the work that the Lord has commanded us to do." So Moses gave command, and word was proclaimed throughout the camp: "No man or woman is to make anything else as an offering for the sanctuary." So the people were restrained from bringing; for what they had already brought was more than enough to do all the work* (Exodus 36:2-7).

As a pastor, I can't even image taking an offering from the congregation and saying, "No, no—it's too much! That's more than enough; we just don't need it, you crazy people, you! You're giving too much!" The thought moves a pastor to tears.

Notice in this passage that there were certain craftsmen who were doing artwork for the Lord's tabernacle, where He will meet them. It wasn't just anyone; it was the ones with the skill and the talent and the creative capabilities for the work. God wants the same from us. He's looking for the right men and women with the creative talent who will give Him *their very best*. God is raising up a new generation of craftsmen, gifted and hard working men and women, to create visual and musical temples where our spirits can encounter the Lord and His marvelous creation.

IS IT OK FOR CHRISTIANS TO SMOKE?

There is nothing in the Bible that talks about tobacco, because tobacco wasn't on the market when the Bible was written. Tobacco grows naturally and is not against any laws. So, sure, I believe it's OK for some to occasionally smoke—as long as, 1) You are willing to play with an incredibly addictive substance, 2) You keep it to a level that doesn't harm your body, and 3) You don't cause others to "stumble" by your actions.

Remember, the ethic of love demands that we do no harm to others and allow no harm to come to others. The Golden Rule of "do to others as you would have them do to you" (Luke 6:31) demands a proactive life. But are we free in Christ, as Paul says, to do *all* things? What is "all"?

In answering these questions, certain foundational constraints must guide us:

1. Love for others.
2. Love of Christ.
3. Stewardship of our body and health.

In the 1960s and '70s we used to say, "Dude, God grew it, so we can smoke it!" True, but he made rattlesnakes too, and you wouldn't suck on one of them, would you? Use a little wisdom with what you indulge in. Some things are fine on their own, but not at all wise for us to get involved with.

Supposedly, Charles Spurgeon, a Baptist from London and one of the great preachers of the last century, didn't like working with Americans because he smoked a cigar and that bugged the Yankees to no end. Americans would ask him, "Don't you think smoking is a sin?"

"Not if it's done in moderation," Spurgeon answered.

"What do you think moderation is?" they asked.

"One at a time," he quipped.

We each have the freedom to do what we think is best for us. We need to wrestle out these types of issues for ourselves under the guidance of the Holy Spirit. If you see somebody standing there with a cigar, or a glass of wine, or a rattlesnake, and you judge them, who are you to pass judgment? You probably need to repent for that. They will stand before the Lord to be judged for what they do or neglect to do (see 2 Corinthians 5:10). However, if you think you have the freedom to drink a glass of wine or puff on a stogie in front of the vulnerable and the weak, and you cause them to stumble, then you stand self-condemned.

As any physician will tell you it is easier physiologically to quit heroin than it is nicotine. I don't think there's anything intrinsically wrong with your having a smoke, but understand what you're dealing with.

My grandfather, a 5' 2" little fireball they called "Shorty," began chewing Copenhagen tobacco when he was in the seventh grade. He was easy to buy for at Christmas when I was a kid—just get him a sleeve of Copenhagen. He was so addicted to chewing tobacco that he tried to take up smoking in an effort to quit chewing—and he failed!

Sigmund Freud died of oral cancer from smoking cigars.

You do have freedom in the Lord, but you just need to know what is most glorifying to God, the best for you, and the most loving to others.

WHAT ABOUT DRINKING ALCOHOL?

There is a passage in the Bible that says that God gave wine to "gladden the heart" (see Psalm 104:15). Great bumper sticker, but what is that verse referring to? In Israel when this passage was written, wine was a part of daily life. It wasn't a part of daily life to go around hammered drunk, but back then water wasn't treated or purified, and there was no telling what it contained much of the time. So, wine was part of daily life.

The number one destroyer of lives today is the abuse of alcohol. There's not even a close second. All the heroin, all the crystal methamphetamine, all the cocaine, and all the marijuana combined do not come close to the destruction caused by alcohol.

When my father-in-law was in Vietnam in 1964, he became an alcoholic. He became such a street drunk, he said that if the military hadn't thrown him in jail, he probably would've died. He went to Alcoholics Anonymous after they booted him out, and he found the Lord and dried up.

There is a theory that once you're an alcoholic, you're never supposed to touch a drink again. And there's another theory that you might be able to have limited drinks now and then. But I was told that if you've ever been an alcoholic, you would never go near it again even if you wanted to, because one drink is too much and a hundred are not enough. I also know of someone who, after 15 years of sobriety, took a drink…and ultimately proceeded to drink himself to death—after being 15 years sober.

Proverbs 31:4-5 warns rulers not to desire strong drink or else they will drink and forget what has been decreed by God and will pervert the rights of the afflicted. And Proverbs 20:1 warns us that wine is a mocker and strong drink is a brawler, and that whoever is led astray by them is not wise.

If you have an addiction, get help. Fight through it. Go to Christ and say, "Lord, bring some people into my life to help guide me through this."

For those who do not have an addiction, use your freedom in the Lord wisely. Be sensitive to people out there who may be vulnerable in areas where you may be strong.

God wants us to enjoy everyday pleasures—so long as they don't distract from our love, obedience, and worship of Him, or lead others away from His Son. Life doesn't have to be eight decades of mundane drudgery. God made the world, and He declared it "good." Enjoy it within His parameters, and you will experience a life filled with the joy of the Lord.

ENDNOTES

1. James Dixon, *Virtue and Vice.*
2. See http://www.csun.edu/science/health/docs/tv &health.html.

CHAPTER 19

Issue Twelve—Choosing Employment and Careers

What Should I Do With My Life?

In the Introduction to this book, I told you about my friend Brad, a man who is as smart and gifted as a person can be. He left his employer after they wanted to transfer him, and he launched into his own business with some friends from college. But the business never really took off. His debt skyrocketed. His wife and kids began to feel the strain. His marriage is near collapse, with his wife the only one really working. And now, Brad is too angry with God to even mention His name.

What went wrong?

Certainly you've felt stress in your career—and in life in general. Your decisions can dramatically affect the future course of your life. Where should you go to college? What profession should you choose? Should you go into full-time ministry? Is that lucrative business opportunity the best investment for your family and finances? These are crucial decisions that come with life-impacting ramifications.

To make matters worse, there can be times when you've searched the Scriptures, and they just don't give you that specific answer you're looking for. Well-meaning friends who say they've "heard from God" for you chime in with messages that seem to totally contradict His Word. Add to that all those around you who live their lives as if they know exactly what God has planned for them. Or those who seem to be perfectly happy following their own futile career reasoning.

THE RIGHT DREAM NEEDS THE RIGHT BOAT

Everyone has certain skills, talents, and abilities. We also have deep dreams of what life should be about. This dream is more than a wish list or a daydream. It's the deep things that we think make life worth living. These elements of the dream travel with us our whole lives. Maybe a happy family, or a certain amount of money, or some public recognition. What we do is hold this dream in one hand and start to negotiate with reality in the other hand concerning how to launch our heart's dream. We try and build a career boat to float this dream. We try to get life to validate and reward our skill set so we can achieve the dream.

What happens when we see our job or career opportunities sink? Were we off in understanding God's call on our lives? Not necessarily. Sometimes God says, "Right dream, just the wrong boat." When the job or career doesn't succeed, it may not be that the dream was wrong, but the boat or career vehicle was the wrong one. Don't walk away from the dream, just start building a new boat. (I love the truth that the Titanic was built by experts but Noah's ark was built by an amateur. The same can be true in lots of areas.) Knowing that we are called first to the Person of Christ, and secondarily to whatever task or mission we have is a crucial key to finding fulfillment in our jobs.

There is a way out of this spiritual maze. It's found where Scripture and life intersect within your own heart.

According to the famous Westminster Catechism, "Man's chief end is to glorify God, and to enjoy Him for ever." To best do this, we need to develop spiritual intelligence in life callings. First, we are called to a Person—Jesus Christ. Then, we are called to be good stewards of whatever God have given us, including opportunities made available to us. In making wise choices, we have the four sentinels at our disposal: Scripture, Reason, Wise Counsel, and the Inner Voice of the Holy Spirit. However, the Bible can be frustratingly nonchalant about career and job decisions throughout life.

One way to find this wisdom is by following King David's three-step process:

1. *Trust* in the Lord.

2. *Delight* yourself in the Lord.

3. *Commit* your way to the Lord.

Let's take a look at each.

Trust in the Lord

Do not fret because of evildoers, nor be envious of the workers of iniquity. For they shall soon be cut down like the grass, and wither as the green herb. Trust in the Lord, and do good; dwell in the land, and feed on His faithfulness (Psalm 37:1-3 NKJV).

As hard as we try, it is difficult not to compare our situation with that of others. But such comparisons rarely bring comfort. We see crooked CEOs, drug-gulping professional athletes, disgruntled employees, and young Hollywood celebrities—all raking in millions of dollars (and squandering it, in many cases). It seems that the problem is twofold—the wicked reap insane profits while the righteous seem to barely scrape by. King David, Job, and Jeremiah recognized all this.

Lord, how long will the wicked, how long will the wicked triumph? (Psalm 94:3 NKJV)

Why do the wicked live on, reach old age, and grow mighty in power?...They spend their days in prosperity, and in peace they go down to Sheol. They say to God, "Leave us alone! We do not desire to know your ways" (Job 21:7,13-14).

Why does the way of the guilty prosper? Why do all who are treacherous thrive? (Jeremiah 12:1)

We must remember that wealth does not necessarily equal God's blessing. We often equate happiness, contentment, and blessing with money, even though we know rationally that money cannot buy these things. Look deeper into the lives of the wealthy, and you often find stories of heartache and pain.

King David suggested that we need to have an eternal perspective on life. Psalm 37:2 gives us such a perspective by reminding us that our days are short and that both rich and poor will soon wither as the green herb. All that is left then, according to the psalmist, is to trust in the Lord, to live in the land, and to enjoy our security (see Psalm 37:3).

To "trust in the Lord" literally means to "lean on Him." It is not a partial thing, but a total letting go. It you've ever tried to get into a hammock, you know that you cannot partially sit on one. It's an all-or-nothing thing. To enjoy the rest of a hammock is to completely lean back, trusting it to support you.

Trusting people is much different. Trust between people only comes from knowing them and understanding the desires of their heart. With God it's no different. You can't really trust in God unless you begin to know God. How do you do that?

Fortunately, God did not leave us in the dark or hide from us. He gave us His Word, the Bible. The more you know God's Word, the more you'll understand God's heart. And the more you understand God's heart, the easier it is to put your trust in Him. Read God's Word and you'll realize that you can always trust Him to act according to His desires. God will not act in a way that pleases the crowds or panders to His critics. He only acts according to His will.

You cannot trust God if don't know what He's asking you to do. And reading God's Word reveals what He requires from you. Here's how one great theologian put it:

> Trust in yourself, and you arc doomed to disappointment; trust in your friends, and they will die and leave you; trust in money, and you may have it taken away from you; trust in reputation, and some slanderous tongues will blast it; but trust in God, and you are never to be confounded in time or eternity.
>
> —*Dwight L. Moody*[2]

Of course, fully trusting is much easier to talk about than to put into action. We Americans are brought up to be independent and self-sufficient. We hold on to things, determined to fix them on our own. To trust in God means to give it over to Him.

Many of us in this world are slaves to our situations because we have such a tight grasp on them. We are afraid to let them go. We don't realize that there is freedom in letting go and trusting God, who is faithful to answer our call and able to work for good in our lives to His glory.

Delight Yourself in the Lord

Delight yourself also in the Lord, and He shall give you the desires of your heart (Psalm 37:4 NKJV).

There is a story of an old Scottish woman who went from home to home across the countryside selling thread, buttons, and shoestrings. When she came to an unmarked crossroad, she would toss a stick up in the air and go in the direction the stick pointed when it landed. One day, however, she was seen tossing up the stick several times.

"Why do you toss the stick more than once?" a passerby asked her.

"Because," replied the woman, "it keeps pointing to the left, and I want to take the road to the right." She then dutifully kept throwing the stick into the air until it pointed the way she wanted to go.

I have seen far too many believers treat the will of God in a similar fashion. They make up their mind first, and then seek only the kind of guidance that supports their decision. Because they have already made up their mind, they are not really interested in hearing God's mind on the matter—they merely want to bend His will to their way. They don't have an attitude that is receptive to wise counsel. They even go so far as to engage in dazzling verbal gymnastics of misquoting Scripture to justify their ways. In the end, all they want is for God to simply bless their decision, because they're going to do it their way anyway.

Many of us won't inquire of God because we fear His will is in opposition to our desires. In fact, many avoid Christianity because they believe that to follow Christ is to suppress or live contrary to their natural desires. They don't realize that true Christian growth and maturity is in allowing God to make our desires His desires.

Are you willing to let the Lord make Himself as desirable to you as the world is? To be a Christ-follower does not mean shunning a life of prosperity for a life of poverty and lack. Biblical Christianity is about developing a passionate hunger for God Himself and for the things that He desires. Then He promises that you will forever be satisfied and that He will give you the desires of your heart (see Psalm 37:4).

There are times when God's will is pretty cut and dry. For instance, "abstain from the desires of the flesh that wage war against the soul" (1 Pet. 2:11); or, "abstain from fornication" (1 Thess. 4:3); or even, "go out and encourage your men" (2 Sam. 19:7 NIV). It's not difficult to understand those words. For some, however, following God's will in that area may be extremely difficult—even though His will in the matter is not hard to determine. At other times God's will is more mysterious...more of a path or a process than a proclamation...more of a circle than a dot. Sometimes what pleases us, pleases the Lord. Do we pray about what clothes to wear today? No. Why? Because the Lord would probably say something like, "I don't care. Whatever pleases you pleases Me. Do put something on that won't offend everyone around you, but whatever your delight is." Other times, God's will is very specific, as in the Ten Commandments and the Golden Rule.

When we finally arrive at the place where we want the Lord's will over and above our own, when His desires truly become our desires, then we are able to remove our hands from the steering wheel of our life and let Him fully guide us. Then we can say, without reservation, that we want His will more than that job, that date, that house, that business deal. We will trust in His will and not fight for our own justice or recognition.

When we get to that place, we will find that God does not necessarily write the answer on wall—but upon our heart. Then we are free to move forward in the knowledge that He is leading us.

God's will, although sometimes difficult, is never miserable. It brings incredible peace knowing that He can use your life to bring glory to Himself, blessing you in the process.

Commit Your Way to the Lord

Commit your way to the Lord; trust in Him, and He will act. He will make your vindication shine like the light, and the justice of your cause like the noonday. Be still before the Lord, and wait patiently for Him (Psalm 37:5-7).

To "commit your way to the Lord" is much more than committing just one decision to Him. It is a total surrender of your life's entire decision-making process. That means that we trust not only in God's decision, but also in His timing and His methods, knowing that His thoughts are not like our thoughts, nor are His ways like our ways (see Isaiah 55:8).

After years of service in South Africa, the famous missionary Robert Moffat returned to Scotland to recruit desperately needed workers to join the cause. One cold, wintry night he arrived to speak at a church but was dismayed that only a small number of people had come out to hear him. What bothered him even more was that the only people in attendance were women! Although grateful for their interest, he had hoped to challenge men to answer the call. He had even chosen as his text Proverbs 8:4, "Unto you, O men I call."

In his discouragement, Moffat failed to notice one small boy in the loft, pumping the bellows of the organ. Moffat felt frustration as he gave his message, for he realized that very few of these women could be able to undergo the rigorous life of the undeveloped jungles. But he had forgotten one thing: God works in mysterious ways!

Although no one volunteered that evening, the young fellow assisting the organist was deeply moved by the challenge. As a result, he made a vow to God that he would follow in the footsteps of this missionary pioneer named Moffat. When the young lad grew up, he remained true to that vow and went to Africa to minister to the unreached tribes. His name was David Livingstone. Robert Moffat never ceased to wonder that his appeal, which he had intended for men, had stirred a young boy who was eventually used mightily by the power of God.

How Do I Know What God Wants?

King Solomon was given a choice that other men could only dream about. God said that Solomon could ask Him for *anything*. This was the magic ticket! Solomon could have asked for great wealth. Or power. Or influence. Or even worldwide domination had he wanted to. But Solomon asked instead for wisdom, and God granted his request:

> *God answered Solomon, "Because this was in your heart, and you have not asked for possessions, wealth, honor, or the life of those who hate you, and have not even asked for long life, but have asked for wisdom and knowledge for yourself that you*

may rule My people over whom I have made you king, wisdom and knowledge are granted to you. I will also give you riches, possessions, and honor, such as none of the kings had who were before you, and none after you shall have the like" (2 Chronicles 1:11-12).

Solomon knew that wisdom was the key to all good things in life. What does God want for you in your career? That question may be the toughest of all of life's mysteries for adults. Here's the great news: you don't have to be 100 percent sure about your every career decision. You merely need to trust in the Lord, delight yourself in Him, work diligently where He has placed you for now, and commit your way to Him even when it makes no sense to human wisdom to do so. Then you can be 100 percent sure in your heart that God will move on your behalf and use you to His glory.

We each want to be happy, productive, fulfilled, and appreciated. If we strive to please the Lord first and foremost, then all these things will fall into place.

Remember, you are not in a job primarily to earn money. You are there to influence people for God—it's a temporary assignment. Thus, the questions we should be asking ourselves at our job are: "Who here does God want me to touch? Who can I learn from? Who can I reach and influence for the Kingdom of God on earth?"

To God, the question of *what you do* is not nearly as important as the question of *who you are*. He is more concerned with who you are trusting and following, and who you are becoming in the process. His desire is for you to experience the faith and peace and confidence that come from believing that He will be true to His Word. Then you will take new turf and be used to influence those around you.

ENDNOTE

1. Quoted in "Hezekiah: A Portrait of Trust," by Dr. Brian Allison;http://www.briceandbensa.com/HezekiahAPor traitofTrust.htm.

SECTION D

*Life in the Spiritual World—Discerning
Truth From Error*

Introduction

Summon the courage to wander outside of the unity and intellectual protection of your local church, and you won't get too far before running into some very different beliefs and ideas.

Speak of religion and of faith, and some will look at you in a patronizing manner and ask, "Aren't all religions really the same? You all have your little imaginary gods."

Others will take a more accusatory tone, saying, "The problem with the world today is religion itself. It's religion that spawns all our wars and hatred. We don't need freedom of religion—we need freedom *from* religion!"

As mentioned previously, the world we live in today is more diverse in race, creed, and culture than ever before. Because of this, it has never been more important to be able to represent your faith before others in a loving and respectful manner.

The first century city of Colosse was not unlike our world today—a literal crossroads of commerce, Eastern religions, and pagan doctrines. The fledgling Christian church there was faced with an onslaught of ungodly influences from the outside, as well as the creeping presence of false teaching from within. The apostle Paul, writing to them from his prison cell, looked back and, under the inspiration of the Holy

Spirit, tried to summarize the veracity of the true gospel and the identity of this great Christ whom they worshiped.

> *He is the Image of the invisible God, the Firstborn of all creation; for in Him all things in Heaven and on earth were created, things visible and invisible, whether thrones or dominions or rulers or powers—all things have been created through Him and for Him. He Himself is before all things, and in Him all things hold together. He is the Head of the body, the Church; He is the beginning, the firstborn from the dead, so that He might come to have first place in everything. For in Him all the fullness of God was pleased to dwell, and through Him God was pleased to reconcile to Himself all things, whether on earth or in Heaven, by making peace through the blood of His Cross* (Colossians 1:15-20).

Is it possible that we hear Scripture so much that we forget just how radical these claims about Jesus of Nazareth really are? According to that passage, He is either the most wonderful thing to ever hit this planet, or He is the most bizarre lie and illusion ever perpetrated upon humankind. And among the most radical of all His claims is this thing called *grace*—the unmerited favor from a holy God given to humankind.

It is important to remember the fundamental doctrines of Christianity, such as grace. Christians hardly have a corner on the market of kind and wonderful people. There are some intelligent, amazing, and loving people within many other faiths—Hinduism, Buddhism, Judaism, Islam, Mormonism...the list goes on. But the idea we are saved on the basis of what someone else did for us is unique to the Christian faith. We agree with the other great faiths in that our actions and behaviors *do* matter. The difference is that we do them on the basis of *already being* accepted, not *to* gain acceptance. I wanted my children to behave when they were growing up, not so I could learn to love them, but on the basis that I was already crazy about them.

What we are talking about is not individual behavior of different people. We're talking about the teachings themselves. And as we take a closer look, we begin to realize that, contrary to popular belief today, all religions are not just different ways of getting to the same objective.

CHAPTER 20

Issue Thirteen—Ghosts, Angels, and Demons

Unlocking the Supernatural

Worldwide, there is an obsession with the spiritual realm and the supernatural. We see it woven throughout the fabric of our society—from television shows like *The Ghost Whisperer* and *Medium*, to movies like *Ghost* and *Sixth Sense*, to the local palm reader. Can we contact the dead? Are demons or angels real?

ANGELS

There has always been a fascination with angels. Depictions of angels range from chubby little flying cherubs to your average "man on the street." Are there angels out there guiding and protecting us and carrying out the plans of God?

The answer is yes, and Scripture is filled with numerous accounts of the supernatural. While it's important to know the ministry and activity of angels in the life of the believer, we are not to be obsessed with them.

Hebrews 1:14 says, "Are not all angels spirits in the divine service, sent to serve for the sake of those who are to inherit salvation?" The Hebrew word for *angel* is *malak*, which means "an agent or messenger." The good angels (the "angelic" as we call them) are those who are concerned with our welfare. These angels are given to protect and to guide us.

God is the King of His Kingdom, and within His Kingdom there is a divine order. Therefore, there is a divine order of angelic beings. There seems to be two classifications of angels: cherubim and seraphim (see Genesis 3:24 and Isaiah 6:2). There are three archangels mentioned in the Bible: Michael, Gabriel, and Lucifer (a cherubim; see Ezekiel 28:14).

A misconception about angels is that when you and I cross over into eternity, we will become angels. That is untrue. Instead, we will actually judge and rule over angels (see 1 Corinthians 6:3).

Angels are invisible, but at times they enter our time-space continuum and become visible to human eyes.

Do not neglect to show hospitality to strangers, for by doing that some have entertained angels without knowing it (Hebrews 13:2).

There are many examples of angelic intervention into the affairs of humankind, in both the Old and New Testament. Abraham entertained some of the angels of the Lord (see Genesis 18:2). Jacob experienced the ministry of angels (see Genesis 28:12). Elijah was strengthened by an angel who brought him food and drink (see 1 Kings 19:5-7). And Daniel was protected by an angel in the lions' den (see Daniel 6:22).

There are also many references to angels during the life of Jesus. Angels spoke to Mary, Joseph, and the shepherds (see Luke 1:26–38; Matthew 1:20–21; Luke 2:13–15). Angels ministered to Jesus after His temptation in the wilderness (see Matthew 4:11). And two angels were present at Jesus' empty tomb after His resurrection (see Matthew 28:2–7).

In the early church, angelic ministry also frequently occurred. An angel opened the prison doors releasing the apostles (see Acts 5:19). An angel told Cornelius to send for Peter so that he could share with him the gospel (see Acts 10:3, 30–32). And Herod was struck down dead by an angel for his pride (see Acts 12:23).

As hinted at in the Bible, each person has a guardian angel:

Take care that you do not despise one of these little ones; for, I tell you, in Heaven their angels continually see the face of my Father in Heaven (Matthew 18:10).

KINGDOM OF DARKNESS

For our struggle is not against enemies of blood and flesh, but against the rulers, against the authorities, against the cosmic powers of this present darkness, against the spiritual forces of evil in the heavenly places (Ephesians 6:12).

As real as the presence of angels is, so too is the presence of demons. Isaiah and Revelation insinuate that satan rebelled against God and convinced one-third of the angels to join the rebellion and follow him (see Isaiah 14:12; Revelation 12).

His tail swept down a third of the stars of Heaven and threw them to the earth... (Revelation 12:4).

Lucifer (which means "light one," a term from the Middle Ages) was originally an archangel before he struck against God and became satan (which means "accuser," from the Bible), the adversary of God. Of course he lost that battle quickly and was ejected from Heaven, along with his followers. They set up shop on earth, where their chief occupation is to keep our attention away from God (see Isaiah 14:12).

DEMON POSSESSION

People who play these satanic-type games and attempt to "contact the dead" are really saying that they want to be controlled by those demonic forces. When you start playing around with things you shouldn't be involved with, pretty soon you are walking away from God's protection. If you think you can live life all on your own and away from God's Word and ways, then you are setting yourself up for other powers to influence you. The difference between prayer and magic is that magic tries to control the divine powers, whereas prayer submits to them. As C.S. Lewis wrote in *The Problem of Pain*, "Heaven is where we say to God, 'Thy will be done.' Hell is where God says to us, 'Your will be done.'" Striving to control life by spells, incantations, potions, or contacting the "other side" is a dangerous game of magic. It knocks on the wrong door.

The extent of satan's kingdom depends on the extent to which he is free to exercise his dominion on the earth or in a person's life individually. This is important, especially with regard to the question, "Is there demonic possession?" The answer is yes—but it's not as common as some would have you believe.

Can a Christian be possessed? The idea of being "possessed," in the sense of a spirit entity taking over a person's body, does not appear in the Old Testament. In the New Testament, the word *possessed* comes from the Greek word *daimonizomai*, which means "being demonized" or a process of "another personality taking up residence." The term appears a dozen or so times in various related contexts in the Books of Matthew, Mark, Luke, and Acts.

I personally do not believe that Christians can be possessed. This is based on the passage in First John that says that greater is He who is in us than he who is in the world (see 1 John 4:4). The theological statement that "a Christian can be oppressed, but not possessed" may be accurate, but there is no biblical reference for it.

There is no record in the New Testament of a Christian living under the control of a demon. Yet Judas became one of only two people in history ever to have been possessed by satan himself (not just any demon). The other person will be the antichrist, who will be possessed in the last days.

HEALING THE POSSESSED

How can you tell if some broken soul is under demonic attack versus emotional distress or even a psychotic episode? It's not easy to discern—and it's something that should be handled by a professional who specializes in that particular area.

You cannot "repent" of an emotional illness. It must be dealt with medically for physical healing and emotionally for psychological healing. If it's possible to medicate the symptoms, like hearing voices, then you're probably not dealing with the demonic.

But conversely, you cannot merely "treat" demonic activity as if it were something biological. It must be prayed for and repented of. To mistreat a spiritual illness as something psychological is as wrong as mistreating an emotional or mental illness as a spiritual problem. The encouraging news is that the power of Christ is available to heal both. Only when you experience the healing and freedom of the Lord are you truly free (see John 8:36).

TEMPTATION

Even though a Christian cannot be possessed by a demon, we do need to be on guard against temptation. When temptation comes, you can overcome it through the power of God. James 4:7 says, "Resist the devil, and he will flee from you."

There's a difference between the tempter and the temptation. You resist the tempter, and you flee the temptation. When you experience temptation to do wrong, you don't respond by saying, "I'm not gonna give in"—you get out of there! That's why it's important to be connected with other godly believers who can help you withstand temptation.

Satan and his evil spirits are neither omnipresent nor omniscient. When faced with temptation, just say, "Satan, go! In the name of Christ, get out of here." Ever notice how in the midst of a temptation the last thing your old nature wants to do is mention Christ? Because there is power in His Name. You'll know when it's gone too, because the atmosphere will change as the temptation to do wrong leaves. That doesn't mean you're not drawn to it anymore, but there is a sort of "chemistry change" in the situation.

GHOSTS AND POLTERGEISTS

Demons have no real power over the saved, but they are still determined to harass, destroy, mislead, and attempt to frustrate the plan of God. John 10:10 says, "The thief comes only to steal and kill and destroy. I came that they may have life, and have it abundantly." Heaven is all about giving; hell is all about taking.

Interestingly, there is no biblical record of the demonic ever actually taking on flesh and blood and becoming human in appearance as the angelic do at times. There is no record of the dead interacting with this world, other than that strange passage where King Saul sought out a spiritist at Endor to summon up the spirit of the prophet Samuel after his death.

It was against the law in the Old Testament to go to a medium or to a spiritist to try to and contact the dead. Yet in this passage, Saul disguised himself and went to the medium at Endor, who had a reputation for supposedly contacting the dead. Saul, at this point, had turned away from God and could no longer hear from God. But he was supposed to go out and battle the Philistines again—and the mighty prophet Samuel was dead. So look what Saul did:

> *Saul disguised himself and put on other clothes and went there, he and two men with him. They came to the woman by night. And he said, "Consult a spirit for me, and bring up for me the one whom I name to you."...Then the woman said, "Whom shall I bring up for you?" He answered, "Bring up Samuel for me." When the woman saw Samuel, she cried out with a loud voice; and the woman said to Saul, "Why have you deceived me? You are Saul!" The king said to her, "Have no fear; what do you see?" The woman said to Saul, "I see a divine being coming up out of the ground." He said to her, "What is his appearance?" She said, "An old man is coming up; he is wrapped in a robe." So Saul knew that it was Samuel, and he bowed with his face to the ground, and did obeisance. Then Samuel said to Saul, "Why have you disturbed me by bringing me up?"...* (1 Samuel 28:8,11-15)

What do you do with *that* passage? First, definitely don't take it as an invitation to go out and conjure up the dead! But was God letting them see and know that it was Samuel? I don't know. Was it some demons messing with Saul? I don't know—though that's entirely possible, because Second Corinthians 11:14-15 says, "Even satan disguises himself as an angel of light. So it is not strange if his ministers also disguise themselves as ministers of righteousness." The central lesson is to leave the dead to God and to the dying. As Jesus said, "Let those without eternal life [the spiritually dead] concern themselves with things like that" (Luke 9:60 TLB).

Yet many people throughout history have believed that the dead can contact this world. A teaching of the Roman Catholic Church is that the dead pray for us and intercede on our behalf. From writings such as Homer's *Odyssey*, we see that the Greeks thought that death meant a person was "half-alive," and that the dead were always trying to come back to this world.

I disagree. I don't believe the dead can come back or contact the living. In fact, I don't think they even want to. The other side of death, that is, being in the Lord's presence, is more real and wonderful than this side. I also think that the reason many of those who leave their bodies for a few minutes in "near death experiences" find it to be a wonderful experience—even for the lost—because the great Judgment Day has not yet happened yet.

I don't think there are ghosts right now that are haunting hotels or graveyards or tourist spots. I don't believe that the dead contact this world. As the passage in Luke 16:26 said, "Between you and us a great chasm has been fixed."

Now I imagine that it's not impossible that sometimes God might give us strange "hugs" to let us know that things are all right on the other side. Sort of unusual reassurances. For instance, I once did a funeral for a woman's dad. She loved him very much. She said to me once, "He put on too much Old Spice cologne all the time." Well one day she was driving along, and all of a sudden she caught a strong whiff of Old Spice. What do you do with things like that?

But remember, death is a one-way ticket. Hebrews 9:27 says, "And just as it is appointed for mortals to die once, and after that the judgment." There are no repeat rides.

The only people recorded in the Bible who returned from the dead were Moses and Elijah, when they appeared on the Mount of Transfiguration talking with Jesus (see Matthew 17:1-8). But there's even an element of mystery surrounding the death of Moses, because the Bible records that God Himself buried Moses, and no one to this day knows the location of his grave (see Deuteronomy 34:6), although the devil himself disputed over his body (see Jude 1:9).

The idea of poltergeists, haunted houses, graveyards, or "making peace with the spirits before passing over" is all medieval theology and Hollywood imagination—and has no biblical basis. Instead, those departed souls outside of God's grace are waiting to appear before Him to give an accounting of their earthly deeds. And those who are saved are celebrating and cheering us on, because they know what is waiting for us.

In saying all that, it doesn't mean that demonic spirits imitating the dead are not attempting to influence people in this world. Therefore, when people think they are communicating with the dead, it can only be demon spirits imitating departed loved ones (see

Deuteronomy 18:11; 1 Chronicles 10:13-14; Isaiah 8:19). When you open yourself up spiritually to communication with the spirit realm, then satan will gladly accommodate your desire for the supernatural and lead you down that slippery slope.

AUDIENCE IN THE HEAVENLY REALM

Remember, we are not alone. The Lord has given us spiritual help and has surrounded us with an audience in the heavenly realm. When you get to Heaven, you may find out how the Lord watched over you during those times when you should have been hurt or even killed, but you weren't.

I hear all the time from people who sensed they were being protected. There is no doubt that there have been numerous instances when God has watched over you and you never even knew about them. In fact, when you stand before the Lord, He may reveal to you how He used you on earth. He'll say, "Look at all these people I touched through you." And you'll respond, "Wow! I never knew!" And He'll say, "Of course not, if you knew, you would've gotten in the way and messed it up!"

> *Therefore, since we are surrounded by so great a cloud of witnesses, let us also lay aside every weight and the sin that clings so closely, and let us run with perseverance the race that is set before us* (Hebrews 12:1).

CHAPTER 21

Issue Fourteen—Christianity and Islam

Confronting Islam With the Love of Christ

The common thread among most religions of the world is that you are saved through your own good, dedicated, well-meaning efforts. Christianity, on the other hand, has the audacity of *grace*! God did it on our behalf. In order to interact with other religions intelligently and respectfully, you and I need to understand the basic tenets of their faith, how it corresponds to our faith—and thereby be able to boldly share the unique hope that we have in Christ.

With that in mind, I want to first set the stage for what God's Word says concerning the teachings of "any other gospel," as written by the apostle Paul to the Galatians.

I am astonished that you are so quickly deserting the One who called you in the grace of Christ and are turning to a different gospel—not that there is another gospel, but there are some who are confusing you and want to pervert the gospel of Christ. But even if we or an angel from Heaven should proclaim to you a gospel contrary to what we proclaimed to you, let that one be accursed! As we have said before, so now I repeat, if anyone proclaims to you a gospel contrary to what you received, let that one be accursed! Am I now seeking human approval, or God's approval? Or am I trying to please people? If I were still pleasing people, I would not be a servant of Christ (Galatians 1:6-10).

First, let me say, contrary to common belief, you and I, by interacting with Muslims, have the opportunity to associate with some of the most loving people we will ever meet. The dry cleaner I go to is owned and operated by a devout Muslim, and he is one of the nicest, most fun people I have ever met. Yet it is not hard to find pictures on the Internet of fanatical Muslim terrorists who have the blood of innocent people on their hands.

Why this dichotomy? Let's begin by looking at the birth of Islam.

THE NUMBERS

The name *Islam* means "submission." Muslims are "those who have submitted," or those who have accepted Islam. Up to one-fourth of the entire world are Muslims. There are an estimated 1.5 billion Muslims worldwide.[1] The following is a breakdown of world religion adherents:

- ◆ Christianity: 2.1 billion
- ◆ Islam: 1.5 billion
- ◆ Secular/Nonreligious/Agnostic/Atheist: 1.1 billion
- ◆ Hinduism: 900 million
- ◆ Chinese traditional religion: 394 million
- ◆ Buddhism: 376 million
- ◆ Primal-indigenous: 300 million
- ◆ African Traditional & Diasporic: 100 million
- ◆ Sikhism: 23 million
- ◆ Juche: 19 million
- ◆ Spiritism: 15 million
- ◆ Judaism: 14 million
- ◆ Baha'i: 7 million
- ◆ Jainism: 4.2 million
- ◆ Shinto: 4 million
- ◆ Cao Dai: 4 million

- Zoroastrianism: 2.6 million
- Tenrikyo: 2 million
- Neo-Paganism: 1 million
- Unitarian-Universalism: 800 thousand
- Rastafarianism: 600 thousand
- Scientology: 500 thousand

Percentage-wise, the world's major religions are represented as:[2]

- Christians: 33.32%
- Roman Catholics: 16.99%
- Protestants: 5.78%
- Orthodox 3.53%
- Anglicans 1.25%
- Muslims: 21.01%
- Hindus: 13.26%
- Buddhists: 5.84%
- Sikhs: 0.35%
- Jews: 0.23%
- Baha'is: 0.12%
- Other religions: 11.78%
- Non-religious: 11.77%
- Atheists: 2.32%

HISTORY

Muslims believe in one god, Allah (Arabic for "god"), and his prophet Muhammad, who is to be the final prophet in a long list going back to Abraham, whom Muslims view as the very first Muslim. The Qur'an says the world was originally monotheistic, but that it lost the truth and served many false gods, so Muhammad was sent to restore the one true faith. Muslims view the time before Muhammad as "the time of ignorance," when the Jews and the followers of Jesus distorted the original truth of Abraham.

Muhammad was born in A.D. 570 in Mecca, a city of trade and commerce. The great Ka'bah stone (the stone where Muslim pilgrims today walk around its circumference, in prayer) was already a religious site by the polytheistic Arab tribes. Muslims claim that it was a meteor that fell during the time of Adam.

Muhammad was born to the Quraysh tribe, of the clan of Hashim, known as custodians of the sacred places of Mecca. There were many deities worshiped there, as well as planets, and one unapproachably holy god named Allah.

Muhammad's father died when he was born, and his mother died when he was only six. He went to work for his uncle Abu Talib, with little time for school. This is important to Islam because Muhammad was illiterate, and yet he miraculously received the Qur'an. At the age of 12, Muhammad was exposed to Jewish and Christian beliefs. This led him to question many of the beliefs and customs he had come to know, specifically his belief in many gods (polytheism). At age 40 he claimed to have seen visions of the archangel Gabriel during the night of the 26th of the month of Ramadan, thereafter called the "night of Power." He therefore came to the conviction that he had been called to be a prophet of Allah and received his revelations and the Qur'an.

During a difficult period of his life when he was undergoing much persecution, he experienced the "Night of Ascension," when he is said to have traveled from Jerusalem into God's presence and to have met the prophets who had gone before him, from Adam to Jesus (this is said to have happened at the Dome of the Rock site in Jerusalem, Islam's third holiest site after Mecca and Medina).

Before Muhammad's death in 632, the expansion of the new religion of Islam was unparalleled in history. Muhammad never gave instructions about who was to succeed him, so his close friend Abu Bakr was elected as the first caliph. This decision was hotly contested, with Shi'ite Muslims believing that the true successor was Mohammed's cousin and son-in-law Ali (who was married to Muhammad's daughter Fatima).

Sunnis (or "people of the *Sunnah*" tradition) make up 80 percent of the world's Muslims. Though many Muslims are peaceful and very moderate, Daniel Pipes of the Middle East Forum suggests the likelihood that 10-15 percent of Muslims are radical in conviction (that's approximately 150 million), and at least 30 percent (around 500 million) identify and sympathize more with Osama bin Laden and the Taliban over the actions and policies of the United States in Muslim countries throughout the world.

BASICS OF ISLAMIC FAITH

Qur'an means "recites," and the book is generally referred to as "the noble Qur'an." "The enlightened Qur'an" is a moniker that came later. It is called the Qur'an because you "recite" its passages over and over. It contains 119 chapters, called *surahs*, which reveal the teachings of Allah as allegedly told to Muhammad by the angel Gabriel.

At first Muhammad faced opposition over his newly founded religion. He would counter objections with debates over the validity of the Qur'an (Koran), which is an amalgamation of his personal beliefs, the Torah, and Christian teachings. Years later he adapted his teaching to include *jihad*, which literally means "struggle in the way of God."

> In broader usage and interpretation, the term [*jihad*] has accrued both violent and non-violent meanings. It can refer to striving to live a moral and virtuous life, to spreading and defending Islam, and to fighting injustice and oppression, among other usages. Jihad is also used in the meaning of struggle for or defense of Islam. The primary aim of jihad is not the conversion of non-Muslims to Islam by force, but rather the expansion and defense of the Islamic state.
>
> —*Jihad* definition[3]

As a result of *jihad*, Islam spread through conquest and persuasion throughout Indonesia, Europe, and China. Instead of sharing his religion, Muhammad now claimed that Allah would only forgive if a person admitted that the Qur'an and the recitations of Allah were the only way to live—and only then could a person live also.

Islam teaches that there is one message for every nation—believe in one god (Allah) and be fair to each other. Muslims claim that the laws of Moses and the Gospels of Jesus are sacred to them, but are only "complete" in the Qur'an.

The Qur'an states that there are "five pillars" of Islam:

- ◆ Pillar 1: All true believers must declare their faith in Allah and Muhammad before their community; and in the *shahadah* prayer they must pray, "There is no God but God, and Muhammed is the Messenger of God."

- ◆ Pillar 2: Muslims must pray five times a day on their knees, no matter where they are, facing toward Mecca; this is called the *salat*.

- ◆ Pillar 3: The *zakat* says that Muslims must give 2.5 percent of their annual income in support of their religion by helping the poor.

- ◆ Pillar 4: *Sawm* means that Muslims must fast for a specific period of time during the month of Ramadan.

- ◆ Pillar 5: The *Hajj* means that at some point in their life, all Muslims are expected to make a pilgrimage to Mecca, where the prophet Muhammad was born.

To further understand the evolution of Islam, let's look at the lineage of Abraham, according to the Bible:

Now Sarai, Abram's wife, bore him no children. She had an Egyptian slave-girl whose name was Hagar, and Sarai said to Abram, "You see that the Lord has prevented me from bearing children; go in to my slave-girl; it may be that I shall obtain children by her." And Abram listened to the voice of Sarai. So, after Abram had lived ten years in the land of Canaan, Sarai, Abram's wife, took Hagar the Egyptian, her slave-girl, and gave her to her husband Abram as a wife. He went in to Hagar, and she conceived; and when she saw that she had conceived, she looked with contempt on her mistress. Then Sarai said to Abram, "May the wrong done to me be on you! I gave my slave-girl to your embrace, and when she saw that she had conceived, she looked on me with contempt. May the Lord judge between you and me!" But Abram said to Sarai, "Your slave-girl is in your power; do to her as you please." Then Sarai dealt harshly with her, and she ran away from her (Genesis 16:1-6).

Prior to this story, Abraham was called to be the father of many nations; but up to this point, he and his wife Sarai (later renamed "Sarah") had not yet had a child. Sarah was getting on in years, so she decided that maybe she and Abraham should help God get the process going through her slave Hagar. She gave her slave Hagar to Abraham, and Hagar became pregnant. But Sarah quickly decided that her idea wasn't as great as she once thought it was, and she was cruel to Hagar until Hagar finally ran away.

The story continues:

> *The angel of the Lord found her by a spring of water in the wilderness, the spring on the way to Shur. And he said, "Hagar, slave-girl of Sarai, where have you come from and where are you going?" She said, "I am running away from my mistress Sarai." The angel of the Lord said to her, "Return to your mistress, and submit to her." The angel of the Lord also said to her, "I will so greatly multiply your offspring that they cannot be counted for multitude." And the angel of the Lord said to her, "Now you have conceived and shall bear a son; you shall call him Ishmael, for the Lord has given heed to your affliction. He shall be a wild ass of a man, with his hand against everyone, and everyone's hand against him; and he shall live at odds with all his kin." So she named the Lord who spoke to her, "You are El-roi"; for she said, "Have I really seen God and remained alive after seeing Him?" Therefore the well was called Beer-lahai-roi; it lies between Kadesh and Bered. Hagar bore Abram a son; and Abram named his son, whom Hagar bore, Ishmael. Abram was eighty-six years old when Hagar bore him Ishmael* (Genesis 16:7-16).

Muslims believe this was reversed and that Ishmael was actually the promised child. Islam, Christianity, and Judaism all trace their roots back to Abraham and his seed. The claims of Judaism and Christianity are that the promise of God to Abraham is passed on through Abraham's son Isaac. But Islam claims that the promise was passed on through Ishmael, and that he holds preeminence as Abraham's firstborn son. As Christians, even though we believe it was through Isaac that the Messiah would come, God did promise to bless Ishmael in his own way (see Genesis 17:20).

SIMILARITIES BETWEEN CHRISTIANITY AND ISLAM

What do Christianity and Islam have in common?

Similar to Christianity, Muslims believe that Allah is merciful and that there is no greater joy to him than to forgive someone who sincerely repents. The majority of Muslims are also taught that to kill one person is to kill all of humanity, and that violence toward women makes someone the least of any Muslim.

Muslims believe that there is one god, that he is Allah, and that Muhammad is his only prophet. This is a part of the great prayer every Muslim prays five times a day.

Muhammad was raised in an extremely pagan, polytheistic land in Arabia in the sixth century A.D., and when he received his so-called "divine revelation," he came up with the idea that there is only one god—an idea that is common to Christian and Jewish beliefs.

Another belief we have in common is that there is a right way to live. You and I live in a culture where it doesn't matter what you believe as long as you're "sincere." But sincerity doesn't mean innocence—and it certainly does not mean accuracy. A Muslim, however, says that it *does* matter how you live—a belief they share with Christians.

There is a right way to live and behave. The Bible shows that way.

THE DIFFERENCES BETWEEN CHRISTIANITY AND ISLAM

There are many differences between Christianity and Islam. For one, Islam comes very close to worshiping the Qur'an itself—the actual, physical *book*. The book was supposedly given directly from Allah to Muhammad. As children, Muslims are taught how to properly carry the Qur'an. When they enter a mosque, they are never to carry it below the waist. They must also kiss it three times and then tap the top of their head. When packing a suitcase, the Qur'an is to be placed on top of the clothing. When a Muslim opens the Qur'an, there can be no other books around it.

In the 1960s a famous boxer converted to Islam and changed his name to a Muslim name. When he visited Saudi Arabia, everyone was excited to meet him because he had converted. He carried a copy of the Qur'an with him, and when people wanted his autograph, he would sit down and put the Qur'an next to him on the ground—which is strictly forbidden in Islam. People were so upset that it practically incited a riot, and his tour had to be cut short.

In the religion of Islam, salvation is obtained by human works, not by redemption through a gracious God's own sacrifice. There is much debate within Islam about who will and who will not make it to Heaven.

One time on an airline flight, I was writing a funeral sermon while sitting next to a Muslim. The man said to me, "You Christians are so arrogant."

"Well, thank you," I said. "That's good to know."

"You are going to claim this person is in Heaven," he persisted. "How do you know? Only Allah can assign that." He said that because his religion is a belief of human works and not of divine grace—and you never know if you've done quite enough work to measure up and earn yourself a slot in Heaven. It truly is a fear-based religion.

Islam also rejects the biblical doctrine of the Trinity since Muslims claim that Jesus is not the Son of God. Moses and Jesus are respected as great prophets, but they teach that Muhammad is the last and greatest of the prophets. However, we know from the Bible that rejecting Christ as Messiah is anathema to God—the sin unto death (see 1 John 5:16).

After Jesus was resurrected and before He ascended to Heaven, He told the apostles and disciples to preach the gospel:

> *And Jesus came and said to them, "All authority in Heaven and on earth has been given to Me. Go therefore and make disciples of all nations, baptizing them in the name of the Father and of the Son and of the Holy Spirit, and teaching them to obey everything that I have commanded you. And remember, I am with you always, to the end of the age" (Matthew 28:18-20).*

For centuries after Christ's resurrection and ascension, Christians traveled the Mediterranean world preaching the gospel—without violence. However, Muhammad launched the very first holy war, long before the western Europeans then responded with the Crusades. At the beginning of Muhammad's life, before he had control, the Qur'an was more peaceful in overall tone. After Muhammad established his "new revelation" he became more hostile toward Jews and Christians (which explains the presence of both kind and harsh words and attitudes in the same book) and during the ten years that he lived in Medina, he either authorized or participated in more than 70 raids, battles, and skirmishes.[4]

While they believe there is some validity to the Jewish and Christian Scriptures, Islam claims that only the Qur'an has absolute authority. A major problem with that for the Christian is that the Qur'anic surahs seem to advocate warring against Christians and Jews. For example, Surah 9 of the Qur'an is Muhammad's last revelation in its entirety before he died. He commissioned his followers to wage war on Jews and Christians (who Muslims call "the People of the Book"[5]):

> Fight against those who believe not in Allah, nor in the Last Day, nor forbid that which has been forbidden by Allah and his messenger (Muhammad) and those who acknowledge not the religion of truth (Islam) among people of the Scripture (Jews and Christians) until they pay the *jizyah* with willing submission, and feel themselves subdued.
>
> —Surah 9:29, the *Qur'an*[6]
> (insertions in parentheses by Hilali and Khan).

This surah, which commanded battle against Christians and Jews, was all about theology and belief—a "spiritual" war. It said nothing explicit about responding to real, physical harm done to Islam.

In late A.D. 630, Muhammad launched his Tabuk Crusade against the Byzantine Christians. He had heard a rumor that an army was mobilizing to invade Arabia, but the rumor was false. So instead, his 30,000 *jihadists* imposed a *jizya* tax on the northern Christians and Jews, giving them three options: 1) Fight and die, 2) Convert to Islam, or 3) Submit and pay the second-class-citizen *jizya* tax for the "privilege" of living under Islam.[7]

> The Jews call Uzair a son of Allah, and the Christians call Christ the son of Allah. That is a saying from their mouth; (in this) they but imitate what the unbelievers of old used to say. Allah's curse be on them: how they are deluded away from the Truth!
>
> —Surah 9:30, the *Qur'an*[8]

As this passage states, the idea that Jesus is the Son of God is blasphemous to Muslims, who feel that anyone who claims this should be cursed. Muslims believe Jesus was a loving prophet, and they respect His teachings—but they would never worship Him.

For Christians, as proven through His miracles, His resurrection, and through the change of hearts and lives as evidenced in the acceptance of His work of redemption on the Cross, Jesus was much more than a mere prophet. He is God the Son. We don't just have a prophet, we have a Savior, and He's the *only* way to Heaven. The Muslim view of the Qur'an being eternal and preexistent is so close to the truth of the existence of the Eternal Logos, or Word of Christ, that it is a great starting point in sharing Christianity with a Muslim.

If you're a Muslim, there's an element of uncertainty regarding your entrance into Heaven. Maybe your good deeds will be enough to get you in, maybe they won't. However, if you're slain and die, then Allah's forgiveness and mercy will grant you entrance into Heaven. This is why the motivation to blow oneself up is so strong, because Muslims believe that this is an automatic ticket into Heaven. Evil has such a way of twisting truth and misleading people.

Christianity also disagrees with Islam on the nature of salvation—by grace, not by works. We believe that we cannot achieve our own salvation. It is entirely by God's grace, through the gift He gave in sending His Son to the Cross. Ephesians 2:8 says, "For by grace you have been saved through faith, and this is not your own doing; it is the gift of God." Many of the surahs of the Qur'an begin with, "In the name of Allah, the merciful and compassionate." Muslims so long for grace, yet sadly, their belief does not permit it.

Finally, Christianity disagrees with Islam's insinuation that conversion can result from coercion. Many Muslims believe that *jihad* means that they are called to "struggle" only in their minds and hearts, through good deeds, yet many others misinterpret Surah 9:29 to be a call to violence.

It is imperative that we stress the uniqueness of Christianity, the only religion that teaches salvation by grace alone, and the only religion that proclaims a Savior. Apart from Jesus and the belief in His crucifixion, death, burial, and resurrection, Christianity could not exist, nor would there be any hope of salvation. We must show grace in our personal lives to all Muslims, so that they can understand this grace of Christ.

We must also defend the Gospel boldly and know what our faith teaches. We are called to love, to stand firm in our faith, to know the truth, and to follow it. Do you have a Muslim friend? If you don't, you need to befriend a Muslim and show them how you love them and how you love Jesus.

You celebrate the fact that you don't need to enforce God's laws—just show His grace. We don't need to subjugate our culture—we need to transform it, and only Christ can do that. We need to show others what true love through Jesus Christ is all about. We need to love them with His unyielding love.

ENDNOTES

1. http://www.adherents.com/Religions_By_Adherents. html (accessed April 22, 2008).

2. https://www.cia.gov/library/publications/the-world-fact-book/geos/xx.html (updated April 15, 2008).

3. http://en.wikipedia.org/wiki/Jihad (accessed February 6, 2007).

4. http://www.answering-islam.de/Main/Authors/Arland son/contrast.htm.

5. Ibid.

6. Ibid.

7. Ibid.

8. http://www.usc.edu/dept/MSA/quran/009.qmt.html.

CHAPTER 22

Issue Fifteen—Christianity and Judaism

I write about Judaism with reverence, for several reasons. First, Judaism was the vehicle for the Kingdom of God, culminating for us in the person and work of Jesus Christ.

Second, I come to the topic of Judaism a bit biased. My grandmother was Jewish. Also, my spiritual father, Eliazer Urbach, was a Polish Jew, a survivor of the Nazis, and a strong crusader for the birth of the nation of Israel.

On top of this, I work with many Jewish leaders on a daily basis in Southern California, and I am a regular guest at one of the Rabbinic counsels in Los Angeles. (L.A. is the third largest Jewish city in the world, with New York being number one and Tel Aviv number two.)

Understanding Judaism is important to Christians because our faith springs from it. We cannot fully appreciate Christianity until we completely comprehend Judaism. And even beyond that, we cannot reach out to the Jewish people with the love of God through Jesus until we understand who they are as a people, what they believe about God, and their expectations of the Messiah.

I'd like to devote this chapter to exploring who the Jewish people are and how we, as Christians, are called to relate to them—which, as you'll see, is with the utmost respect, love, and honor, as we should people of all faiths. We don't need to compromise on the truth of the

257

Gospel, but we shouldn't negate the truth of Jesus Christ by our bad behavior and attitudes.

Whose Scriptures Anyway?

Most Christians are caught off guard when they start sharing Old Testament passages with their Jewish friends. Their Jewish friends either, 1) don't know the Bible (much like many Christians), or 2) deeply disagree with how we understand them. Most of the Messianic prophesies they will say apply to the Nation of Israel and not necessarily the actual Messiah Himself. But here is just a smattering of why we understand Jesus to be the fulfillment of God's prophecies:

Hosea 11:1 prophesied that God's Son (Messiah) would be *"called"* out of Egypt. Matthew 2:13-15 reveals that Jesus spent His formative years, shortly after birth through a few years old, in Egypt, before returning to Jerusalem.

Matthew 1:1-17 gives the exact genealogy of Jesus of Nazareth, right back to Abraham, and includes all of the patriarchs. (Even the genealogies Joseph *and* Mary, Jesus' earthly "parents," trace directly back to King David in Luke's account.)

Micah 5:2 prophesied that Messiah would be born in the city of Bethlehem in the county of Ephrathah, when a bright star appears (Numbers 24:17). This was fulfilled by Jesus' birth in Bethlehem, as noted in Matthew 2:1-2.

Isaiah 7:14 said it would be a miraculous, virgin birth. This was fulfilled with Jesus, as noted in Matthew 1:18-23 and Luke 1:27-35.

Isaiah 35:5 said the eyes of the blind would be opened and the ears of the deaf unstopped. Jesus did these as listed in Mark 8:22-25 and Mark 7:32,37 (see also Matthew 11:5). Messiah was to calm the sea (Psalm 107:29) and cause the mute to talk (Isaiah 35:4-6), which were fulfilled by Jesus in Mark 4:39 and Matthew 9:33.

Isaiah 53 said that Messiah was to become man's sin offering and that He would arrive in Jerusalem on a donkey amidst praises (Zechariah 9:9). This was fulfilled by Jesus as noted in Matthew 21:2-5.

Psalm 41:9 said that Messiah would be betrayed by a friend, which was fulfilled when the apostle Judas betrayed Jesus in John 13:18-31 for 30 pieces of silver—exactly as prophesied in Zechariah 11:12-13. Later Zechariah said that 30 pieces of silver would be thrown on the floor of the temple and would eventually go to purchase a "potter's field," which is precisely what occurred in Matthew 27:5-7.

Isaiah 53:7 said that, at His trial, the Messiah would not defend Himself and would say nothing. This was fulfilled by Jesus, who stood silent before the inquisition of Pontius Pilate, as noted in Mark 14:60-61.

Messiah was to be crucified, with His hands and feet pierced (Zechariah 12:10 and Psalm 22:16), which was fulfilled by Jesus as noted in John 19:18.

Psalm 22 said that Messiah's enemies would encircle Him, mock Him, and cast lots for His clothing. He would call to God, asking why He was "forsaken." He would be offered gall and wine (Psalm 69:20-22). He would die with thieves, but unlike the thieves, none of His bones would be broken. His heart would fail, as indicated by blood and water spilling out from his side when pierced with a spear (Zechariah 12:10 and Psalm 22:16). The Scriptures said that He would be buried in a rich man's tomb (Isaiah 53:9) and that on the third day He would rise from the dead (Psalm 16:10). All of these prophesies were fulfilled by Jesus as noted in John 19:34-42 and First Peter 2:22-24.

Isaiah 53:12 said Messiah would die with evildoers. John 19:18 and Mark 15:27-28 describe this concerning Jesus.

The Messiah would then ascend to Heaven (Psalm 68:18), which was fulfilled by Jesus as noted in Luke 24:51 and Acts 1:9.

Isaiah 8:14 said that Israel would reject Messiah. This was fulfilled by the Jewish leaders, who handed Jesus over to the Roman governor to be crucified. Though most Jewish men and women cannot see the huge evidence of Jesus in the Old Testament, thousands of them have found the Messiah in Jesus Christ (and wonder how they ever missed Him).

JEWS TODAY

The Jewish nation and the "Second Temple" (the first was the temple built by Solomon) were destroyed when the Jews rebelled against Rome in A.D. 70 and in A.D. 143. In 1948 came the rebirth of the nation of Israel.

Of the six billion people who live on planet Earth as of 2006, up to five billion are estimated to practice one of the five major religions—Judaism, Christianity, Islam, Hinduism, and Buddhism. Of these, three sprang from Abraham, the father of Israel: Judaism, Christianity, and Islam (the newcomer). Of those, only 12 to 14 million are Jews.

Of all the faiths, Judaism is unique in that it is not defined by religion alone. In fact, a surprisingly high number of people of Jewish descent do not believe in their religion at all.[1] Over half of all Jews in Israel today call themselves "secular" (which basically means "atheist"). For those who do believe, however, the Torah is their Holy Scriptures. Just who is a "Jew" is a huge debate today. It can refer to either a religious affiliation, or to a genetic classification, or to cultural identity, or to all three.

As a core faith, Jews share many basics with Christianity, such as the nature of God and the sinful nature of man. In Judaism, however, actions are far more important than beliefs. Judaism focuses on relationships, primarily the relationship between God and humankind. And with this relationship comes mutual obligation. These are played out in many rituals, such as Torah readings, *bar* and *bat mitzvahs* (for sons or daughters "of the commandments"), *seders* (or Passover, which is one of the holy feasts), and the upholding of the Sabbath.

Orthodox Jews believe in a Messiah who has yet to come. They believe the Messiah will be a great political leader descended from King David and that he will be a unique human being, but not God incarnate.

The Jews are a nation, a deep-rooted community with a common history and destiny. Within this extended nation are four basic movements, ranging from conservative to liberal. These include the orthodox, reformed, conservative, and reconstructive Jews.

THE ORTHODOX

The Orthodox believe that the 613 individual commands of the Torah (called the *mitzvahs,* or the *halika*) are the divine teaching of the Jewish law. They also believe not only in the written Word that

God gave to Moses, but also in oral traditions that God gave, which tells humankind how to live, what to believe, and how to act.

Orthodox Jews live "by the book." They're the fundamentalists. They're the ones who are more likely to be "kosher." (The word *kosher* comes from Deuteronomy 14:21, which says, "Do not cook a young goat in its mother's milk." That was because the Canaanites did that, and the Jews were forbidden from following the customs of the non-believing nations. Jewish people who are *kosher* will never mix dairy and beef products—not for health reasons, but simply because God said not to.)

There's a reason why you see many orthodox Jewish people walking to synagogue on Saturdays. They walk because *Shabbat* (Sabbath) is the underlying law for them. They make their meals ahead of time, and they don't do any work on the Sabbath.

To "make a fire" is against the laws of Sabbath. When automobiles were invented, the rabbis would come out and ask, "Are you making a fire?" That's why they walk on the Sabbath. A person can live wherever they want, but they're going to have to walk to synagogue to worship. So they buy houses near their places of worship. How many Christians choose to buy a house near their church because God is so important to them? The Orthodox accept the teachings of all of the *Tanak* (which is an anachronism of the three groups of Scripture: *Torah*, or first five books of Moses; *Nevi'im*, or the prophets; and *Ketuvim*, or the writings like the Psalms).

Rabbinic Judaism was developed when the captives in Babylon could no longer sacrifice or go to the Temple of Solomon. Things such as synagogue worship, liturgical prayer, and strong ethical behavior replaced the offerings and sacrifices. The Rabbinic teachings (or *Midrash*) created dual ways of interpreting how to live: *Halakhah* sought to focus on proper living, and *Haggadah* focuses on historical stories and wisdom folklore.

There is great debate among the Orthodox about the legitimacy of the nation of Israel, because they claim that the Messiah alone will be the one to create the new Israel.

THE CONSERVATIVES

Conservatives also believe that the Torah is from God, but they feel it needs to adapt a bit to today's culture. They still maintain its integrity, however, and believe it should not be compromised. Conservatives aren't necessarily looking for a personal Messiah as the Orthodox still are, but rather see "living the righteous, caring life" as being messianic to the world on God's behalf.

It is very difficult for an orthodox or conservative Jew to accept Jesus as Messiah, because to be baptized is often to be dead to your parents relationally.

THE REFORMED

Next are the reformed Jews. They are the more liberal Jews. Any time you hear the word "temple," it's not coming from an orthodox Jew, because the Orthodox believe that there is only one temple, and it was in Jerusalem and has been destroyed. The reformed Jews, however, often call synagogues temples.

THE RECONSTRUCTIONISTS

Finally, there are the Reconstructionist Jews. They seek to preserve Judasim in the face of secular rationalism and try to harmonize scientific thought with natural religious truths. The current fad with the Reconstructionists is *kabala*, a sort of the New Age mystic Judaism. The Reconstructionists don't know if God is personal or not, but they believe that there are ways to get rid of one's sins by oneself—sort of a "do-it-yourself" offshoot of Judaism.

AN INCREDIBLE PEOPLE

To say that the contribution of Jews to the world has been enormous would be an understatement. It's impossible to exaggerate the contribution of the Jewish people to the sciences, to math, to the arts, to literature, to music, and to entertainment.

Just think of their contributions to film, television, and entertainment in general. There have also been some extremely funny Jewish comedians over the decades.

Henny Youngman said, "I wanted once to become an atheist but I gave up because they have no holidays."

Mel Brooks, who is also Jewish, said, "The remarkable thing about my mother is that for 30 years she served nothing but leftovers. The original meal has never been found."

Golda Meyer, Prime Minister of Israel and standup comic that she was, said, "Let me tell you one thing I have against Moses: he took us 40 years in the desert in order to bring us to the one place in the Middle East that has no oil!"

A rabbi once told me that one of his older congregants said to him, "Rabbi, I want to be cremated. Is that alright?"

"Yes, yes," the rabbi told her, "it's OK. You can be cremated. What shall we do with the ashes?"

"I want them sprinkled in Bloomingdale's," she responded.

"Why in Bloomingdale's?" he asked.

"Because then I'll know that at least twice a week my daughter will come see me, that's why."

Where does all that wonderful humor come from? Very much from the painful history that belongs to Judaism. They've developed the paradoxical ability to be funny in the midst of great hardship. A rabbi friend of mine shared with me that the "whining" within the Jewish culture is *really waiting for the other shoe to drop.* In Jewish e-mails, you read, "Start worrying—details to follow." They've experienced tremendous sorrow, sadness, and pain from persecution throughout the ages—and yet they have this incredible ability to still smile, laugh, and rejoice.

HISTORICAL BARRIERS

Many Christians realize that all the pain the Jewish people have experienced was often at our own hands—from the Inquisition (when the Catholic Church literally burned Jews alive if they refused to confess Jesus), to the Tsars (who slaughtered Jews in the name of Russian Orthodoxy), to the Holocaust (when the Nazis ruthlessly slaughtered the equivalent to half of all of the Jews living today). They don't blame the Church or Christians for Nazi atrocities, but are deeply resentful at the silence of the Church against Hitler.

This is a natural barrier whenever we, as Christians, try to talk to someone who is Jewish. Everything that the Church has done to the Jews throughout the ages is a horrible, unbelievable story, and we have to overcome it each and every time we try to develop a friendship with a Jewish person.

Never say to somebody, "Well, that's not my fault—it wasn't me who did that to your people." Instead, stand with them and say, "Forgive us, please, for what the Church has done to you."

If you still don't think Jews have been a persecuted people, think again. Jerome, who translated the Scriptures into Latin, said, "God hates the Jews. Therefore, I hate the Jews." Boy did he get the translation wrong!

Cyril Patriarch Alexander said he fell upon the synagogues with armed force and gave their wealth to "the true people of God," the Church. He was plundering the synagogues!

Richard the Lionheart, King of England in 1189, expelled all the Jews from Great Britain because he said they were causing earthquakes and famines.

In the Middle Ages, Thomas Aquinas said, "It is perfectly within the law to hold the Jews accountable because they crucified our Lord."

After the Crusades, after fighting against the Muslims, the Christian crusaders thought they'd be welcomed by the Jews. When the Jews didn't welcome them, the crusaders herded them into synagogues and burned them alive while they sang Christian hymns outside!

Yes, the Jewish people have been through it.

Don't get me wrong. Many Christians through the years have stood up for the Jewish people. Many Christians stood up against Nazi Germany, for instance. My wife's great aunt, in fact, died in a death camp, a Lutheran Christian standing up against Hitler.

All of that history is often still in the back of your Jewish friends' minds whenever you bring up the subject of Christianity and conversion. They think of the people who persecuted them or their ancestors, or of those who stood by while others did.

Ultimately we know that it was satan who spearheaded the murder and mayhem against God's chosen ones, using the Church's lack of spiritual intelligence to do his evil work. But we have to do all we can to overcome those memories for the Jewish people and to paint for them a new picture of our belief, which is an extension of theirs.

A LOT ALIKE…YET VERY DIFFERENT

Where does Christianity agree with Judaism? The answer is, more than two-thirds of the Bible. That's how much we agree with each other.

Most people are fairly ignorant as to what Jews or Christians believe, including most Jews and Christians! But the entire Bible was written by Jews (except for the physician Luke). We need to understand one thing—if Jesus is not the Jewish Messiah, then there is no way that He is the Gentile Messiah.

What we call the Old Testament, the Jewish call the Torah or the Tenak.

We agree with the Jews that the Bible reveals who God is. God is not hiding from us. In fact, our culture has it backward. Many think that we understand ourselves and that God is a mystery. In the Bible, the reverse is true. God *can* be known and we're the mystery—why we behave the way we do (which is because we have a disease called "sin").

But despite these similarities between Christianity and Judaism, there are still many differences. A lot of these differences are based on misunderstandings, but some of them are genuine, legitimate differences.

First of all, many Jewish people think Christians believe in three gods. Of course, we don't; we believe in one God embodied in three persons—a mystery.

The Jews also say that the virgin birth could not have taken place (even though our shared Scriptures of the Old Testament mentions it in Isaiah 7:14). Well, it certainly doesn't happen a lot (just as an 85-year-old woman named Sarah giving birth doesn't happen a lot, either), but that doesn't make it untrue. God will move at times. He'll break human protocol and even set biological precedent.

Jews also believe that Jesus violates the Law; when, in actuality, He came to *fulfill* it. And most Jewish people think that if you ask them to become a Christian, they'll have to become a Gentile first and give up being Jewish. Wrong! They don't have to become Gentile any more than we have to be Jewish. It's merely a matter of accepting the fact that their own long-awaited Messiah has come, and that they need to accept Him. Jesus came, and He is the Sacrifice—their Passover Lamb.

Our Jewish neighbors believe that when the Messiah comes, the Kingdom will be ushered in with all the promises of God. "Where is the Kingdom?" they ask. What happened was that a piece of God's future invaded the world in the Person and work of Christ. All the spiritual promises of complete forgiveness, acceptance, adoption, etc., are now available to *individuals* who yield to Christ.

> "For Christians, a 'splinter' of the future has invaded the present. Some of the blessings of the 'age to come' are available right now through Christ. But the complete presence of the Kingdom is yet to be realized. We live in a time of fulfillment without consummation."
>
> —*Dr. George Eldon Ladd*

SIN: THE PRIMARY ISSUE

Judaism says that the primary problem with people is the sin in our hearts. God created us in a perfect environment (the world was not always the way it is today), and humankind chose to rebel against God, thereby making ourselves slaves of the Lower Laws. Christianity agrees with this.

But Jews are perplexed at Christians because Christians have a mindset that people like to sin and God likes to forgive. Jews disagree with that point of view. They say that your actions are more important than your heart. The primary issue for Judaism is not whether a person is truthful but whether that person is righteous. It's not what you *believe*; it's how you *behave*.

It's like a space shuttle returning to earth. On a trip in 2003 everything looked fine, but the integrity of the hull had been breached by the loss of a small portion of the outer insulation shield. As they were reentering the earth's atmosphere, the sudden heat hitting the craft caused it to burn, and the ship disintegrated. Likewise, Jewish theology contends that we are just cruising along, thinking everything is fine—but someday we're going to stand in front of a holy God, and our sin is going to be revealed as a big problem. Christians would agree with that. But here's where we disagree—a Man named Jesus.

Most Orthodox rabbis won't use the word *Y'shuah* (Hebrew for "he will save"—what the name Jesus means). They say He was a Jewish man who had Jewish followers, but He didn't follow the Torah. They feel the same way about Jesus as Christians might feel about Jehovah's Witnesses or Mormons: they got some of it right, but they've stepped out so far that they're not even part of the faith anymore. That's how the rabbis characterize Jesus. They'd say, "This guy's followers grafted the Gentiles in—and they eat pork!"

A standard Jewish apologetic against Jesus goes like this: "You take Jesus. I'll take God." Their primary argument is that if Jesus really was the Messiah, then where is the Kingdom that Messiah was supposed to usher in? The Bible says that when Messiah comes, the Kingdom comes. The Jews say, "So, where is the Kingdom?"

Even Paul couldn't understand this at first. He said, "To hang on a cross means to be cursed, and God would never let Messiah be cursed" (see Galatians 3:13). But the Scriptures finally all came together for Paul and he realized that Jesus came to take care of the primary issue—sin. He came to be the ultimate sacrificial Lamb for our sins, as our Savior, and He's coming again someday, as the Lion of Judah, to vanquish the devil and sin, and to set up His eternal Kingdom.

A DONE DEAL

The splendor of our future illuminates what we do now. It's as if the missile has left the silo, but it just hasn't hit yet. And there's no calling it back—the first stage is done, and it's all moving forward. Christ fulfilled all the Messianic prophecies from the Old Testament, but the ultimate consummation has not totally taken place yet.

But it will.

If you've ever had surgery, you wake up in the recovery room and the surgeon says, "The surgery was a success." Yet you're laying there feeling like somebody backed a truck over you, and it doesn't feel much like a success. But it was. And you heal. And in time you realize that it truly was a success. In the spiritual realm, it's the same. The surgery took place when Christ came to earth, died on the Cross, and rose again as the propitiation for our sins. When He comes back the second time, *then* we will be fully healed. Even though one of Judaism's great calls is to study, some of the Rabbis are so afraid of their people leaving their faith for Jesus that they keep them from ever studying alone (not all of them, but definitely some of them). They are afraid we Christian are telling the Jews to become Gentiles like us. Nothing is further from the truth. We just want them to find their own Messiah. His name is *Yeshua*. We call him Jesus.

In Christianity, we are encouraged to read and study Scripture, not only in church or in Bible studies or classes, but also on our own. It also helps to compare the Bible to the other so-called "holy books" of the other religions, because it becomes obvious how radically different the New Testament is and how powerful the truth is to change lives.

We go after truth and read the Bible not because a pastor tells us to, but because when we read it, the truth clearly stands out and changes our hearts, our minds, and our very lives.

GRACE, GRACE, GRACE

We Christians disagree with Judaism about sacrifices. After the Babylonians and the Assyrians took the 12 tribes of Israel captive, the Jews could no longer do blood sacrifices. So what would stand in for their sin? That's when the synagogue was born, to bring the people together, and the "essence" of the sacrifice became the focus—which means prayer, good deeds, repentance, and turning away from bad deeds. They say, "We'll do it this way until we can do blood sacrifices again some day."

Today's practicing Jews go to the synagogue on the holy days. They believe that what saves them is repentance, prayer, and doing good works (*mitzvahs*). In other words, it's *primarily* up to their own human efforts, with little acknowledgement as to the importance of humbly accepting the unmerited grace and forgiveness of God, and not trying to "relate" to Him through intellect and action alone. As a consequence, Judaism takes the concept of repentance very seriously. They confess sins we'd probably never even think to mention. The reason is that due to their experiences of sin and all of our failure to overcome it in our own power. We tend not to be fully confident in God's forgiveness purely by grace. Though there are great teachings of grace in the Old Testament, most of Judaism's belief system was built around the legal blood sacrificial system. So now they're left just hoping and hoping that their actions are enough. They don't know all that sacrificing was just a foreshadowing of the once-for-all atoning death of Jesus.

It all comes down to grace, God's unmerited favor. God says that it's not dependent on your being a better man or a better woman, and it doesn't come down to your good deeds outweighing your bad deeds. No, it's all based on His love. He picked up the bill for your sins—not because you or I earned it or deserved it, but because He is just that good and that loving and that gracious. We can either accept it or reject it, but it is His love that is trying to chase us down to pay your tab. God's grace will lead you to a life of honoring Him and loving others (and it means you live with a mindset of being accepted, not *trying* to be accepted).

Believe it or not, this isn't a New Testament concept. God's grace and unmerited favor is woven throughout all of Scripture—Torah included. Father Abraham himself was a man of faith, and it was his faith—not his actions!—that was credited to him as righteousness:

> *What then shall we say that Abraham, our forefather, discovered in this matter? If, in fact, Abraham was justified by works, he had something to boast about—but not before God. What does the Scripture say? "Abraham believed God, and it was credited to him as righteousness." Now when a man works, his wages are not credited to him as a gift, but as an obligation. However, to the man who does not work but trusts God who justifies the wicked, his faith is credited as righteousness* (Romans 4:1-5 NIV).

HOW THE GENTILES FIT IN

What about the relationship between the Jews and the Gentiles? Paul has something to say about this in Romans:

> *Brothers, my heart's desire and prayer to God for the Israelites is that they may be saved. For I can testify about them that they are zealous for God, but their zeal is not based on knowledge. Since they did not know the righteousness that comes from God and sought to establish their own,*

they did not submit to God's righteousness. Christ is the end of the law so that there may be righteousness for everyone who believes (Romans 10:1-4 NIV).

The Romans wanted to know if Jesus was actually the Messiah or not, because they were responding to the message of Christ and wanted to know why the rest of Israel wasn't reacting well to the message of Messiah's arrival. Paul responded that keeping the Law is not bad—but it can't save a person either. No one can ever be saved by human efforts.

He continued by warning that the Gentiles who understand this message should be careful not to boast, because God is working a specific plan:

I do not want you to be ignorant of this mystery, brothers, so that you may not be conceited: Israel has experienced a hardening in part until the full number of the Gentiles has come in (Romans 11:25 NIV).

What Paul said in this verse was powerful. It was this: God allowed (didn't put a stop to, didn't interfere with) the hardening of the hearts of the Jewish people so that the gospel would go forth and be shared with the Gentiles as well. Inherent in this message is the fact that someday, in God's perfect timing, Israel will respond and be saved. I fully believe that.

DUE RESPECT

The Rabbi Saul of Tarsus, a Hebrew of Hebrews, trained under the venerable Rabbi Gamaliel, said, "I am not ashamed of the gospel; it is the power of God for salvation to everyone who has faith, to the Jew first and also to the Greek" (Romans 1:16). That's a bold statement from a man who went about giving Christians up for killing.

I speak the truth in Christ—I am not lying, my conscience confirms it in the Holy Spirit—I have great sorrow and unceasing anguish in my heart. For I could wish that I myself were cursed and cut off from Christ for the sake of my brothers, those of my own race, the people of Israel. Theirs is the adoption as sons; theirs the divine glory, the covenants, the receiving of the law, the temple worship and the promises. Theirs are the patriarchs, and from them is traced the human ancestry of Christ, who is God over all, forever praised! Amen (Romans 9:1-5 NIV).

In this passage, Paul said that the great advocate, the Law, has not been negated but rather fulfilled.

What do we Gentiles owe to the Jews? According to Paul, the answer is *everything*. Gentile means "brought in by the blood of Christ." Our Christian faith springs from the Jewish faith, and it is we Gentiles who have been "brought in." The Jews were in God's family first.

Paul was a Jew of Jews. Every time he went through a city, he stopped at the local synagogue, where his people were, so that he could preach to them until they beat him or left him for dead or ran him out of town. He said we owe the Jews everything—and he lived it out, too.

God worked with the Ethiopians, the Egyptians, and even the hated Philistines—God was in all of their histories. But Israel was special. Israel had the Abrahamic covenant, where God said:

I will make of you a great nation, and I will bless you, and make your name great, so that you will be a blessing. I will bless those who bless you, and the one who curses you I will curse; and in you all the families of the earth shall be blessed (Genesis 12:2-3).

God extended that covenant in First Chronicles 17 with the Davidic covenant. God said to David, a man after His own heart, that He would make sure that somebody from David's lineage would always be on the throne of the Kingdom. What God was foretelling was the story of a little Jewish girl named Mary. The angel Gabriel came to her and said, "Hail Mary, blessed are you among women, for from you shall come the promised One and Messiah, the Anointed One shall be born" (see Luke 1:28-33).

It was through Mary's Son, the Anointed One, that we Gentiles can now be "grafted" in to the family of God.

If some of the branches have been broken off, and you, though a wild olive shoot, have been grafted in among the others and now share in the nourishing sap from the olive root, do not boast over those branches. If you do, consider this: You do not support the root, but the root supports you. You will say then, "Branches were broken off so that I could be grafted in."

Granted. But they were broken off because of unbelief, and you stand by faith. Do not be arrogant, but be afraid. For if God did not spare the natural branches, He will not spare you either (Romans 11:17-21 NIV).

Again in this passage, Paul reminds the Roman Gentiles that they have now been embraced into the Kingdom of God through Christ—but that this is not cause for arrogance or self-righteousness.

We need to be careful about how we view the Jews. We have been grafted in because of their disobedience, but *they* were the root. Are they right in rejecting Jesus as Messiah? Absolutely not. Do they need Jesus? Absolutely yes. And you and I are called to tell them the Good News.

Not long ago I heard about a lawsuit that was filed. A man was in line to buy a Powerball ticket, and he had waited for two hours in line and stepped out briefly to use the restroom. He was next in line to buy, and the person behind him bought the ticket that he would have bought—and that's the ticket that won. So now he's suing the man who has what he claims is rightfully his ticket.

It's similar to when the Jews were waiting and waiting for Messiah, and out of rebellion they stepped out of line, and we Gentiles were handed the Powerball ticket called Jesus. But according to Paul, be very careful about thinking that you deserve that ticket—because you don't. That ticket is a gift from God, just like it is to the Jews, and we Gentiles are called now to go back and share the wealth.

JUSTICE OR FORGIVENESS?

We tend to take lightly what it is to know the meaning of freedom and grace. We know that the righteousness of God is not on the basis of works—it's on what *He* has done. But we've become so familiar with that fact that often we don't fully appreciate it.

In a moral universe, if I step on your foot on purpose, you have two choices—you can practice *justice* and step on my foot (that's where *I* pay for my sin), or you can practice *forgiveness* (that's where *you* pay for my sin). God had the same two choices: *justice* or *forgiveness*. God is a Holy God, so justice is required. Yet He loves us so much that He desired to extend forgiveness. And being God, He found a way to implement both. It's as if God said, "I love you so much; and yet I'm a holy God, so somebody must pay." The astounding thing is that *He* was the one to pay! He came to earth, as God the Son, and paid *our* price on the Cross.

SHARING THE GOOD NEWS

We are called to share this Good News with those around us, including God's people, the Jews.

What about those who have never heard the good news of Christ? What happens when they stand before the Lord? God says, "Stand according to the light that is shown you. To whom much is given, much is required" (see Luke 12:48). Conversely, to whom little is given, little is required.

So then, following this logic, why even tell people about Jesus? If they don't know, they won't be accountable. Right? Wrong. We tell people the good news of Christ because it's true and because God told us to tell it. He loves the Jewish people with all of His heart, and He tells us to, "Go, tell them the truth." And so we must go.

I read an article recently about the Ebola virus breaking out in Africa. What a terrible virus. When it first hit some of the villages in eastern Africa, near Tanzania, there were some women who survived, but the terrible virus destroyed almost all of the children and men.

Can you imagine if someone had the cure for Ebola but just held onto it and said, "Well, some of them might figure out how to make it. Let's see who does and who doesn't"? God have mercy on our souls if we have that attitude! The truth is that this is the way many of us Christians behave. We have the spiritual antidote for the problems of sin in this world, and yet we don't share it!

This doesn't mean you have to sneak Jesus into every conversation. But at some point you can be close up. Do you have a Jewish friend? Get one. I highly recommend it. Not for the sake of converting them and scalping them for Jesus, but for the sake of befriending them. And if you love them, you'll give them the antidote.

There's almost a "spiritual Darwinism" in Christian society today that refuses to preach the gospel to the Jews—as well as to anybody else that we're so-called "respecting" for their personal views! But when we don't offer the antidote, the good news of Jesus, we're not truly respecting them—we're disdaining them and abandoning them. Christ did not abandon you.

God alone is judge. You and I are called to love and to share, because there are real issues at stake—including *eternity*.

A FLOOD IS COMING

What a great time to be alive. God is going to do some great things with this generation. What wonder and what beauty. But there are some real floods coming.

When Hurricane Katrina came there was true horror, as many could not escape and many perished. I saw one gentlemen being interviewed on CNN, and he was sitting there just beside himself, wracked with grief as flames and dead bodies drifted all around. The reporter asked, "So, why are you so upset, sir?" And all the man kept saying was, "Dear God, forgive me. I could've gotten out of town. I've been here before. But I didn't get out. I should've listened, I should've listened, I should've listened."

God is speaking—a flood is coming! But it's not just a flood of judgment against the wicked and those who've rejected God and lived for themselves. It's also a flood of joy and peace and righteousness for those who leave their ways and embrace Jesus.

Our relationship with our Jewish friends should be one of respect and love—just as it should be with all people. And part of that is telling them that we have a Savior. His name is Jesus.

KNOWING IT ALL ALONG

When Helen Keller was young, she was hit with a terrible fever that left her blind, deaf, and mute. She couldn't speak during most of her life, and she lived in a world of darkness and deafness, in a tragic state somewhat like a caged animal.

Then a woman named Anne Sullivan, who was learning a new language called Braille, began working with Helen when she was 12. Anne took Helen's hand one day and put water on it and made a sign of the letter "W"...and then did it again...and again...and again...until it finally connected with Helen and she realized that someone was *communicating* with her! Helen Keller went on to finish college and write several books.

One day Anne Sullivan asked Helen through Braille what her beliefs were and if she knew about God. She took Helen to see Phillip Brooks, a famous pastor, who sat down with Helen. Through Anne, Phillip Brooks asked her, "Helen, have you heard of a God who loves you? A God who is holy and perfect and who gave His Son because He loves you so much?" Helen answered, "Yes. I've known for a long time. What you said makes sense, because I've always known He would be that way." Even in her darkness, Helen Keller knew the Truth that is out there.

I believe that perhaps it will be much the same way when our Jewish friends come to accept Jesus as the Messiah. It will be as if a light bulb goes off and they'll say, "You know, I've known this for a long time. Jesus is the missing piece. It all makes sense now." We must be persistent in telling our Jewish friends about Jesus. God has chosen to let us be part of that process—and it is a privilege, not a chore.

However, evangelizing doesn't mean being a pest. I never have to "sell" Jesus, because the Holy Spirit is in charge of that part. And if God could show Himself to me and change *my* heart, then I know He can change anyone! Just learning to share interest in their *Seder* or Passover meal, and its connection to Jesus, or showing interest in their (or anyone's) religious customs, breaks down barriers.

We are not called to "save" anybody. That's the Holy Spirit's job. We are not called to convict people of sin. That, too, is the Holy Spirit's job. We are called to love and to help and to show others God's love through our words, our faith, and our actions.

CURRENT EVENTS AND POLITICS

What about the contemporary relationship we have with the Jewish nation? I believe we should be friends with Israel. Period. It is in the strategic interest of the United States to support the only democracy in the Middle East.

However, I don't believe in all the policies of Israel. Eighty percent of the people in Israel are agnostic or atheist. So many Jewish Israelis don't believe in God because of what they see around them daily. And it's against the law to share Christ in Israel—you cannot evangelize there.

Even though I don't agree with all of the policies, I believe in supporting Israel 100 percent. I believe that they are as blessed of the Lord as those who embrace the Lord. But that doesn't mean they're not going to be held accountable for their rejection of God's Son.

How can 6 million Israelis hold off 220 million hostile Arabs? It's not only a miracle of God's hand, it's also because God has used America to help defend Israel. It is wise for us to do so. I may not agree with everything that the Knesset and the Likude do over there. And there is terrible oppression of the Palestinians. But on the other hand, I do believe that supporting Israel is a wise move on America's part. I believe that God's hand is very much involved in current events in Israel.

I also think we should support the Palestinians. I have a Christian brother who is a Palestinian who lives on the Mount of Olives. Israel doesn't like him because he's an Arab, and the Arabs hate him because he's not a Muslim. We need to help the Christian Palestinians, and all of the Palestinians.

A HUMBLE, GRACIOUS RESPONSE

In closing, I'd like to encourage Christians to think differently about Judaism. Israel was the vehicle for the kingdom of God to be set up and ushered in. *They* are the root, and *we* have been grafted in—not the other way around.

When the Messiah came, He founded a church that has no walls and no dividing lines. Jews and Gentiles, blacks and whites, male and female, slave and free are all brothers and sisters in the Lord. And someday, the Kingdom itself will break into this world when the King of Kings comes back. And then the real adventure begins!

ENDNOTE

1. A 2003 Harris Poll revealed that 79 percent of American adults said they believe in God. In an updated survey done in 2006, the number went down to 73 percent. Forty-two percent admit they are not "absolutely certain" there is a God, while 15 percent are only "somewhat

certain." Eleven percent think there is probably no God at all, and 16 percent aren't sure. Only 76 percent of Protestants, 64 percent of Catholics, and 30 percent of Jews say they are "absolutely certain" there is a God. On the other hand, 93 percent of Christians who describe themselves as "born again" are absolutely certain there is a God. Yet, only 26 percent of those who say they believe in God attend religious services once a week or more, 46 percent attend services just a few times a year, and 18 percent never attend at all. See: http://channels.isp.net scape.com/news/package.jsp?name=fte/notbelieveingod /notbelieveingod. Also see Theology Matters: Understanding Key World Religions Around Us by Dr. Randall Otto (Number IV, January 2008).

CHAPTER 23

Issue Sixteen—Christianity and Hinduism

BASICS OF HINDUISM[1]

Hinduism is arguably the most complex of the great faiths on this planet, dating back to the third millennium B.C.

More than 95 percent of the one billion followers of Hinduism live on the subcontinent India. Many of the tenets of Hinduism are laced through cultures around the globe, including America. In fact, many of the ideas of Hinduism are found within the New Age movement of the last two to three decades. Hardly the latest fad, however, Hinduism is considered to be the world's oldest religion—besides Judaism and its daughter, Christianity.

The term "Hindu" was not a common term until as late as the 1800s, when, for the purpose of British census taking, it referred to the people in the Indus River Valley of India. It was first used by the Muslim conquerors when these people would not convert.

Hindus is a complex worship of a single deity, yet simultaneously has over 330 million individual gods and goddesses. They believe these other gods and goddesses reflect certain aspects of that one god. The holy writings of the *Vedas* (Sanskrit for "knowledge") came from central Asia. The people groups of the *Aryans* (which Hitler misrepresented as being the northern European race) and *Davidians* were language groups. While Hindus prefer to call their religion

Santana Darma (eternal religion) and use the Vedas, they also use the *Upanishads* (written around 400 B.C.) as scriptures, which are basically ways of how to live and how to offer sacrifices to the deity.

Although the key concepts of *karma* (judgment for how a life is lived), *samsara* (the fallen illusionary world), and *reincarnation* (living over and over again) do not appear in the older Vedas, the Upanishad writings summarize the religious use of all of these concepts. The focus for Hindus is how to achieve *moksha* (deliverance) from the world of pain through physical, mental, and spiritual exercises.

The divine that is worshiped depends on the individual worshiper. For example, Brahman is called "the creator." Vishnu, also known as Krishna, is "the preserver." Shiva is called "the destroyer."

Hindus believe in multiple reincarnations. They also believe in "karma," a cycle of cause and effect in which the way a person acts and thinks comes back on the individual, be it for good or for bad. According to Hindu teachings, once one has learned all the lessons life can teach, the soul will eventually reach "true enlightenment" and become "one with god."

It was this belief in reincarnation that led to the caste system, in which the entire society is broken down into five categories, ranging from those closest to enlightenment (the priests) to those furthest from it (the "untouchables").

Among the most distinguishing physical features of a Hindu follower is the red dot often worn on the foreheads. This is called a *bindi*, and it is traditionally worn by married women, but everyone can. The area between the eyes where it is worn is said to be the "sixth chakra," or the seat of "concealed wisdom." Among other things, Hindus believe that the *bindi* helps to increase spiritual concentration and protect against demons.

FINDING COMMON GROUND

Unfortunately, a great deal of intolerance and conflict in this world has resulted from the followers of various religions focusing only on the differences between faiths. Real dialogue and understanding only comes when we first recognize the common ground we have with other religions. Having a high SQ (spiritual intelligence) is to be secure enough in communicating "you don't have to believe the way I do for us to be friends. Of course, since you are my friend, I would love for you to know my Savior." And believe it or not, there is common ground between Christianity and Hinduism. For instance, Christianity would agree with Hinduism that life consists of more than merely the physical.

The belief system of today's secular, materialistic culture would suggest that what you see and touch is pretty much all there is—that the cosmos originates in the physical, and when the physical is over, everything is over. Hinduism would disagree with that line of thinking. Hindus believe that there is something beyond the physical, something spiritual—and Christians agree with that. In Hinduism, however, "god" is relegated to the background and is, at best, some kind of impersonal substance or force.

The Upanishads, a part of Hinduism's sacred Vedic literature, were written in eighth century B.C., around the same time that the prophets Amos and Hosea were recording their Scriptures. In this selection from the Upanishads, there is a sense of where reality comes from:

> As the spider moves along the thread it produces, or as from a fire tiny sparks fly in all directions, even so from this Atman come forth all organs, all worlds, all gods, all beings.

> —*Brihadaranyaka Upanishad Selections 1:20*

Atman is a term identifying the Brahman, or the all-pervading soul of the universe. It is not a personal entity, but merely a kind of impersonal substance that exists beyond the physical realm. Part of the goal of Hinduism is to detach the soul from this physical world, awakening it to the unseen spiritual realities beyond. In fact, there are several traditional Hindu stories that portray this. One story holds that if your child is having a nightmare in which they are being eaten by a tiger, you must wake them up and bring them back to reality. Likewise, we who become attached to this physical world need to be enlightened by the fact that this world is fading and that there something better coming.

A second point of agreement between Christianity and Hinduism is that there are consequences for moral behavior. Our modern, secular culture claims that there is no longer sin or rebellion—just pathologies, disorders, and syndromes. Hinduism would disagree. They would say that there is sin and that there are consequences for the moral decisions people make—and we Christians would agree with that.

Since Hindus are accepting of many religions, and Jesus is another one of the *avatars*, or manifestations of the Divine, there is a real opening for discussing the Incarnation.

But the similarities break down there. As a Hindu, you must live through many lifetimes in order to overcome sin. Part of the theory of reincarnation is that if you really blow it in this life, you will come back in an even worse form. You might come back as a dog or a bird or a bug. This is why all life is sacred to the Hindu. Don't squash that insect—it might just be your brother.

There is a saying among Hindus: "Just as a calf will find its mother among a thousand cows, so your sins will find you out after a thousand rebirths." This is the Hindu concept of karma—good karma or bad karma. If you have done good deeds, good will come back to you; if you have done evil, evil will come back to you.

Samsara is the Hindu term for the ongoing cycle of birth, death, and rebirth. It is the concept of being attached to this world and yet wanting to escape from it. *Dukkha* is the Hindu word for *suffering*. In our culture, a criminal might "suffer" arrest, confinement, and prison—and we wouldn't interfere because that criminal would be suffering for their "sins" against society. Likewise, in some forms of Hinduism, if someone is experiencing suffering in their life, at times you must not interfere because they are merely experiencing karma. To interfere would be to get in the way of cosmic justice—and then *you* would pay for meddling.

Even the untouchables, the outcasts of society, are not allowed to be helped. It is said that if even their shadow passes over you, it taints your life! This is why there is great oppression within the caste system of southern Asia. It is not necessarily out of callousness, but out of the belief that there are consequences for moral behavior, and that it's not a matter of "forgive and forget" but of "that's the way it is."

WHERE WE DIFFER

He is the image of the invisible God, the Firstborn over all creation. For by Him all things were created: things in Heaven and on earth, visible and invisible, whether thrones or powers or rulers or authorities; all things were created by Him and for Him (Colossians 1:15-16 NIV).

Ultimate reality for the Christian is not some impersonal Brahman. As the apostle John explained, "In the beginning was the Word, and the Word was with God, and the Word was God. ...And the Word became flesh and lived among us, and we have seen His glory" (John 1:1,14). Our ultimate reality is found in a personal, relational God—One who did not create the world and then play "hide and seek," but who put on flesh and bone and dwelled among us so that we might know Him completely.

In Hinduism, the original creation came from the "Hiranyagarbha" (sometimes depicted in paintings and artwork as a golden egg), the original being that spawned all the gods. These gods manifest themselves in different ways according to Hinduism. The most familiar for Americans might be Krishna (as in the Hare Krishnas). Krishna is the seventh avatar of Vishnu, which is really just a manifestation of one of their ultimate gods.

For the Christian, however, behind this whole universe is a *personality*, not an impersonal substance. For us, the mystery of the triune God is the Father, Son, and Holy Spirit. For us, behind the physics of trying to find the unified theory of the universe is not some new kind of subatomic formula, but rather the person of the Father who loved His Son and gave Himself to the Son, and the Son who gave Himself, and the Holy Spirit. All of creation—the entire physical cosmos—is simply a response to this relationship.

Another important difference between Christianity and Hinduism centers on the essence of suffering and sin. For the Hindu, the problem of the human condition is ignorance and the solution is enlightenment. For the Christian, the problem is rebellion and the solution is repentance. In other words, it's not that we're ignorant and don't know what to do—on the contrary, we know what we should do, but we chose not do it. The Bible calls such rebellion sin. God calls to us, but we deliberately rebel against Him. We have a congenital condition that has no cure apart from God's intervention.

Christianity disagrees with Hinduism in our view of salvation. For the Christian, salvation is from outside of ourselves, not from within. It is from grace, God's grace through His Son. In basic Hinduism, however, you live life trying to inch yourself up from one level to the next. To do that, you might live a life of devotion as practiced by the Hare Krishnas, who often chant their *maha-mantra* over and over. This is because the Hare Krishnas believe that, through devotion, one can work themselves up to another level. The one syllable word "AUM" you hear as a mantra is an acronym for the wrongly described "Hindu Trinity." A= Brahman, the god of creation; U= Vishnu, the god who preserves creation; and M= Mahadved, or Shiva, which is the god of destruction who is at the end of all things and reduces everything to its essence. Meditation and fasting are ways out of this world of samsara.

Hindus teach that another way to move oneself up is through selfless living, or *karma-marga*, which is where a person runs around doing good deeds in the hope that good karma will come back to them. There is also the practice of asceticism, which is the denial of any kind of physical pleasure.

For the Christian, however, the most radical truth is that we have been saved by God's grace and Christ's blood and not by anything we do. Krishna never sacrificed himself for anyone—Christ did. Jesus also conquered death and rose from the grave—another thing that Krishna or Brahman or Shiva never did. In fact, they didn't even exist.

Finally, Christianity and Hinduism differ in their understanding of truth and the way to salvation. Hindus often have no problem coming into our churches and watching us worship. They rationalize that Jesus might be one of the avatars, a manifestation of one of their gods. But Jesus didn't say, "I know the light." He flat out said, "I am the light" (John 8:12). And Jesus didn't say that He is *a* way; He said He is *the* way (see John 14:6). Jesus isn't just one of many gods—He is the one and only true God, who came to earth as a man, not just to show us how to live, but also to die for our sins.

Rabi Maharaj descended from a long line of Brahmin priests. He trained as a yogi, and after a search for "truth," he found Jesus Christ and became a Christian. In his book *Death of a Guru*, Maharaj says, "Just as those who do not know the field walk up and over the hidden treasure of gold and do not find it even though all the creatures go here day after day into the Brahma-world, and yet do not find it, for they are carried away by untruth."[2]

AMAZING GRACE

There is a God who loves us more than anything we can ever imagine. We can only imagine what it must be like for Muslims, Orthodox Jews, Hindus, or Buddhists who go to bed each night wondering if they are good enough to "make it." But we have a God who loves us so much that He said, in effect, "*I* will pay for your sins."

In high school, my daughter Rachel was in a surfing accident. She dove off the board and it came back and slashed the right side of her face. Thankfully, a great plastic surgeon was on duty at the hospital and stitched her back together. As a parent, there is nothing worse than holding your child and seeing their wounds. You swear that you would bear the wounds instead if you could. That is exactly what God did. He took the wounds—even for those shaking their fists in His face. He said, "I love you so much that I will pay for your bill." This is the kind of God that we Christians serve.

John Newton, a slave trader in the 18th century, was in the middle of the horror of taking families from Africa to the United States to sell them as slaves. Half of the slaves would die each time his ship made this errand of horror and insanity. One night, in the middle of a storm, he thought he was going to die in the Atlantic and he fell on his knees. He cried out to Christ and afterward penned these words: "Amazing grace, how sweet the sound that saved a wretch like me. I once was lost but now am found, was blind but now I see." No one has expressed it more clearly since.

ENDNOTES

1. Facts about other religions come from my own research and exposure over the years. A recent source includes "Theology Matters: Understanding Key World Religions Around Us" by Dr. Randall Otto, PhD, publication number IV, January 2008.

2. Dave Hunt and Rabi R. Maharaj, *Death of a Guru* (Eugene, OR: Harvest House Publishers, 1984).

CHAPTER 24

Issue Seventeen—Christianity and Buddhism

Forty years ago, Hinduism and Buddhism were just a couple of mysterious but distant Asian religions. Most Americans had heard *of* them, but didn't know much *about* them. Some saw them as part of the historical past of Asian nations. Others saw them as simply religions—the Methodists or Presbyterians of Asia. Few would have been able to tell you much about them other than that Buddhists had the statue of that rotund man and Hindus worshiped cows and wore red dots on their foreheads. That was about it.

Today, ease of travel and communication have made the world we live in a melting pot of different cultures. Nowhere is this more evident than in the area of spirituality. So many who are approaching spirituality for the first time take a "smorgasbord approach." They take what they like of several religions, leaving behind the things they don't care for—a dab of Catholicism here, a smidge of Buddhism there, and a dollop of Christianity—mix it all together and hope for the best!

Amid this environment, it is more important than ever that we Christians understand not only the tenets of our faith, but how our beliefs line up with those of other faiths.

A BRIEF HISTORY

Buddhism began as an offshoot of Hinduism in southeast Nepal sometime between 500-400 B.C. While Hinduism acknowledges aspects of Buddhism, seeing the Buddha as a facet of the incarnation of the god Vishnu, Buddhism differs from Hinduism in its emphasis. Buddhism is pretty disinterested in the whole divine thing, obsessing instead on the transitory nature of all things. It's all passing away, including ourselves and creation. Another difference is that Hinduism isn't tied to any historical person or event that took place. Hinduism is more a collection of very ancient teachings. Buddhism, on the other hand, is very much linked to a gentleman who lived in the sixth century B.C. by the name of Siddhartha Gautama. Though many Buddhists claim Siddartha was one of a long line of 24 previous Buddhas, he is the one who is the most well known "enlightened one." The name *Buddha* in Sanskrit means "enlightened one" or "savior." It was a title, in the same way that *Christ* means "Messiah" or "the Anointed One."

Along with Hindus, Buddhists believe in reincarnation, or multiple rebirths, where a person lives many consecutive lives over and over until they finally arrive at a state of perfect peace and enlightenment and blessedness, which they call "nirvana." Some of the most gentle, loving human beings you will ever meet are Buddhists, because of their belief that emotions such as anger, vengeance, and greed bind people to this world and keep them from achieving enlightenment.

Born in what we now call Nepal, Siddhartha was a young prince who lived in the foothills of the Himalayan Mountains and was raised as a Hindu. Being immersed in Hinduism, he believed in thousands of gods and that you had to be reincarnated thousands of times in order to atone for past sins.

Siddhartha's father, Suddhodana, was chief of the Shakya nation. Siddhartha's mother was Queen Mayadevi, a Koliyan princess. According to legend, Siddhartha's parents had long struggled to have a child, when one night she had a dream that an elephant had entered into her right side and that she was going to become pregnant, which she did. After giving birth, they named their child Siddhartha, which means "all desires fulfilled." Siddhartha's mother died when he was a young boy, leaving a scar on his life that intensified with age, just as the scar on a tree that is damaged in its youth grows more pronounced with time.

A story is told of when young Siddhartha was out playing and helping a little caterpillar along when a bird flew down, snatched it, ate it, and flew off. Siddhartha was struck in that moment by the fact that everything that lives must endure suffering.

Trained in the military sciences, Siddhartha was in line to become king of his little province. At the age of 19, a bride was chosen for him. He married princess Yasodhara, and ten years later they had a child, whom they named Rahula. Although his family and position ensured that he had everything he could want or need, Siddhartha felt that material wealth was not the ultimate goal of life.

Then one day, the story goes, a Hindu mystic came by and told Siddhartha's father that he saw a glow in the palace, and that if the prince remained there, he would become a great king and subjugate the whole world—but that if forsook the court life for the religious life, then he would become the savior of the world, a Buddha.

So Siddhartha left his wife and infant child, feeling that it would help him seek religious enlightenment and figure out how best to deal with issues of human suffering. He lived in the woods for six years with two ascetics, and through painful rituals they tried to rid themselves of all desires in order to achieve enlightenment. Although he reached high levels of meditative consciousness, he was still not satisfied with his path.

Then one day a woman gave him a cup of milk. His ascetic companions were shocked that he'd let a woman give him something to drink, and so he told them he'd find his own way, and he left them.

At last, at the age of 35, after traveling throughout northeast India for six years, Siddhartha (at this point renamed Buddha) discovered the path to enlightenment, which he called the "noble eightfold path."[1] He taught that one reaches *nirvana* (the Buddhist equivalent of Heaven) by practicing these eight so-called *paths of correct living*, which (among others) include proper behavior, discipline, and wisdom (or "insight into truth"). Once a person has successfully followed the eightfold path and has eliminated all the cravings of this life, that person reaches nirvana.

Buddha preached his eightfold path for 45 years. When Buddha was 80 years old a blacksmith gave a meal in his honor, but Buddha contracted food poisoning and fell deathly ill. He went into the forest, and there, sitting between two great trees, he continued to teach about nirvana until he breathed his last.

A disagreement broke out among his followers as to what they should do with his remains. Eventually he was cremated, and his ashes were divided and put into ten towers in the different provinces, in an effort to avoid fighting among the kingdoms.

The ways of Buddha spread throughout the world. Today, Buddhism is practiced by 350 million people in Sri Lanka, Southeast Asia, and Japan, as well as by more than three million followers in the United States.

There are different schools of Buddhism. Theravada Buddhism is fairly agnostic. They believe that there *might* be a god out there—a Vishnu, or whoever else—or there might not be. It doesn't really matter, they say. Mahayana Buddhism states that there is no personal god, just a state of nirvana.

Often you will see statues of a serene and smiling Buddha. That represents Siddhartha when he finally achieved enlightenment—he's smiling because he got rid of all desire. He could have stayed in this perfect state of enlightenment in the eternal realm, but they say he came back into this world of suffering to teach "the middle way" or "eightfold path to enlightenment."

Have you ever been to a place where you were so close to the Lord that you just kind of smiled? For the Christian, there is a point when we get so close to God that we just want to smile. Not because we have rid ourselves of all desire, but because all of our desires have been *fulfilled* by Christ—in the way that they were intended to be.

WHERE CHRISTIANITY AGREES WITH BUDDHISM

The first point of agreement between Buddhism and Christianity is in the belief that life can be a painful journey. Job said, "Human beings are born to trouble just as sparks fly upward" (Job 5:7). Jesus put it this way: "In the world you will have tribulation; but be of good cheer, I have overcome the world" (John 16:33 NKJV). The

Bible also says, "All who want to live a godly life in Christ Jesus will be persecuted" (2 Tim. 3:12). And the apostle Paul wrote, "I wrote you out of much distress and anguish of heart and with many tears" (2 Cor. 2:4).

We all suffer tribulations in this world. On that point, we Christians agree with the Buddhists. The apostle Paul said that we can't even see reality sometimes because our tears are so much in front of our face. Yes, we will have tribulations.

A second point of agreement between Christianity and Buddhism is that our corrupted, fleshly desires create much of the misery in our lives. We would agree with Buddha that a lot of our desires cause a lot of our pain.

Here is a reading, taken from the teachings of Buddha, that talks about desire and what it is like to be alive:

> Behold this painted body, a body full of wounds, put together, diseased, and full of many thoughts in which there is neither permanence nor stability. This body is worn out, a nest of diseases and very frail. This heap of corruption breaks in pieces, life indeed ends in death. What delight is there for him who sees these white bones like gourds cast away in the autumn? Of the bones a citadel is made, plastered over with flesh and blood, and in it dwell old age and death, pride and deceit.
>
> —*Dhammapada*, 147–150

I like Siddhartha's honesty. He says, in effect, "You see all this happiness we have? It's all an illusion—it passes away." In fact, as a young man, Siddhartha wrote, "Luxuries of the palace, healthy bodies, rejoicing youth! What do they mean to me? Some day we may be sick, we shall become aged, from death we cannot eventually escape. Pride of youth, pride of health, pride of existence, all thoughtful people must cast them aside as the illusions they are."

TEACHINGS OF BUDDHA

What Siddhartha was saying is that there's not really a "you"—you are an illusion, and if you can get over that, you won't hurt as much. He talks about the problem of being able to walk through life:

"There is grief but none suffering, there is no doer but there is action, there is quietude and none being quieted, there is a path but none going along the path." He was saying that your existence is an illusion, so get over it. Do good. Purify your mind. Love others. And someday, finally, as a drop of water goes into the ocean, you will be taken care of.

A third point of agreement is that there is a place of contentment and fulfillment. For Buddha, this state was called *nirvana*. For the Christian, however, the place of contentment and fulfillment is in life with Jesus.

WHERE WE DIFFER

A major source of disagreement is that, while Siddhartha may have been a great seeker of truth, to the Christian he was not "the savior of the world." That Person is only Jesus Christ. How interesting it would have been if these two men could have met and broken bread together. I think that, if Siddhartha had met Jesus, he would have become a follower of Christ, because his entire life was spent in the pursuit of truth, and Jesus made it very clear that *He* was the truth—and that He was also God:

> *Jesus said to him, "I am the way, and the truth, and the life. No one comes to the Father except through Me. If you know Me, you will know My Father also. From now on you do know Him and have seen Him"* (John 14:6-7).

Another difference between Christianity and Buddhism is that Buddha's goal was not to get rid of wrong desires, but to get rid of *all* desires. Nirvana is not the fulfillment of your desires, but a complete *absence* of desire itself. Christianity, however, is about the fulfilling of God-given desires and the crucifixion of selfish desires.

While we agree with Buddhism about the destructive force of sin and desire, we also differ on how to treat those maladies. According to the "theology" of Buddha, if you saw all of the lives that you would have to live, if you piled up all of the ashes of your remains from all of the funerals you were going to go through, it would be as high as the Mount Everest! That's how many thousands of lifetimes it would take to reach nirvana. On the other hand, if you "pay" in the next "lifetime" for the things you did in this one, then if you're human you could be piling up "sin debts" that would take you forever to pay off!

Christians, however, believe that one day we're going to stand in front of the Lord and face judgment (see Ecclesiastes 12:14 and 1 Corinthians 5:10). When we stand in front of the Lord, we'll instantly discover that death will not change the direction we were headed in—either in the direction of Christ and truth or away. At that time, whatever a person has sown, they will reap (see Galatians 6:7). And the only thing that will have saved us is not the karma of a thousand lifetimes finally lining up just right, but the grace of God. After all, if we could simply work our way to God, we wouldn't need a Savior—He would only be a referee, there to keep score in our efforts to achieve perfection.

> *There is no one who is righteous, not even one; there is no one who has understanding, there is no one who seeks God. All have turned aside, together they have become worthless; there is no one who shows kindness, there is not even one* (Romans 3:10-12).

We know that this grace is not from ourselves but that it is a gift from God:

> *For by grace you have been saved through faith, and this is not your own doing; it is the gift of God—not the result of works, so that no one may boast* (Ephesians 2:8-9).

Not only are we saved only through the work and person of Jesus Christ, but Scripture is clear that there are no redos, no multiple reincarnations.[2] This is wonderfully explained in the Book of Hebrews, where Paul has just been referencing the Old Testament practice of offering sacrifices over and over again for sin:

> *For Christ did not enter a sanctuary made by human hands, a mere copy of the true one, but He entered into Heaven itself, now to appear in the presence of God on our behalf. Nor was it to offer Himself again and again, as the high priest enters the Holy Place year after year with blood that is not his own; for then He would have had to suffer again and again since the foundation of the world. But as it is, He has appeared once for all at the end of the age to remove sin by the sacrifice of Himself. And just as it*

is appointed for mortals to die once, and after that the judgment,
so Christ, having been offered once to bear the sins of many, will
appear a second time, not to deal with sin, but to save those who
are eagerly waiting for Him (Hebrews 9:24-28).

The idea of multiple reincarnations may sound enticing, but according to the Bible, you've got one race to run, and you're running it right now—so run it well (see 1 Corinthians 9:24-27). No flaking out at the halfway point because you figure you've got another shot at a makeover in your next "physical incarnation." Run it well now.

When my wife and I dropped our oldest off at college some years ago, I had to write a bunch of checks for books and tuition and dorms and meals. As I wrote my checks, I was sitting there next to a gentleman who was frowning at his checkbook. He looked up at me and said, "If I come back in the next life, I want to come back as my son!"

The truth is, many of us would relish a second chance at life. We'd love to hit the reboot button on the computer of life if we could. But the Bible says there is but one life to live, and then we are going to stand before the Lord. When the game's over, the game's over. It's not the end of your existence, but it's the end of your life here on earth and the beginning your eternity somewhere else.

Where will you be spending your eternity?

IS THERE ANOTHER WAY TO GOD?

Any discussion about other religions eventually comes down to one crucial question—what will it be like when individuals of other religions stand before the Lord? To put it another way, is Jesus Christ really the *only* Way? Is there any hope at all that those outside of Christ will be saved?

These questions are being asked more and more as those of other faiths are living closer together. Many of us know some great, kind, and giving people who belong to other faiths. Is there any hope for them at all?

The apostle Paul touched on this issue when he explained how nature displays God—and what happens to people who place creation above the Creator:

*For **since the creation of the world His invisible attributes are clearly seen**, being understood by the things that are made, even His eternal power and Godhead, **so that they are without excuse**, because, although they knew God, they did not glorify Him as God, nor were thankful, but became futile in their thoughts, and their foolish hearts were darkened. Professing to be wise, they became fools, and changed the glory of the incorruptible God into an image made like corruptible man; and birds and four-footed animals and creeping things* (Romans 1:20-23 NKJV).

All who have sinned apart from the law will also perish apart from the law, and all who have sinned under the law will be judged by the law. For it is not the hearers of the law who are righteous in God's sight, but the doers of the law who will be justified. When Gentiles, who do not possess the law, do instinctively what the law requires, these, though not having the law, are a law to themselves. They show that what the law requires is written on their hearts, to which their own conscience also bears witness; and their conflicting thoughts will accuse or perhaps excuse them on the day when, according to my gospel, God, through Jesus Christ, will judge the secret thoughts of all (Romans 2:12-16).

What Paul is saying in these passages is that, first, there is something beyond the physical matter we see—God is out there! And second, he's saying that it's not what people believe that condemns them, it's what (or Who) they reject.

I believe that someday when we stand before the Lord, we will be judged according to the light that was shown to us. Will there be Buddhists who make it into Heaven? Very possibly—not because they're Buddhists, but only because they were exposed to the pre-gospel and responded to whatever truth they had been exposed to. We know that God alone will judge who gets to spend eternity with Him in Heaven or not. Say you were raised on a desert island and came to believe that there is a great God out there, and you called Him "Bahunga." And one day you died in battle and suddenly found yourself standing before Jesus. You would say, "You're the great Bahunga!" And Jesus would respond, "Well, actually my name is Jesus."

At that point you would have two choices. You can either say to Jesus, "It wasn't fair in my life! I wasn't given the right village! My parents never told me! Other people were stronger and faster! I tried to be good! I deserve jungle paradise!" Or you could say, "I failed in my life. I did not do what was right, even though I wanted to. If You will let me into Your paradise, it is simply on Your grace that I will be allowed." That is not a "second chance"; that is a fulfillment of God's promise to those who believe, whether they know Him as Jesus, or Jehu, or Christ, or Messiah.

You and I have the Truth. We have a Book that is historically documented and backed up by thousands of years of facts. Can you imagine what it's like for the people going to bed tonight who think they have to reincarnate a thousand times in order to get better? You and I can tell them there's a way out.

As Buddha was dying, he said he was still seeking "the way." Jesus said, "I am the Way, and the Truth, and the Life. No one comes to the Father except through Me" (John 14:6). I don't have to sell Jesus to anybody. If He could show Himself to me, He can show Himself to anybody who truly has a hunger to know Him.

There are some things we can learn from our Buddhist friends. The Bible says that, as believers, we are called to confront evil. But it wouldn't hurt us to take notice of the Buddhist ways that are gentle and peaceable. Hatred has never defeated hatred, neither has vengeance overcome vengeance.

In the time of the early Roman Empire, the Romans would send convicted criminals to work the copper mines. They would take a "C-clamp," put it through the Achilles tendon, attach it to a chain, and send them into these mines where they would work for several months until they died. Once they went in, they would never come out again.

Do you know what some of the early Christians did? They sold themselves into slavery to work the mines in order to bring the light of Christ into that dark hole. Knowing they would never come out, they took the good news of Christ into that world. Why would they do that? Because they were already forgiven—they belonged to the Lord and they knew they would live forever with Him in eternity. And because they had received grace, they could give grace. Since they gave Him their all, they had nothing left to lose in sacrificing for those who knew Him not.

We need to wake up to reality and give up our little addictions and our bitter, petty jealousies and competitions, as well as the little self-worship games we play all day long. We need to let them go and give them up. We need to learn how not to merely fulfill our desires but to change our desires. Life is no game, and there are no do-overs. We need to constantly remember that, when we come before the Lord, if it was up to us to pull ourselves out of our sin, we could never do it. We are lost. But thanks be to God, this grace that is given to us is a grace that we can give to others.

ENDNOTES

1. Many Buddhists today have an eight-spoke wheel, which visually depicts the eightfold path and is a symbol of great meaning for them (just as the Cross is for Christians).

2. Christians agree that we are born twice—once in the flesh and once when we are reborn into life in Christ (see John 3:3,7 and 1 Peter 1:23), which is our new birth into His resurrection—but that we die only once (see Hebrews 9:27).

CHAPTER 25

Issue Eighteen—Christianity and Mormonism

But I am afraid that as the serpent deceived Eve by its cunning, your thoughts will be led astray from a sincere and pure devotion to Christ. For if someone comes and proclaims another Jesus than the one we proclaimed, or if you receive a different spirit from the one you received, or a different gospel from the one you accepted, you submit to it readily enough (2 Corinthians 11:3-4).

The subject of Mormonism is a huge can of worms. In fact, the average Mormon doesn't know much about the deeper teachings of their own religion.[1] Christianity actually has more in common with Islam than with Mormonism! Muslims at least believe in one god, while Mormons believe that we will all eventually become gods, and that at one time their present god was once a normal man just like us.

We hope that no one goes to hell—not even Osama Bin Laden. But God is very clear. To reject the truth of Christ is to leave God with no option but to banish that person from His presence *forever.*

THE ORIGIN OF MORMONISM

Mormonism, also known as The Church of Jesus Christ of Latter-Day Saints, was founded by Joseph Smith Jr. in 1830. At the age of 15, Smith claimed to have had a personal visit from God, whom

Smith claimed later introduced him to Jesus. During this alleged conversation, Jesus told Smith that all churches were wrong, "that their creeds were an abomination in the sight of God, and that those professors (Christians) were all corrupt."[2] Three years later, Smith claimed to have had an encounter with an angel named "Moroni," who told him about certain gold plates that contained so-called scriptures and ancient writings of previous settlers in the Americas. In 1827, Smith allegedly found these golden plates and began to translate them into what is now known as the *Book of Mormon.*

Later Smith became a proponent of polygamy, believing it to be an essential part of Mormonism. He also furthered the teaching that humans, through what he called "eternal progression," could ultimately become gods.

Like many other cults and religions whose main doctrinal teachings are based upon their founders' personal ideas, Smith was surrounded by controversy. He continually changed the Mormon doctrines to accommodate changes in his own personal belief system and "new revelation" that he supposedly received from God. A *Newsweek* article once said of Smith, "Prophet and polygamist, mesmerizer and rabble-rouser, saint and sinner: Joseph Smith is arguably the most influential native-born figure in American religious history, and is almost certainly the most fascinating."[3]

MORMON CHURCH DOCTRINE

To properly answer our family, friends, coworkers, and acquaintances concerning our faith and to effectively refute those who would contradict the true Word of God, we must examine and understand the teachings of Mormonism.

Mormonism treats all of its so-called "sacred texts"—such as the *Book of Mormon, Doctrine and Covenants,* and the *Pearl of Great Price*—as continuing revelation added to the Bible. For Christians, however, the Bible is the only sacred text, and God commanded that we must not add anything to it nor take anything away from it (see Deuteronomy 4:2, 12:32). This is a big logical hole that Mormons often either overlook or are unaware of.

Mormonism flatly rejects the teaching of the Trinity. They do not believe that the Father, Son, and Holy Spirit are both individual *and* One, but rather that They are three distinct beings who are united as one in purpose. Christianity, on the other hand, teaches that the Father, Son, and Holy Spirit are three unique Persons—and yet are also One.

With regard to Christ's life, many Mormon teachings are the same as Christian teachings—on the surface. They believe that the prophets predicted His birth, and they accept the reality of His crucifixion and bodily resurrection. However, Mormonism does not agree with Christianity in that Jesus is the eternal Word of God, or God Himself (see John 1:1).

Instead, Mormonism teaches that Jesus was a "created spirit" and that He is not equal with God. He was "a" son of God, not *the* Son of God, and in this way, according to Mormons, He was like all individuals of humankind before receiving physical bodies.

According to the *Book of Mormon*, satan and Jesus were brothers who vied for the right to receive a body and to become the redeemer for humankind, with Jesus ultimately winning the competition. Mormons also contend that God the Father is not only Jesus' heavenly Father but also His natural father, because, according to Mormons, God and Mary engaged in sexual intercourse.

Joseph Smith wrote, "The birth of the Savior was a natural occurrence unattended by any degree of mysticism, and the Father God was the literal parent of Jesus in the flesh as well as in the spirit."[4]

Christians, however, believe that Christ walked the earth as a man and yet is all God, and that He is the second person of the Trinity. John 1:1-3 says, "In the beginning was the Word, and the Word was with God, and the Word was God. He was in the beginning with God. All things came into being through Him, and without Him not one thing came into being."

The teaching of original sin and the fall of man is also discounted by Mormons. Instead, they teach that it was God's plan for Adam and Eve to eat of the forbidden fruit from the Tree of Knowledge of Good and Evil, so that humankind could become more like Him. This teaching is in direct contradiction to God's Word, which teaches that Adam and Eve, of their own volition, chose to eat of the tree in violation of God's plan:

Now the serpent was more crafty than any other wild animal that the Lord God had made. He said to the woman, "Did God say, 'You shall not eat from any tree in the garden'?" The woman said to the serpent, "We may eat of the fruit of the trees in the garden; but God said, 'You shall not eat of the fruit of the tree that is in the middle of the garden, nor shall you touch it, or you shall die.'" But the serpent said to the woman, "You will not die; for God knows that when you eat of it your eyes will be opened, and you will be like God, knowing good and evil." So when the woman saw that the tree was good for food, and that it was a delight to the eyes, and that the tree was to be desired to make one wise, she took of its fruit and ate; and she also gave some to her husband, who was with her, and he ate (Genesis 3:1-6).

According to Mormons, the purpose of Jesus' incarnation was to teach about God and to provide a model for right living. This is similar to the Christian faith, except that we realize Jesus came for so much more than to just provide a good example. He came to reveal God directly to humankind, to establish personal relationships with individuals, and to die as the one perfect and final Sacrifice for our sins.

Mormons believe that salvation comes through a combination of faith *and* works—with more emphasis placed on works than on faith. Christianity, however, teaches that no amount of good works can earn a person's way to Heaven—it is by faith alone. Works are simply a complement to true, genuine, believing faith (see Hebrews 11:6). As Paul said to the Ephesians,

Even when we were dead in trespasses, made us alive together with Christ—by grace you have been saved. ...For by grace you have been saved through faith, and that not of yourselves; it is the gift of God, not of works, lest anyone should boast (Ephesians 2:5,8-9 NKJV).

Mormons also teach that, after death, there is a time of learning and preparation during which men and women have a second chance to be redeemed. Christian theology teaches that there are no second chances, that we die only once (see Hebrews 9:27), and that our eternal destination is at that point fixed.

Mormons also believe that humans existed as spirits before this life. They believe that salvation is a return to God after this life, and that the spirit is not rejoined with the body until the resurrection. Christianity, however, believes that the souls of the wicked are sent to hell for eternity and that believers go to Heaven. Mormons also believe that hell is only a "state of being," in which there is torment, but from which there remains a possibility of escape if you repent. The Bible, however, teaches that hell is an eternal place of judgment, torment, and separation from God with no hope of acquittal.

> *The wicked shall depart to Sheol, all the nations that forget God* (Psalm 9:17).

In summary, Mormonism teaches that salvation can be obtained by believing in God (as one of many gods) and in Jesus (as one of many sons of God), and that we each can attain "godhood" by performing good works, by developing moral character, by repenting of sins and asking forgiveness, by being baptized and participating in other Mormon ordinances, and by spreading the teachings of Joseph Smith, Brigham Young, and the Mormon faith. By faithfully practicing these means, one can eventually achieve the status of a god.

They Shall Know You by Your Fruit

Whether Mormons should be considered "Christians" is a controversial issue in some Christian circles. Many Catholics and Protestants do not consider Mormons to be Christians because they believe the differences in doctrines are more divisive than those between Christian denominations. On the other hand, some people categorize Mormons as Christians because Mormons themselves believe that they are Christians. (At the same time, it should be noted that Mormons consider themselves to be distinct from Catholics and Protestants, whose faiths they view as corruptions of true Christianity.)

Becoming a Christian is contingent upon the acceptance of Christ and His redemptive work. As Paul wrote to the Romans:

> *If you confess with your lips that Jesus is Lord and believe in your heart that God raised Him from the dead, you will be saved. For one believes with the heart and so is justified, and one confesses with the mouth and so is saved. The Scripture says, "No one who believes in Him will be put to shame." For there is no distinction between Jew and Greek; the same Lord is Lord of all and is generous to all who call on Him. For,*

"Everyone who calls on the name of the Lord shall be saved" (Romans 10:9-13).

The question is, "Can one accept Jesus while *also* accepting another creed such as Mormonism? It would be very difficult to integrate the teachings of Mormonism and an honest reading of the Bible. I know they do it every week, but listening halfway to most Mormon teachings and you discover that they are loaded with contradictions and half statements. Besides, a true Christian is a person in whom Christ's Spirit dwells as the result of asking His forgiveness for sins, putting faith and trust in Him and *Him alone,* and then accepting Him as the *one and only* Lord and Savior—not "one among many."

The byproduct of salvation is the joy of having a personal relationship with Jesus Christ and being able to commune with Him through prayer and His Word on a daily basis.

Again, our purpose in tackling the tough issue of Mormonism is not to become confrontational with our faith nor to attack theirs, but to display Christ's love to them. Jesus said, "By this everyone will know that you are my disciples, if you have love for one another" (John 13:35). We must conduct ourselves wisely toward outsiders, making the most of the time and making sure that our speech is always gracious and seasoned, so that we may know how to answer everyone who inquires about our faith (see Colossians 4:5–6; 1 Peter 3:15). Only then shall we be known as Christ's, when the fruits of love, joy, and peace are evident in our lives.

ENDNOTES

1. Sadly, many Christians don't know much about the deeper teachings of Christianity, either. However, an in-depth study of Mormonism reveals that it is impossible to integrate the teachings of the Bible with the *Book of Mormon* or the *Pearl of Great Price,* or to accept such concepts as Jesus and Lucifer being brothers (as Mormonism teaches).

2. Joseph Smith, *Pearl of Great Price,* 2:18-19.

3. Elise Soukup and Jon Meacham, "Solid, Strong, True," Newsweek, Oct. 17, 2005.

4. Joseph Smith, *Religious Truths Defined,* 44.

CHAPTER 26

Issue Nineteen—Heaven and Hell

THE REALITY OF HEAVEN AND HELL

One of the many questions I get from people when it comes to subjects such as death and dying, disease, abuse, starvation, and wars is, "How can God allow such pain and injustice?" Take that question to its extreme, and you're confronted with the final challenge—is there an actual Heaven and a real hell?

We live in a time when Heaven and angels are cool, and hell and the devil are passé. Spirituality is in; Christianity and traditional faiths are out. The numbers show this trend: 79 percent of Americans believe there is a Heaven and think that's where they're going when they die, while only 27 percent believe there is an actual hell and don't know of anyone personally who believes they are going there.

What does the Bible teach about the idea of a literal Heaven and a literal hell? Before we answer that question, we first need to consider the topic of death and dying.

DEATH: A ONE-WAY TICKET

Today 153,000 people died.[1] That's the average number of people who breathe their last on this planet *every day*. By the time you finish reading this page, more than 100 people will have stepped into the presence of the Lord to face their eternity. Thousands every single hour—nearly two people every second! That fact begs a question: Where are they now?

When you look out at the ocean and it looks peaceful and serene, periodically you might glimpse a dorsal fin breaking the surface of the water, which reminds you that there is a whole world under those waves. So too is there a place lurking just beneath what we perceive on earth. Once in a while the spiritual breaks through into our time-space continuum, and we're reminded that the veil between us and the spiritual world is not as thick as we thought. Just because you've never seen it doesn't mean it doesn't exist. Hell is very real—and it is real horrible.

OK, let me lighten it up a bit. Not long ago I was invited by the White House Office of Faith-Based and Community Initiatives to meet the president. I had been at the White House before for a faith-based initiative. This time, the president told me he liked Presbyterians. Of course it was an election year. He would probably have told me he liked Martians had I been one.

While there, I had my first chance to spend some time with Bishop Charles E. Blake, who pastors one of the larger African-American churches in Los Angeles. Bishop Blake had heard about my church's mission of getting churches of different denominations together, and he wanted to be involved.

Then I spent about a half-hour with Dr. Robert Schuller and his son Robert Jr. (who was in one of my classes when I went to Fuller Seminary). And I asked Dr. Schuller if he'd ever heard of the story where satan one day announced that he was tired of the fight. It goes like this:

Satan went up to Saint Peter and said, "You know what? I'm tired of the hassle of bickering with all you Christians down on earth. Why don't you just give me three of your top guys and I'll call it a truce for awhile?"

Peter responded, "Well, I don't know if I can do that."

"Look," satan cut in, "Just give me Billy Graham, Oral Roberts, and Robert Schuller, and I'll quit harassing all of the rest of the Christians all over earth."

Peter thought a moment, then said, "That's not a bad idea. OK. Let's try it for awhile."

So off went Graham, Roberts, and Schuller to hell. About a month later, satan came stomping back up to Peter in a bad mood, and Peter said, "You don't look too happy. How's it going in hell?"

"The deal's off!" satan yelled. "You can have them back!"

"What? What happened?" Peter asked.

"What happened?" satan shot back. "Are you kidding me? First of all, everybody in hell is now a Christian—thanks to Billy Graham, who converted them all! Second, nobody down there has anymore diseases or problems now—because Oral Roberts healed them all!"

"Wow," Peter retorted, "that doesn't sound like a problem to me. What happened with Schuller?"

"Schuller? He's the worst of the lot!" satan yelled. "He raised enough money to air condition all of hell!"

All joking aside, I want to propose to you a very important point: death is a one-way ticket—and hell is no picnic.

> It is appointed for men to die once, but after this the judgment (Hebrews 9:27).

WHAT HAPPENS?

What happens when we die?

Christ loved to teach the truth through life—sometimes through parables, sometimes through events. One time Jesus answered His critics on this issue of death, Heaven, and hell with a marvelous story about a rich man and a beggar, found in Luke 16.

In this account, a rich man dressed in his fine purple linen, had feasted sumptuously every day. At his gate lay a poor man named Lazarus, who was covered with sores and longed to satisfy his hunger with what fell from the rich man's table. Even the dogs would come and lick Lazarus' sores. You know what that meant for a Jew? Having a dog lick you meant that you were unclean—indicating that the man was always *unclean*. He led an unbelievably horrid life.

In verse 22, the poor man died and was carried away by the angels to be with Abraham. The rich man also died and was buried in hades, where he was tormented continually. And he looked up and saw Abraham far away, with Lazarus by his side. Jesus picks up the story:

> *The rich man also died and was buried. In hades, where he was being tormented, he looked up and saw Abraham far away with Lazarus by his side. He called out, "Father Abraham, have mercy on me, and send Lazarus to dip the tip of his finger in water and cool my tongue; for I am in agony in these flames." But Abraham said, "Child, remember that during your lifetime you received your good things, and Lazarus in like manner evil things; but now he is comforted here, and you are in agony. Besides all this, between you and us a great chasm has been fixed, so that those who might want to pass from here to you cannot do so, and no one can cross from there to us." He said, "Then, father, I beg you to send him to my father's house—for I have five brothers—that he may warn them, so that they will not also come into this place of torment." Abraham replied, "They have Moses and the prophets; they should listen to them." He said, "No, father Abraham; but if someone goes to them from the dead, they will repent." He said to him, "If they do not listen to Moses and the prophets, neither will they be convinced even if someone rises from the dead" (Luke 16:22-31).*

The point in the story of Lazarus is that what the rich man did that was so wrong wasn't that he lied, or that he was abusive, or that he cheated, or that he stole. What he did that was so wrong was to *live only for himself.* He was self-absorbed.

Not long ago I was in Colorado and ran into an old friend who is about 20 years older than me and whom I had not seen in quite some time. He's a good-looking guy, and he's a Christian—but he was always in a bad mood. When I saw him, it almost took my breath away. The last 20 years of bitterness had taken a toll on his appearance. The wealth of looks had faded way.

The wealth of fame and talent diminish with time, as well. I saw an interview a while back with Muhammad Ali, the greatest boxer of all time. The guy was unbelievable in his day. And here he was on television, just shaking with Parkinson's disease, reduced to a shell of who he once was. He used to say, "I'm the greatest in the world!" Not anymore.

The point is, death comes to us all. I'm going to die, and you're going to die. In fact, as far as we know, only two people in history ever got out alive—Enoch and Elijah (see Genesis 5:18–24; 2 Kings 2:11–12; Hebrews 11:5). So if you're not Enoch or Elijah, then one of these days you're going to put on your socks and shoes for the last time. If Christ returns and takes us to be with Him in the Rapture, then we won't have that physical death, but if that doesn't happen, then we're going to die. We can't avoid it.

Woody Allen once said he doesn't mind dying—he just doesn't want to be there when it happens! And there's good reason why—because death is the great equalizer.

Alexander the Great had all the greatest minds of Greece tutoring him. One day one of the great philosophers of his day was peering at some bones and Alexander asked him, "What are you looking for?" The philosopher responded, "That which no man can find: the difference between your father's bones and the bones of his slaves." In other words, when you're lying there dead, you've been equalized—you're no different than everyone else.

Death "Fixes" Us

Death doesn't change us, it fixes us. It sets us firmly where we chose to be all along.

Notice in the Luke 16 parable that even in death the rich man was ordering Abraham around like he was some kind of bum. "Hey Abe, send Lazarus down here because I'm miserable, will ya?" "Hey Abe, have Lazarus gimme some water so I can at least dip my finger into it, will ya? 'Cause I'm really thirsty here!"

When you die, it forever fixes you in the direction, the final destination, that you've been heading toward your entire life. You're either going to continue in a direction away from God (if you've rejected Jesus), or you're going to continue in the direction toward God (if you've accepted Jesus), growing more into the image of Christ.

That's why you notice that when people reject the Lord, they fall in on themselves more and more—and then it's permanent. Fixed forever.

No going back. God is not roasting them over a spit—although some-day they will wish that it were only that nice—but they find that it is a horrid existence, a world completely devoid of Jesus.

JUDGMENT

All of us must appear before the judgment seat of Christ, so that each may receive recompense for what has been done in the body, whether good or evil (2 Corinthians 5:10).

The word *judgment* in this Scripture is from the Greek word *bema*. The *bema* in Greece was a platform used by judges at Greek games. It was at the *bema* where one decided the winners and the losers. Sometimes the *bema* was also used as a place for civil proceedings. What Paul was alluding to in this passage is that we Christians, although saved, will stand before the Lord at the *bema* of Christ and give an account for what we have done with the life we were given.

In First Corinthians 15:51-52, Paul said that, "we will all be changed, in a moment, in the twinkling of an eye, at the last trumpet. For the trumpet will sound, and the dead will be raised imperishable, and we will be changed." Like the snap of your fingers or the blink of an eye is how fast it will take for you to stand in the glorious presence of the Lord where there is joy, fellowship, and celebration forever.

SAY GOOD-BYE TO YOUR BODY

Another point regarding the dead is that they do not have bodies. Their bodies are located in a cemetery somewhere, or reduced to ashes scattered on the wind. However, we do know that the new bodies believers will be given at the end of history will be just like Christ.

When the rich man discovered the horrors of hell and separation from the Spirit of God, he wanted someone to warn his brothers. Have you ever noticed that everyone in hell is really missions-minded? But that was an impossible mission, because, as we saw earlier, Abraham said, "Between you and us a great chasm has been fixed" (Luke 16:26). There is a great gap between the dead and the living.

With that foundation, I'd like to take a look at two key questions:

What is death like for the lost?

What is death like for the saved?

The reason we need to know about Heaven and hell is that we are currently at the precipice of these destinies. The great news is that Christ came not just to get us into Heaven, but to get Heaven into us.

WHAT IS DEATH LIKE FOR THE LOST?

Do not fear those who kill the body but cannot kill the soul; rather fear him who can destroy both soul and body in hell (Matthew 10:28).

Hell is the dwelling place and final punishment of the unredeemed, or the lost.

Just as God has a place of rest and happiness for the redeemed of the Lord, so does He have a place for those who have rejected Him—a place called hell. Jesus spoke more about hell than all other Bible writers. I believe it was because He loved and cared so much for dying humanity that He wanted everyone to know what it was like, in the hope that all would accept His love and forgiveness and escape that horrible place.

Some ask how a loving God could send anyone to hell. The reality is that He doesn't. Hell was not made for you and me but was prepared for the devil and his fallen angels. Jesus said:

Then he will say to those at his left hand, "You that are accursed, depart from me into the eternal fire prepared for the devil and his angel's ...And these will go away into eternal punishment, but the righteous into eternal life" (Matthew 25:41,46).

Those who traverse the dark domains of hell are those who have willfully rejected God's love and salvation through His only Son, Jesus Christ.

We saw from the story of Lazarus and the rich man that the lost are in misery since hell is a place of eternal torment:

There will be weeping there, and gnashing of teeth, when you see Abraham, Isaac and Jacob and all the prophets in the kingdom of God, but you yourselves thrown out (Luke 13:28 NIV).

Contrary to what other religions might teach, hell is not some holding place for temporary punishment. The punishment for the unpardonable sin of deliberately rejecting God's Son is everlasting separation from the presence of God—and continuous torment forever.

> *These will suffer the punishment of eternal destruction, sepa-rated from the presence of the Lord and from the glory of His might* (2 Thessalonians 1:9).

No appeals can be made to the court of Heaven for a stay of exe-cution once a person enters hell. Hell is self-chosen and self-inflicted, brought upon by sin. God is not willing that anyone should perish, but desires that everyone be saved and come to the knowledge of His truth (see 1 Timothy 2:4). At the same time, God will not coerce or force anyone to accept salvation and go to Heaven against his or her will. Because we are free moral agents, we have the freedom to choose between Heaven and hell—and here is how God clearly wants us to choose:

> *I call Heaven and earth to witness against you today that I have set before you life and death, blessings and curses. Choose life so that you and your descendants may live* (Deuteronomy 30:19).

WHAT IS DEATH LIKE FOR THE SAVED?

Just as hell is an actual place, so too is Heaven; it's the eternal dwelling place of the redeemed. Jesus said that He was going to pre-pare a place for His own, so that where He was there they would be also (see John 14:3). Wherever Jesus is, that will be Heaven. Heaven is a place of life, love, joy, peace, health, happiness, and service. There will be no sin, hate, sickness, disease, or death.

Heaven is a place where we will know things that we're not even able to comprehend here on earth. The apostle Paul said, "For now we see in a mirror, dimly, but then we will see face to face. Now I know only in part; then I will know fully, even as I have been fully known" (1 Cor. 13:12).

There is incredible fellowship there, closer than any intimacy here on earth.

THE MEANING OF SALVATION

In examining the truths of Heaven and hell, we must first understand the meaning of salvation. Matthew 1:21 states, "And you are to name Him Jesus, for He will save His people from their sins."

A word can be so familiar that is never explained. Many who hear the word "salvation" or "saved" do not really understand it. This passage tells us that Christ saved His people *from* sin. He came to seek and to save that which was lost. He bore the punishment of sin in the place of sinners. He paid the price. He accomplished redemption.

The word *redemption* simply means "to buy back, to purchase with a price." Christ has *redeemed* us as sinners from the chains of sin and slavery. Christ became the *ransom*—the "purchase price"—to redeem us and save us from having to spend forever in hell, with its eternal separation from Him.

Being in bondage to sin means that all humankind needs deliverance from satan's dominion, into which we were sold by Adam, since his own blood, which was tainted with sin, was insufficient to pay the price required. Therefore, Christ gave His life freely to buy us back into the Kingdom of God, offering His life as a ransom for us all—if we so choose to claim Him as ours (see Matthew 20:28).

One of the greatest explanations of salvation was given by Jesus to a man named Nicodemus, a ruler of the Jews:

> *Now there was a Pharisee named Nicodemus, a leader of the Jews. He came to Jesus by night and said to him, "Rabbi, we know that You are a teacher who has come from God; for no one can do these signs that You do apart from the presence of God." Jesus answered him, "Very truly, I tell you, no one can see the kingdom of God without being born from above"* (John 3:1-3).

It is not enough to recognize Jesus as a historical figure, just a good man with a heavenly mission. We must attribute to Him His divine Sonship and attest of His death, burial, and resurrection. Then we must acknowledge our own sinfulness and become born again by the power of the Holy Spirit quickening within us our lack of moral fortitude.

PREDESTINED FOR HEAVEN, OR HEADED FOR HELL?

Is salvation predestined, or do we have a choice to make? The answer is "yes." What other way could you express both truths? Our salvation was God's idea first, made possible only by His work, and we were called to Him by His grace…and yet, we individually must respond to this free offer.

There are three main lines of thinking among Christians about how salvation works. These are:

1. God paid the price—and I came to accept the deal.

2. God paid the price—He stopped the river of destruction I was caught in, and I pulled myself out of the water when He called.

3. God paid the price—He stopped the river of sin and pulled me out of the river without anything on my part.

Every manmade "connecting" of the dots has its problems, and this is why we must be careful not to put this mystery into our own neat, tidy box. How salvation can be fully from God while not violating our free will raises many questions—questions that might never be answered until we're face to face with God in Heaven.

The word *predestinate* comes from the Greek word *pro-orizo*, which means "to previously mark out a boundary line, to predetermine or decide beforehand." Because God is omniscient, He knows all things and what will happen ahead of time. Another way of describing this is that God's works are known to Him from the beginning. Yet each man and woman is a free moral agent (which makes humans unique to all other species of beings), and God will not violate our right to choose. Such statements as "the devil made me do it" are ridiculous because he cannot *make* you do anything that you aren't already leaning toward doing. Nor will God *make* you do anything.

DEATH IS NOT TO BE FEARED

No matter how we understand this mystery of predestination and free will, the fact remains that, for those who accept Christ's salvation, death is not to be feared.

The thing Jesus feared most was not the physical torment He would face on the Cross—it was His separation from His Father. Before Jesus took His last breath, He announced to the citizens of Heaven and earth, "It is finished" (John 19:30). The price for your debt and my debt was paid in full, and if you know Jesus, then you're bound for glory with Him. If you've given your heart to the Lord, then you do not need to be afraid of dying.

But if you are reading this book and have yet to accept Christ's love and forgiveness, then fear should come as you grapple with the fact that you will one day stand before a holy God whose grace you once rejected. But it's not too late to get a one-way ticket to Heaven through the blood of Jesus Christ. You can do it right now, where you are, by simply praying, "Jesus, I believe You are the Son of God who came to this earth, lived, died, and was resurrected on the third day. I ask You to forgive my sins and come into my heart. Amen." It's that easy. It doesn't require you to "clean up" first or become a member of a certain church. The Cross is the only road to Christ.

So what do you do in the meantime? You keep your hand to the plow. You keep working and living as though Christ might never come in your lifetime. And you give your all for His glory.

The time is surely coming, says the Lord, when the one who plows shall overtake the one who reaps, and the treader of grapes the one who sows the seed; the mountains shall drip sweet wine, and all the hills shall flow with it (Amos 9:13).

This verse means that when you plant seeds, you must wait a specified period of time before you receive a harvest. From birth to death is a cycle of time involving school, marriage, children, career, retirement, etc. But in today's environment, it seems that events are happening at such an accelerated rate that it's hard to keep up with the blessings you can enjoy right now on *this* side of Heaven.

Yet this world is nothing compared to what lies just beyond the veil in eternity. This world is like a muddy creek compared to a pure spring of joy that's waiting, when we'll drink from the Lord Himself. As Paul said, "It is written: 'Eye has not seen, nor ear heard, nor have entered into the heart of man the things which God has prepared for those who love Him'" (1 Cor. 2:9 NKJV).

315

ENTERING HIS PRESENCE

I've had the privilege of being with people in their dying moments. You can tell when a person's spirit leaves their body. They're not cold instantly—they're still warm. But all of a sudden, they're like an abandoned house whose tenant has left—because the person is gone. Although the dying process may be hard even for a Christian, passing from this life to the next and going into the presence of the Lord is rather easy, because the Lord prepares us.

During her early 20s, Anne Askew, a Christian and a martyr who lived in Scotland during the 16th century, heard about the Reformation and how you couldn't buy your way to Heaven but that a person was saved by faith through grace alone. She subsequently became a convert to Christ and, for her beliefs, was evicted by her husband from her home.

She began to share with others that salvation was by faith in Christ, not by good works. Her "heresy" attracted the attention of the church, and she was arrested, imprisoned, and tortured in an attempt to force her to recant her beliefs. But she responded, "What should move you to judge in me so slender a faith, as to fear death, which is the end of all misery." And on July 16, 1546, at the age of 25, Ann Askew was burned alive.[2]

Another great Christian theologian and Puritan leader by the name of John Owen, while lying on his deathbed, had his secretary write a letter to a friend. He wrote, "I am still in the land of the living." Then Owen told his secretary to stop and change it to say, "I am yet in the land of the dying, but I hope soon to be in the land of the living."[3] God wants you to live a long life, but He doesn't want you to be afraid of death. In fact, Paul said:

> I am already being poured out as a libation, and the time of my departure has come. I have fought the good fight, I have finished the race, I have kept the faith. From now on there is reserved for me the crown of righteousness, which the Lord, the righteous Judge, will give me on that day, and not only to me but also to all who have longed for His appearing (2 Timothy 4:6-8).

The Greek word for *departure* is almost like the French *bon voyage*. A good journey is waiting for us in Christ!

If you only want to enjoy today then buy some flowers, because they don't last very long. But if you want to have a great life, plant a tree because a tree can bless you your entire life. If you want to have a great eternity, love the Lord and love those around you. Keep your hand to the plow, keep loving others, celebrate, and don't despair! There is a home waiting for you that is more splendid and peaceful than words can explain or a mind can comprehend.

And Jesus Himself went to prepare that place for you. It's hand-tailored like a glove, fit just for you. And since He's been gone so long, imagine how much work He has put into making your place beyond stunning! When He has completed it, He will return and take you unto Himself, so that where He is there you may be also (see John 14:2-3). Are you ready for that place?

WHAT ABOUT THOSE WHO HAVE NEVER HEARD THE GOSPEL?

Is someone who has never heard of Jesus going to go to hell? Everyone has the fatal spiritual virus of sin. The debate as to whether God ever administers the antidote of grace outside of the formal gospel message is ongoing among some Christians. God shows many times in Scripture how He used those outside of the people of God—and often they were actually ahead of the "insiders" in spiritual development.

There is a tension between "no man being saved outside the name of Christ" and the mysterious, generous, and sovereign grace and mercy of God. This raises another point—just because a person attends church on a regular basis and hears the gospel does not mean that he or she is saved. This is spelled out in the Gospel of Matthew when Jesus said, "Not everyone who says to me, 'Lord, Lord,' will enter the kingdom of Heaven, but only one who does the will of my Father in Heaven" (Matthew 7:21).

When Gentiles, who do not possess the law, do instinctively what the law requires, these, though not having the law, are a law to themselves. They show that what the law requires is written on their hearts, to which their own conscience also bears witness; and their conflicting thoughts will accuse or perhaps excuse them in the day when, according to my gospel,

317

God, through Jesus Christ, will judge the secret thoughts of all (Romans 2:14-16).

First, we must understand that we will all be judged according to the light we've been shown. In other words, God will do justice. Second, no one goes to hell out of ignorance. The fact is that, for us who know, the all-encompassing call is to share the power and antidote of the gospel with the diseased, broken, and enslaved people whom God loves.

The good news is that God is doing all He can to keep you in His grace—while not treading on your free will. If you're a parent, you know that even when your child does something wrong, that doesn't make him or her any less your child. You still love them and would do anything for them, and you welcome them in your arms no matter what they've done.

> *It's the same way with God. Like a father, He extends His arms of love and mercy to His children. When we fall, His grace picks us up, dusts us off and sets us on the path of righteousness. He's not waiting to beat us down for every mistake we make. So, as His children, we must not be afraid to come to Him, for He commands us, "Come to Me, all you that are weary and are carrying heavy burdens, and I will give you rest"* (Matthew 11:28).

YOU CAN MAKE A DIFFERENCE!

Unfortunately, the church has done more to build up the saved within its own walls than to reach out to the "unchurched" who are truly ignorant of the path to life and increasingly hostile toward the gospel message. We need to become more mission-minded.

If you saw someone trapped in a burning building and you were their only hope, most likely you would run to their rescue. The same holds true with this urgent message we possess. We hold the life-giving, life-changing truth of God's Word, and it's our responsibility to toss this lifeline to those drowning in the sea of sin. We need to go love those in our families, in our schools, and where we work. We need to be a beacon of hope to those we bump into over the course of our lives.

Do we think we love more than God does? Do we think that we know people better than the Almighty does? Do we think that we have the right to give up on anyone? I certainly hope none of us would be brash enough to answer these questions "yes." Instead, we must follow God's call and share His love and grace with those we meet.

Do you have peace with God through Christ, and is His peace reigning in your heart? If so, and if you want to enrich your eternity, then share your Savior with someone. You can make a positive difference in someone's life simply by telling your life's story and how you came to faith in Christ.

ENDNOTES

1. https://www.cia.gov/cia/publications/factbook/geos/xx.html#Intro (accessed January 29, 2007).

2. John Foxe, *Foxe's Book of Martyrs* (1563 ed.), 676.

3. http://www.anecdotage.com/index.php?aid=3622 (accessed January 29, 2007).

CHAPTER 27

Issue Twenty—Miracles

ARE THERE MIRACLES TODAY?

Many of us have experienced answered prayer firsthand, through the intervention of God, or we know someone who has. That answer to prayer may have been as simple as getting to an appointment on time or as extensive as the healing of a family member struck with a terminal illness.

The question that is often asked of me when it comes to God's divine intervention is, "Are there miracles today?" For my definition, *prayer* is when God answers our requests. A *miracle* is one of those rare times when God suspends His normal order of doing things and reveals something of Himself to others. God didn't just part the Red Sea to help out one day; it was God revealing that He is the Redeemer. Christ didn't feed the thousands every day from a boy's lunch; he showed that He is the Bread of life. So my response is yes, although the truly miraculous may not be very frequent. There are, however, no biblical grounds for saying that miracles don't transpire today. They do!

This is evidenced in the story of George Benefield as recounted by Samuel Hole, Dean of Rochester, during the 19th century:

> George Benefield, a driver on the Midland Railway, was standing on the footplace oiling his engine, the train being stationary, when his foot slipped. He fell on the

space between the lines. He heard the express coming on, and had only time enough to lie full length on the "six-foot" when it rushed by, and he escaped unhurt. He returned to his home in the middle of the night and as he was going upstairs he heard one of his children, a girl about eight years old, crying and sobbing. "Oh, father," she said, "I thought somebody came and told me that you were going to be killed, and I got out of bed and prayed that God would not let you die." Was it only a dream, a coincidence? George Benefield and others believed that he owed his life to that prayer.[1]

—E.M. Bounds, *Bounds on Prayer*

God so believes in the mystery of prayer that He has practically confined Himself to it. He awaits the cries of His children so that He can move on our behalf, as witnessed throughout Scripture. Over and over again, you can find the terms "ask," "ask of Me," and "call unto Me" reverberating through the sacred text of the Bible. For instance, Philippians 4:6-7 states that we should:

> *Be anxious for nothing, but in everything by prayer and supplication, with thanksgiving, let your requests be made known to God; and the peace of God, which surpasses all understanding, will guard your hearts and minds through Christ Jesus"* (Philippians 4:6-7 NKJV).

A *miracle* on the other hand is the rare event where God suspends His normal order of doing things. He does this not just to help His people get out of a jam, but to reveal something of who He is to His people. When Christ healed someone, fed 5,000 men plus women and children, walked on water, or raised the dead, He did so not merely to alleviate hurt but to reveal who He is. It was to tell us that, someday, the laws of physics and biology will be null and void, subject to the spiritual realm.

When we pray for people before surgery in a hopeless situation, and the person becomes healed after the operation, I believe that is answered prayer. A miracle would have been if the healing was unassisted, a true intervention beyond the rules of science and biology.

When people say there are miracles every day, what they mean is that God's power is evident continually. If there were miracles every day in the technical sense of the word, it would be a rather unpredictable life of seeming chaos. God likes His normal order of doing things—He thought it all up. Periodically though, even today, God will do things where He suspends the usual laws of science—not just to help, but to reveal more of the nature of His character.

To further understand God's divine intervention in the affairs of humankind, let us delve into the nature of prayer.

DEFINITION OF PRAYER

God answers prayers to the glory of His name and purpose, and to bless His children.

Dr. Martin Luther King Jr. said, "To be a Christian without prayer is no more possible than to be alive without breathing."[2]

Have you ever noticed that there is universality to prayer? Men and women in their greatest hour of need are quick to call upon the name of the Lord for help. You may have heard the World War II truism: "There are no atheists in foxholes." In other words, more often than not, even the staunchest atheist will cry out to the Lord when faced with the possibility of great harm or death. Prayer crosses denominational, cultural, ethnic, and socioeconomic lines, and transcends time and space. And there is not a prayer that you've prayed that God has not already provided the answer for.

Yet what *is* prayer? Prayer is *communing*, or *conversing*, with God. You talk with God just like you would with a close and valued friend. Prayer is also conveying our desires to God, for things in accordance to His will.

This is the boldness we have in Him, that if we ask anything according to His will, He hears us (1 John 5:14).

No one is immune from the need to pray. In fact, I believe it is the most necessary—and most overlooked—duty of the Christian. Prayer is so important to the cause of Christ that He gave us a prayer outline as a brief guide to how we ought to pray:

He said to them, "When you pray, say: Our Father in Heaven, hallowed be Your name. Your kingdom come. Your will be done on earth as it is in Heaven. Give us day by day our daily bread. And forgive us our sins, for we also forgive everyone who is indebted to us. And do not lead us into temptation, but deliver us from the evil one" (Luke 11:2-4 NKJV).

The Lord's Prayer is our model for our own prayer life with our heavenly Father. Just as Jesus prayed to the Father, so are we to entreat Him—for our own needs and desires and for those things that are in alignment with His will.

When we pray, it should be with a heart attitude of forgiveness. Unforgiveness is one of the greatest hindrances to effective prayer. James put it like this:

> *Therefore confess your sins to each other and pray for each other so that you may be healed. The prayer of a righteous man is powerful and effective* (James 5:16 NIV).

Sometimes I wonder how many prayers have gone unanswered because we have allowed resentment or bitterness to fester like an open sore in our hearts.

AN ATTITUDE OF PRAYER

> *...men always ought to pray and not lose heart* (Luke 18:1 NKJV).

To be weak in prayer is to be weak in all other aspects of our spiritual walk. Prayer is the foundation upon which we are to build our daily lives. It can direct the course of our actions and thereby determine our very future. Our attitude in prayer should be one of reverence, birthed from a desire for a continual, up-to-date, growing relationship with our heavenly Father.

Prayer is more than a 911 call to Heaven for God to intervene on our behalf in times of crisis. It is to be a constant flow of communication between us and the Lord at all times—in health, sickness, tragedy, joy, success, or failure. Our approach to prayer should consist less of a self-serving attitude in communicating our own needs to God and should be more intercessory in nature—our petitioning God on behalf of others.

When we pray, we should expect to be heard by the Lord. Jesus said in a prayer to His heavenly Father, "And I know that You always hear Me, but because of the people who are standing by I said this, that they may believe that You sent Me" (John 11:42

NKJV). When your heart is unencumbered by sin and unforgiveness, then you have the ear of God and His desire to grant your petition.

When we begin to foster an attitude of prayer, then it's like bringing Heaven to earth in our daily routine. The Lord becomes a partner with us in bringing to pass His will and purpose in our lives and in the lives of those around us.

THE LORD WILL HEAR AND ANSWER

…You do not have, because you do not ask (James 4:2).

There are times when God will not do anything about an issue until He raises up a group of His women or men to pray for it.

> Prayer is the capital stock in heaven by which Christ carries on His great work upon the earth.[3]

> —*E.M. Bounds*

The Lord very often partners with you and me to accomplish His plans in the earth. God said in Ezekiel 22:30 (NKJV), "So I sought for a man among them who would make a wall, and stand in the gap before Me on behalf of the land, that I should not destroy it; but I found no one." Since God is already in the future, He is actually engineering answers to prayers we haven't even whispered yet. The greatest change that prayer creates is the change on the person who prays. It is mysteriously wonderful and life changing. In fact, He commands: "Call to Me, and I will answer you, and show you great and mighty things, which you do not know" (Jeremiah 33:3 NKJV).

Answered prayer brings hope to the person who has awaited its arrival. It shows to a world of skeptics that there are some things that cannot be explained by scientific or natural means. That's why, when we pray, our prayer should reflect an unshakeable resolve, which will keep us from giving up short of God intervening in our situation. How many times have we caved in just prior to receiving our hearts desire? How many times have we pulled back from our prayer closet, believing the heavens were brass and that our petitions never seemed to make it higher than the ceiling? Like a marathon runner in the homestretch, we cannot give up when our prize is so close at hand.

SOVEREIGNTY OF GOD

God is not a human being, that He should lie, or a mortal, that He should change His mind. Has He promised, and will he not do it? Has He spoken, and will He not fulfill it? (Numbers 23:19)

Science, and at times religion, tries to provide valid arguments against miracles, supernatural revelation, or even life in Heaven or hell. But God, in His sovereignty, does what He wills. So we should guard against putting God in the box of our religious traditions, demanding that He perform according to *our* predetermined formula.

The man with an argument is never at the mercy of a man with an experience. The deciding factor is what you choose to believe. Whether God chooses to answer the requests of His children through prayer or by an unexplainable miracle, we must realize that He will never violate His own Word to do so.

God takes great pride in His Word, for it's the power behind His name. If His Word promises His children something, He will honor it.

Are you in a desperate situation and in need of answered prayer? Have you made supplication to the Lord? God is not withholding His reply. He's just waiting for you to ask.

The eyes of the Lord run to and fro throughout the whole earth, to show Himself strong on behalf of those whose heart is loyal to Him... (2 Chronicles 16:9 NKJV).

ENDNOTES

1. E.M. Bounds, *E.M. Bounds on Prayer* (Whitaker House, New Kensington, PA, 1997), 254.

2. http://thinkexist.com/quotations/prayer/ (accessed February 6, 2007).

3. E.M. Bounds, *E.M. Bounds on Prayer* (Whitaker House, New Kensington, PA, 1997).

Conclusion

It's remarkable how much Christians agree on. Just read the Apostles' Creed and you'll realize that almost every one of the estimated 12 billion people throughout history who have been Christians have affirmed the tenants of this ancient creed. It is impressive how much of the shared core issues the 2 billion people on this planet today who call upon the name of Jesus agree upon.

The early Church creed of decision-making sums it up: "In essentials unity, in non-essentials liberty, in all things charity (or love)." In other words, we are united and unmoving in our essentials of the faith. In the nonessentials, we are free to disagree as long as everything is done in a spirit of love—love for God, love for His Church, love for His Word, and love for one another.

These issues are among the most important challenges we will face in our entire lives. This doesn't mean we will break fellowship over these areas or call those who disagree with us "unsaved." However, they are emotional and bothersome issues that demand a response that honors God and hopefully will give us the peace and confidence we need to face life head-on while allowing God to continue to lead us as we set His examples for a dying world.

Successfully tackling life's tough issues is all about raising your Spiritual Quotient. Anyone who wants to know and love God with deeper intimacy can raise their SQ, which is the only way to increase one's ability to deal victoriously with the ongoing challenges everyone faces in life. Combine the four sentinels of spiritual intelligence—*Scripture, Reason, Wise Counsel,* and the *Inner Voice of the Holy Spirit*—and you simply cannot go wrong in moving through life with purpose, wisdom, strength, and an inner peace that surpasses all understanding.

Your life does not have to be a series of disjointed steps and missteps. It can become a glorious dance of joy and pleasure.

THE DANCE OF LIFE

One Valentine's Day I took my wife out with another couple. We went to dinner at a club. I knew what was coming at the end of dinner, and it made me real nervous—dancing! When we were in college, my wife signed me up for ballroom dance lessons. But I'm about as graceful as a rhino on a bus. When we got there, sure enough the band started playing. You know what they were teaching that night? Tango! So I got right to praying, you know—*Rapture now, Lord. Rapture now. Rapture. Rapture.*

It didn't happen. And my wife looked at me with those kind of pitying eyes. She is such a good dancer. She just says gently, "Come here," then puts her arms around me, and she's so graceful the way she moves that, after a while, her grace just sort of rubs off on me! The next thing you know, I'm dancing!

God shows that same kind of gentle, loving grace to us. One day He saw me lying in the dust, and He didn't say, "Look at you, Brewer—you're a mess!" No. He said, "Come here." And then He stood by me and said, "Let's work on this dance together." He never once said, "You go get yourself cleaned up, then come back to Me." No. He said, "Come here. Will you let Me teach you?" He said, "Let's not march to all these sets of rules and laws...let's dance."

God's grace is finally starting to rub off on me, I think. If you let Him, His grace can rub off on you too...and as your life becomes a beautiful dance, you can extend a hand to others.

What will you do when you're faced with life's tougher issues? At one time or another in your life, you will be confronted with one or more of the situations we've explored, or there will be someone close to you who will. These challenges relentlessly crash in on us all the time in this brave new world in which we live. Will you choose to handle them with spiritual intelligence? We might not be able to do much about our IQ, but we certainly can raise our SQ.

It's all about learning to move among our fellow human beings with God's effortless grace during our short time here on earth.

May you smile at everyone God puts into your life, and with His amazing love say to them…*Let's dance.*

About the Author

Dr. Mark Brewer came to church ministry as a third-generation Presbyterian minister's son. Since June 2001 he has served as senior pastor of the historic Bel Air Presbyterian church in Los Angeles, which had a congregation of 2,000 when he arrived and currently has nearly 5,000 members.

Dr. Brewer received his undergraduate degree in the social sciences from Colorado State University (for which he received the Kodak scholarship for the highest GPA in his field). He earned his master's and doctoral degrees from Fuller Theological Seminary, where he is currently an adjunct professor. He has also completed post graduate work at St. Andrews University, Scotland, as well as at several other seminaries.

Dr. Brewer served as a pastor in Denver, Colorado, for 20 years, building up his church congregation while reaching out to the larger Denver community in creating urban and suburban alliances. Starting with five families in 1980, he became the organizing pastor of Cherry Creek Presbyterian Church in Denver, Colorado, which grew to 5,000 members by 1992.

In 1993 he accepted the call as senior pastor of the 3,000 member Ward Presbyterian in Detroit, Michigan, which he helped relocate to a new, 100-acre campus. While in Detroit, the passion of his life took hold—building relationships between segments of society that had not previously existed. By applying the truths of "family systems" he discovered that it is possible to be effective in cross-racial, cross-denominational, and extremely hostile situations, and still bring true healing to God's children.

Starting with a handful of people in 1994, Dr. Brewer became the organizing pastor of Colorado Community Church, which grew to five thousand members by 2001. While in Colorado he was head of "Denver LINK," an organization that forged close relationships between the spiritual leaders of the city.

Dr. Brewer has received numerous awards and national recognition for his work in uniting churches of different ethnicities and denominational backgrounds. He hosted the popular nationally syndicated radio news show "A New Day for America," a program that seeks to bring urban and suburban churches together.

His passion is in weaving fabrics of friendship across the diverse communities of Southern California. His desire is to equip his missions-minded church with bold and fresh ways of connecting with the city residents.

In 2000 he wrote *A Walk Into the City*, a book that examines the principles of discovering new relationships between urban and suburban churches, bringing to light the attitude of service and reconciliation.

Dr. Brewer has been married to his wife, Carolyn, an occupational therapist, for 27 years. They have three children: Vanessa, recently married; Paul, recently graduated from the University of Colorado in Boulder; and Rachel, recently graduated from UCLA and currently attending medical school.

ALSO BY DR. MARK BREWER

A WALK INTO THE CITY

"Is it possible for the scores of different Christian church denominations around the world to ever see eye-to-eye on the Word of God?"

"Why is there such division on even some of the more basic tenets of Christianity?"

"Is there a way that Christians of different denomination can separate theology from the agapeo love of Jesus and move forward united in Christ?"

A Walk Into the City answers these urgent questions that deeply impact Christian life in the 21st century. Dr. Brewer reveals principles of discovering new relationships between urban and suburban churches, and brings to light the importance of our maintaining an attitude of service and reconciliation—key factors in healing division in the Church today.

With an Introduction by Lloyd Lewan and a Foreword by NBA Hall of Fame pro basketball player Dan Issel, this book is must-have if you desire to learn how to connect with Christian churches of different denominations in your city.

What reviewers are saying about Dr. Mark Brewer's *A Walk Into the City:*

"Mark Brewer knows what ails America and, more importantly, has a lot of great ideas on how to set things right."
—*Former U.S. Senator William Armstrong*

"Articulate. Informed. Passionate. Mark Brewer is the right person to address the underlying ills of American society and to point to possible solutions."

—*Pollster George H. Gallup Jr.*

"What really grabbed my attention about Mark is that he comes to where the Blacks are to listen and to hear what they have to say. He works with us. He doesn't tell us who our leaders should be."

—*Clarence Shuler,* Focus On The Family

"Mark is the most effective Anglo pastor in the nation today."

—*Dr. Acen Phillips,* Vice President,
National Baptist Convention

A NEW DAY FOR AMERICA!

A New Day for America is a nationally syndicated radio news show hosted by Dr. Mark Brewer. With its riveting, informative and though-provoking format, Mark Brewer's *A New Day for America!* radio program provides guests and listeners of opposing theological, cultural and societal differences a platform in which to discuss and "hash out" their views in informative, poignant and often humorous ways.

This unique, popular show's approach to seeking common ground in bringing together the Body of Christ breaks down walls and boundaries between Christians of different denominations, and offers solutions that unite not only the Church, but entire communities and cities.